An Introduction to

An Introduction to 3D AutoCAD
Releases 12 and 13

A. Yarwood

Autodesk.
Registered Developer

Longman

Addison Wesley Longman Limited
Edinburgh Gate, Harlow
Essex CM20 2JE, England
and Associated Companies throughout the world

© Addison Wesley Longman Limited 1996

All rights reserved; no part of this publication may be reproduced, stored in any retrieval system, or transmitted in any form or by any means, electronic, mechanical, photocopying, recording, or otherwise without either the prior written permission of the Publishers or a licence permitting restricted copying in the United Kingdom issued by the Copyright Licensing Agency Ltd, 90 Tottenham Court Road, London W1P 9HE.

First published 1996

British Library Cataloguing in Publication Data
A catalogue entry for this title is available from the British Library

ISBN 0-582-29091-0

Set by 24 in 10/13pt Melior
Produced by Longman Singapore Publishers (Pte) Ltd
Printed in Singapore

Contents

List of plates	ix
Preface	xi
Acknowledgements	xiii

1 Introduction — 1
  AutoCAD Releases 12 and 13 — 1
  The AutoCAD Drawing Editor — 1
  An AutoCAD workstation — 1
  Methods of calling commands — 2
  Selection methods used in this book — 4
  The file acad.pgp — 4
  3D coordinates — 5
  Drawing lines in 3D – the tool LINE — 7
  The tool 3Dface — 10
  The tool Vpoint — 11
  The tool Hide — 16
  The tool Elev — 17

2 3D tools from Surfaces — 20
  Introduction — 20
  The tools 3Dline and 3Dface — 21
  The Surfaces tools — 23
  The tool 3Dface — 25
  The tool 3Dface with the Invisible prompt — 25
  The tool 3Dface and prompt Third point: — 27
  The Surfaces tools — 28
  The tool Edgesurf — 29
  The tool Revsurf — 32
  The tool Rulesurf — 36
  The tool Tabsurf — 38
  The tools 3Dmesh and 3Dpoly — 40
  The tool Pface — 43
  3D Objects — 44

3 The User Coordinate System (UCS) — 50
Introduction — 50
The variable UCSicon — 50
The UCS icon — 51
The variable UCSfollow — 51
The tool UCS — 52
Warning — 55
Calling a new User Coordinate System — 57
An example of a 3D drawing with the aid of the UCS — 57
Notes on the UCS — 59
Exercises — 61

4 Viewports, Tilemode, MSpace and PSpace — 70
The tool Viewports — 70
UCSfollow and Vpoint settings in Viewports — 72
Tilemode — 72
Model Space and Paper Space — 73
Viewports in PSpace and MSpace — 77
Settings viewports in Paper Space — 77

5 3D solid model drawings — 82
AutoCAD Release 12 compared with Release 13 — 82
Loading the Advanced Modelling Extension — 82
The tools in AME — 83
The AME primitives — 83
Prompts and options for the primitives — 84
Wireframes and surface meshes — 85
The Boolean operators — 88
Saving disk capacity — 91
Primitive, extrusion or revolved solid — 95
Constructing 3D models in viewports — 95
Further examples of AME 3D models — 97
Exercises — 97

6 Additional AME 3D tools — 100
Introduction — 100
The AME tool Solcham — 100
The AME tool Solfill — 100
Problems arising with Solfill and Solcham — 102
The AME tool Solmove — 103
The AME tool Solchp — 105
The AME tool Solsep — 106
The AME tool Solpurge — 107

	The AME tool Solucs	107
	The AME tool Solfeat	108
	The AME tool Solprof	109
	The AME tool Solsect	113
	The AME Solvar variables	117
	Exercises	117
7	**3D solid models with Release 13**	**122**
	Introduction	122
	Calling Solids tools in Release 13	124
	Examples of constructing 3D models in Release 13	124
	Exercises	134
8	**The command DVIEW**	**135**
	Introduction	135
	The CAmera option	136
	The TArget option	137
	The POints option	138
	The Zoom option	139
	The Distance option	140
	The PAn option	142
	The TWist option	142
	The CLip option	143
	The Hide option	143
	The Off option	143
	The Undo option	143
	The eXit option	144
	General notes about the DVIEW command	144
9	**AutoVision**	**145**
	Introduction	145
	The command Shade	145
	AutoVision	146
	AutoVision lighting	147
10	**Autodesk 3D Studio**	**160**
	Introduction	160
	Selection device	160
	Cursors	160
	Viewports	161
	Dialogue and message boxes	161
	Icon panel	161
	Calling AutoCAD and AutoSketch from 3D Studio	162

viii   An Introduction to 3D AutoCAD

Programs in 3D Studio	162
Filenames and extensions	163
Notes about speed of rendering	163
The 3D Editor of 3D Studio	164
Method of rendering a 3D model	164
Mapping, applying mapping coordinates and assigning materials	166
Examples of rendering AutoCAD DXF files	168
An example of rendering in 3D Studio	169
Further examples of mapping and assigning materials	175

11 AutoCAD Designer — 179

Introduction	179
Calling Designer commands	179
First example	180
Second example – parametric possibilities	185

12 Examples of 3D models — 190

Introduction	190
Example 1 – a stile	190
Example 2 – a tiled table	191
Example 3 – a machine part	192
Example 4 – a support bracket	192
Example 5 – a machine part	194
Example 6 – 3D AutoCAD	194
Example 7 – a coffee jug	196
Example 8 – a door handle	197
Example 9 – photographic developing tongs	197
Example 10 – pipe grips	199

Index   201

List of plates

Colour plates are between pages 98 and 99.

Plate I An AME solid model ready for rendering in AutoCAD Release 12 for DOS

Plate II The AME model in Plate I rendered against a white background

Plate III The 3D model in Plate 1 rendered in AutoCAD Release 13 for Windows

Plate IV A 3D model constructed with **Surface** commands and rendered using AutoVision within AutoCAD for Windows

Plate V The 3D model in Plate IV rendered in copper using AutoVision within AutoCAD Release 13 (Windows 95 version)

Plate VI Two poppet valves constructed with the aid of **Surfrev** and rendered in AutoCAD Release 13 (Windows 95 version)

Plate VII A perspective view of a 3D garage model ready for rendering in AutoCAD Release 13 for Windows

Plate VIII The result of using the **Shade** command on the garage model in Plate VII. AutoCAD has here been configured to use a background colour other than white

Plate IX The garage model in Plates VII and VIII rendered in the colours used when the parts were drawn

Plate X The garage model rendered using materials added in Autodesk 3D Studio x   An Introduction to 3D AutoCAD

> *Plate XI*   Two solid models created in AutoCAD rendered within 3D Studio against a tiled background
>
> *Plate XII*   A model constructed in AutoCAD using the **Revsurf** command and rendered in 3D Studio
>
> *Plate XIII*   An AutoCAD 3D model rendered in 3D Studio against a brick background
>
> *Plate XIV*   A model constructed and rendered in 3D Studio
>
> *Plate XV*   A 3D model created in AutoCAD rendered against a background in 3D Studio
>
> *Plate XVI*   A 3D AutoCAD model rendered as a variety of materials within 3D Studio

Preface

This book's contents are intended primarily for those using AutoCAD software on a personal computer (PC) working under MS-DOS and Windows. Its contents are however applicable to AutoCAD operating with other platforms.

Throughout the book references will be made to AutoCAD Release 12 and AutoCAD Release 13, usually as R12 and R13. Although most of the illustrations of features using AutoCAD editor screens will be from the Windows versions of these two releases, some illustrations will show the AutoCAD editor screen of MS-DOS Release 12. The MS-DOS version AutoCAD editor screen of Release 13 will not be shown in any of the illustrations because it is similar to that of the Release 12 MS-DOS version. It must be noted however that constructional methods for the MS-DOS version of R13 are exactly the same as those for the Windows version of Release 13.

The book has been written for students and other users of AutoCAD who are already reasonably conversant with AutoCAD for constructing two-dimensional (2D) drawings and who wish to understand the basics of creating three-dimensional models (3D) with the software.

The rendering of 3D models created in AutoCAD allows realistic photographic-like illustrations to be produced in full colour, including realistic representation of the material(s) in which the model could be manufactured. Chapter 9 of this book deals with one rendering programme AutoVision, which runs inside AutoCAD. Chapter 10 deals with another rendering programme, Autodesk 3D Studio, which is a software programme independent of AutoCAD, but which allows AutoCAD 3D files to be loaded into its systems. It must be noted here that descriptions of the facilities available in either of these rendering programmes would require books for each software package. Chapters 9 and 10 are a bare introduction to these two software packages.

Chapter 11 is devoted to an introduction to another Autodesk software package which runs in AutoCAD – AutoCAD Designer. Again, the chapter is only a very limited description of the possibilities available with this package.

Two books by the same author – *An Introduction to 3D Studio* and *An Introduction to AutoCAD Designer Release 1* – give further information about the two Autodesk software packages 3D Studio and Designer.

As this book was about to be published a Windows 95 version of AutoCAD Release 13 was released by Autodesk, which is faster than the existing Windows 3.1 versions.

Two colour plates – Plates V and VI – show renderings of 3D models constructed in the Windows 95 version of Release 13.

A. Yarwood
Salisbury 1996

Acknowledgements

The author wishes to acknowledge with grateful thanks the help given to him by members of the staff at Autodesk Ltd.

Registered trademarks

The following trademarks are registered in the US patent and Trademark Office by Autodesk Inc.:

Autodesk®, AutoCAD®, AutoSketch®, Autodesk 3D Studio®, Advanced Modelling Extension (AME)®.

AutoVision™ is a trademark of Autodesk Inc.

IBM® is a registered trademark of the International Business Machines Corporation.

MS-DOS® is a registered trademark, and Windows™ is a trademark of the Microsoft Corporation.

A. Yarwood is a Registered Developer with Autodesk Ltd.

Autodesk.
Registered Developer

CHAPTER 1

Introduction

AutoCAD Releases 12 and 13

Throughout this book, references will be made to AutoCAD Release 12 as R12 and to AutoCAD Release 13 as R13. Although the illustrations of features from AutoCAD editor screens will be from the Windows versions of both Releases, the text descriptions of constructions will be suitable for either the Windows or the DOS versions of the two AutoCAD Releases.

The AutoCAD Drawing Editor

When AutoCAD is first loaded from disk, the drawing editor appears on screen. Figure 1.1 shows the drawing editor for AutoCAD for Windows (R12). The operator can immediately commence the construction of a drawing in this graphics area of the window.

An AutoCAD workstation

Drawings produced with the aid of AutoCAD are usually constructed with the aid of a computer at a workstation. A simple workstation consists of a computer with hard and floppy disk drives, with various devices connected:

1. A visual display unit (VDU) is provided, on the screen of which drawings and alpanumeric information will be displayed. Sometimes two VDUs are connected – one for displaying the drawing editor, the second for displaying alphanumeric information.
2. A pointing device, usually a mouse, is used to control the position of the cursor on screen when drawing, or to point to select commands or prompts from menus and icons which appear on screen. Other pointing devices may be found in some hardware setups.

2   An Introduction to 3D AutoCAD

Fig. 1.1 The AutoCAD for Windows (R12) drawing editor

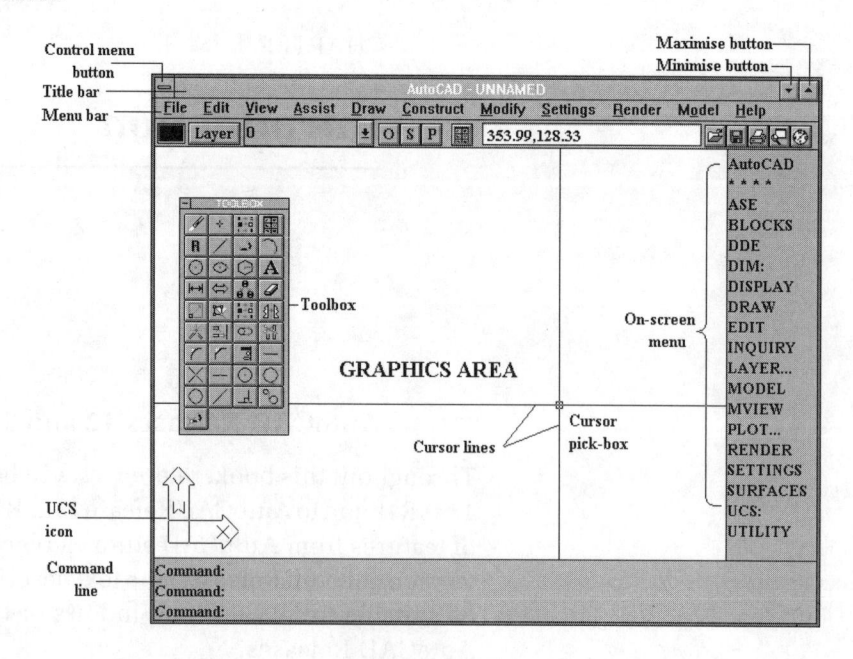

3. A plotter or printer is used for printing drawings on paper, card or tracing material – for producing hardcopy.

Methods of calling commands

In general AutoCAD for Windows provides five methods by which commands (tools) can be called:

1. The tool icon can be selected (picked) from the toolbox with the aid of the mouse. The tool name appears in the Command Line together with prompts.
2. The name of the command may be keyed at the **Command:** prompt in the Command Line of the drawing editor.
3. An abbreviation for the tool name (if available) can be entered from the keyboard in the Command Line.
4. The command may be pointed at and picked from an on-screen menu – usually to the right of the AutoCAD drawing editor. The command name is repeated at the Command Line – if the command name is followed by a colon – e.g. **Line:** – an associated sub-menu replaces the menu from which the command has been picked.
5. A menu name may be *picked* from the Menu bar of the Drawing editor. The tool name may then be selected from the resulting pull-down menu.

Introduction 3

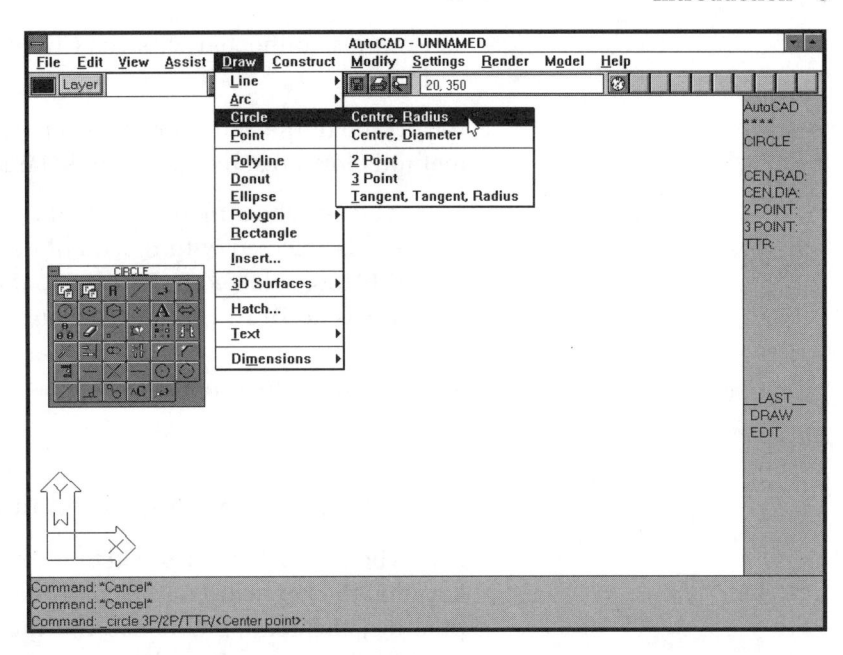

Fig. 1.2 **Circle** selected from the **Draw** menu in AutoCAD for Windows (R12)

Fig. 1.2 shows the tool **Circle** selected from the **Draw** pull-down menu.

Note:

1. If the on-screen menu is showing, the **CIRCLE** sub-menu appears in the on-screen menu area.

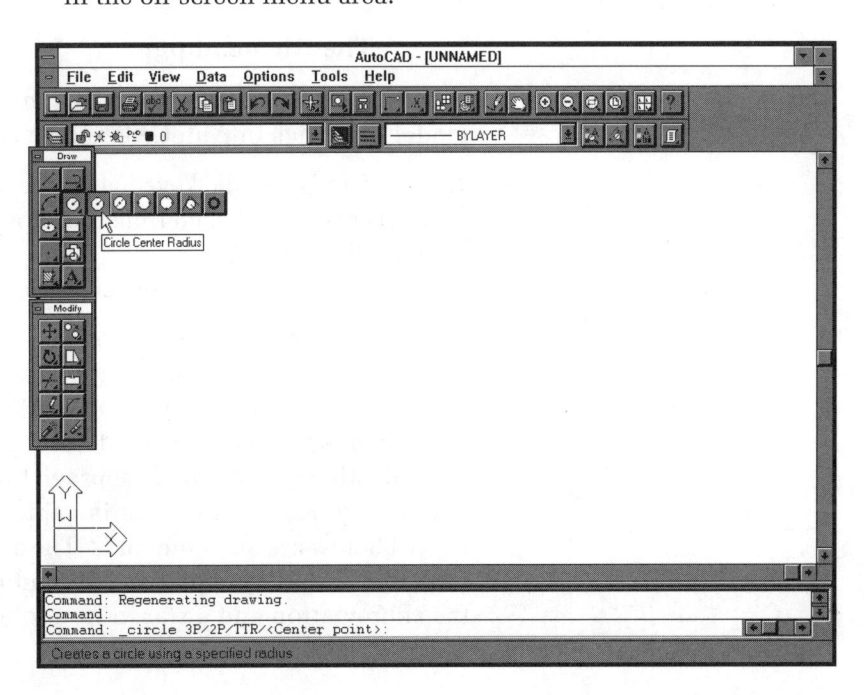

Fig. 1.3 **Circle** selected from the **Draw** toolbar in AutoCAD Release 13 for Windows

2. Prompts connected with the **Circle** tool appear in the Command Line.

If working in the Windows version of AutoCAD Release 13, similar methods for the selection of tools largely applies, except that:

1. Tool icons show in toolbars and each icon shows a tool tip, when a tool is selected with the aid of the mouse. Figure 1.3 shows the **Circle** tool selected in Release 13. Some icons have *flyouts*.
2. There is no **Draw** pull-down menu from which tool names can be selected.
3. It is unusual to have an on-screen menu showing, although one can be configured.

Selection methods used in this book

In this book it will be assumed that commands and their prompts are keyed at the keyboard of the computer using a single VDU setup. In practice, the reader will use the methods best suited to his/her AutoCAD setup – either keying commands or selecting from pull-down menus, toolbox or toolbar. Some will prefer selecting from toolbox or toolbar and keying prompts. However, one of the best and quickest ways for a beginner to learn the AutoCAD tool (command) systems is to start by typing all commands and responses to prompts into the command line of the drawing editor window.

The file acad.pgp

As with other tools (commands), those for constructing 3D solid model drawings in AutoCAD can be called in several ways:

1. Commands may be keyed at the keyboard.
2. Tools may be selected from pull-down menus, from toolbox (R12) or toolbars (R13).
3. The tool name may be selected from an on-screen menu (R12).

Some commands can be keyed at the keyboard in the form of abbreviations. These depend upon the contents of the file **acad.pgp** found in the directory **acadwin\support** (R12) or **acadr13 \common\support**. The standard **acad.pgp** allows the operator to use the following command abbreviations. The abbreviations can be keyed in either lower case or in capitals. Those shown in italics in the list below are 3D commands. The abbreviations are shown in the form in which they appear in the **acad.pgp** file – with a comma after the abbreviation and a star in front of the tool name.

A,	*Arc
B,	*Break
C,	*Circle
CP,	*Copy
DV,	*Dview
E,	*Erase
F,	*Fillet
L,	*Line
LA,	*Layer
LT,	*Linetype
M,	*Move
MS,	*MSpace
P,	*Pan
PS,	*PSpace
PL,	*Pline
R,	*Redraw
Z,	*Zoom
3DLine,	*Line

In addition, the standard **acad.pgp** file of R12 allows many abbreviations for tools for 3D solid model drawings. These abbreviations will be discussed later.

Note that it is comparatively simple to amend the **acad.pgp** file to include any tool abbreviations which the operator is constantly using, or to amend those already included in the file. Information describing such amendments are included with the file.

3D coordinates

All points on any drawing in AutoCAD can be defined in relation to x,y,z numbers in a three-dimensional coordinate system. They can be stated in figures – the distances in coordinate units from an origin defined as $x,y,z = 0,0,0$. Note that with two-dimensional (2D) drawings, the x,y coordinates of the origin are 0,0.

The origin (0,0,0) in AutoCAD is usually at the bottom left-hand corner of the drawing editor graphics area. However, the origin may

6   An Introduction to 3D AutoCAD

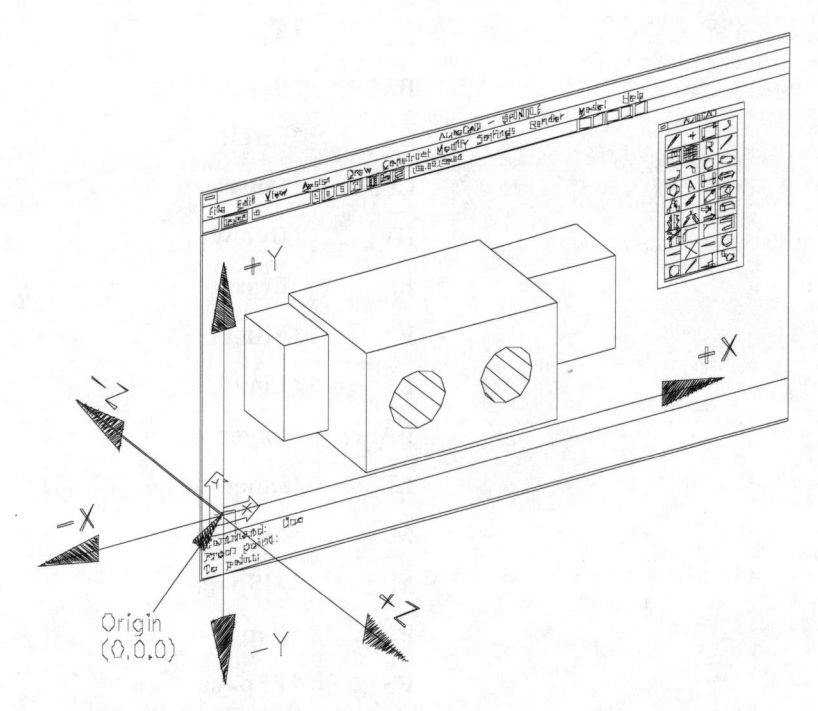

Fig. 1.4 The directions of the AutoCAD *x,y* and *z* axes

be altered, e.g. with the **Pan** tool, or by changing its position when the User Coordinate System (UCS) is in operation. (See Chapter 3.)

The *x* and *y* axes are assumed to be lying horizontally and vertically on the screen surface with the *z* axis lying perpendicular to the screen surface. With the origin (0,0,0) at the bottom left-hand corner of the graphics area, the directions of the *x,y,z* axes are shown in Fig. 1.4. Fig. 1.4 shows the AutoCAD for Windows graphics editor.The relationship between the three 3D coordinate axes is the same in R13.

+ve *x* is horizontally to the right of the origin;
−ve *x* is horizontally to the left of the origin;
+ve *y* is vertically above the origin;
−ve *y* is vertically below the origin;
+ve *z* is as if perpendicular above the origin;
−ve *z* is as if perpendicular below the origin.

The number of coordinate units along each of the *x* and *y* axes available in the AutoCAD drawing editor is determined with the aid of the tool **Limits**:

Command: limits *right-click*
ON/OFF/<Lower left corner> <0,0>: *right-click*
Upper right corner <12,9>: 420,297 *right-click*
Command:

Introduction 7

The drawing editor will not be set fully to these limits until the tool **Zoom** is used to reset the graphics area to the stated coordinate limits as follows:

Command: zoom *right-click*
All/Center/Dynamic/Left/Previous/Vmax/Window/<Scale X/XP>:
   a (All) *right-click*
Regenerating drawing.
Command:

In the given example the limits of the drawing editor were changed from $x = 12$ and $y = 9$ to $x = 420$ and $y = 297$. These new coordinate limits are equivalent to an A3 size drawing sheet in millimetres (420 mm by 297 mm). Thus when drawing within the drawing editor with limits set to $x,y = 420,297$, each coordinate unit can be regarded as one millimetre in order to draw to a scale of full size (scale 1:1) if printing and plotting full size on an A3 sized drawing sheet. Using the **Limits** tool, the drawing editor can be set to allow the operator to draw to any scale and in any dimensioning units – e.g. to draw in millimetres, centimetres, kilometres, inches, feet etc. on any size sheet and to any scale.

Drawing lines in 3D – the tool LINE

There are several methods of drawing lines to defined coordinate lengths in 3D drawings.

By keying or picking absolute coordinate figures

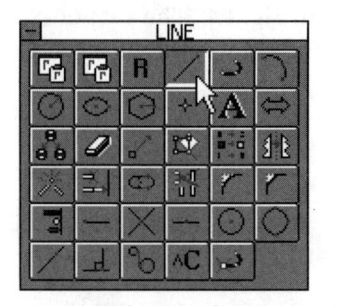

Fig. 1.5 Selecting the **Line** tool icon from the toolbox in AutoCAD for Windows

Because the tool **3DLINE** is included in the *acad.pgp* file as **LINE**, which is also abbreviated to **L**, keying the abbreviation **L** can be used for either **Line** or **3Dline**. **Line** can also be selected from the toolbox (R12) – Fig. 1.5, or from the **Draw** toolbar (R13) – Fig. 1.6 or from the **Draw** menu if an on-screen menu is in use. No matter which method is used, the prompts appearing at the command line will be the same as follows:

Command: l *right-click*
LINE from point: *enter* coordinates at the keyboard or *pick* a coordinate point
To point: *enter* coordinates at the keyboard or *pick* a coordinate point
To point: *enter* coordinates at the keyboard or *pick* a coordinate point
To point:

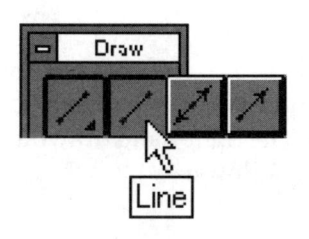

Fig. 1.6 Selecting the **Line** tool icon from the **Draw** toolbar in AutoCAD Release 13 for Windows. Note the *Flyout* and the *Tool Tip*

8 An Introduction to 3D AutoCAD

Fig. 1.7 The **Line** command for drawing 3D lines

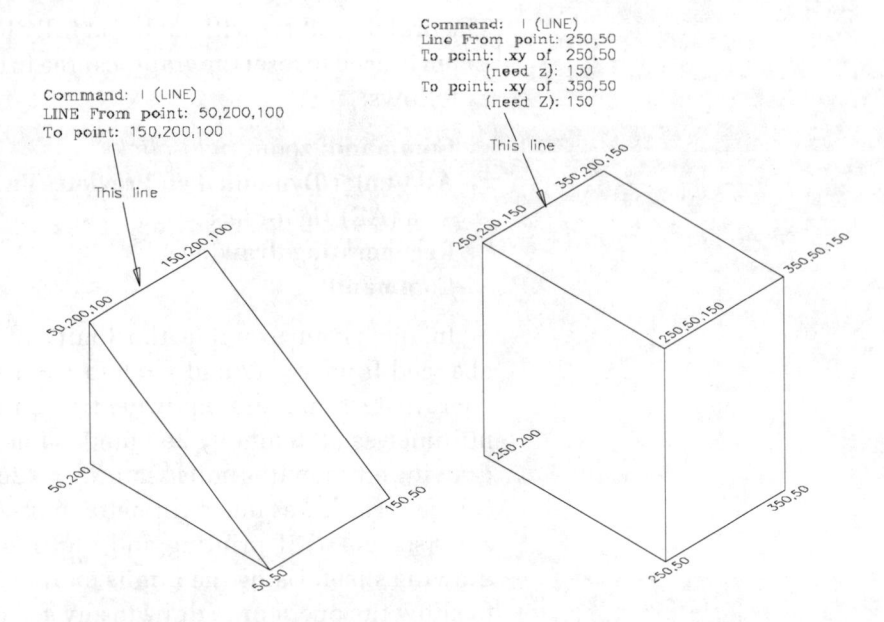

In response to each of these prompts, the operator can key in the required coordinates. An example is given in Fig. 1.7. The sequences for constructing the 3D lines of the left-hand figure of Fig. 1.7 is as follows:

Command: l (Line) *right-click*
Line from point: 50,50 *right-click*
To point: 50,200,100 *right-click*
To point: 150,200,100 *right-click*
To point: 150,50 *right-click*
To point: 50,50 *right-click*
To point: 50,200 *right-click*
To point: 50,200,100 *right-click*
To point: *right-click*
Command:

Using the filter .xy

When using **Line** for 3D drawings, the filter **.xy** can be used to determine to positions of the z coordinates. The right-hand drawing of Fig. 1.7 was drawn using the **.xy** filter as follows:

Command: l *right-click*
LINE from point: 250,50
To point: .xy *right-click*
of 250,50 *right-click*
(need Z) 150 *right-click*

Introduction 9

```
Command: l (LINE)
LINE From point: 70,80
To point: @100,0,150
To point: @0,0,100
To point: @-100,0,0
To point: @0,100,-50
To point: c (Close)
Command:
```

```
Command: l (LINE)
LINE From point: 250,150
To point: @100<45
To point: @100<135
To point: @0,0,100
To point: @100<315
To point: @0,0,100
To point: @0,100,0
To point: c (Close)
Command:
```

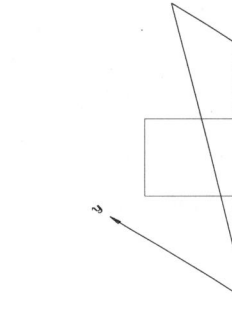

Fig. 1.8 Examples of 3D lines

To point: .xy *right-click*
of 350,50 *right-click*
(need Z) 150 *right-click*
To point: 350,50
To point: 250,50
To point: 250,200
To point: .xy *right-click*
of 250,200 *right-click*
(need Z) 150 *right-click*
To point: .xy *right-click*
of 350,200 *right-click*
(need Z) 150 *right-click*
To point: .xy *right-click*
of 350,50 *right-click*
(need Z) 150 *right-click*
To point: *right-click*
Command:

With relative coordinates

Relative coordinates – those relative in position to the last stated coordinate – can be either keyed or partly picked and partly keyed either with or without the aid of the **.xy** filter.

Relative coordinates are in the form of the following examples:

@100,0,0 – a coordinate position 100 units along the *x* axis relative to the last given position;
@0,100,0 – a coordinate position 100 units along the *y* axis relative to the last given position
@0,0,100 – a coordinate position 100 units along the *z* axis relative to the last given position;
@100<45 – a coordinate point 100 units distant from and at an angle of 45° to the last given point.

Two examples are given in Fig. 1.8. The figures keyed at the command line to obtain these examples are given below:

The left-hand figure

Command: l *right-click*
Line from point: 70,80 *right-click*
To point: @100,0,150 *right-click*
To point: @0,0,100 *right-click*
To point: @-100,0,0 *right-click*
To point: @0,100,-50 *right-click*
To point: c (Close) *right-click*
Command:

Note: The use of negative numbers.

The right-hand figure

Command: l *right-click*
Line from point: 250,150 *right-click*
To point: @100<45 *right-click*
To point: @100<135 *right-click*
To point: @0,0,100 *right-click*
To point: @100<315 *right-click*
To point: @0,0,100 *right-click*
To point: @0,100,0 *right-click*
To point: c (Close) *right-click*
Command:

Note: The use of relative angular coordinate numbers (e.g. @100<45).

The tool 3DFACE

Many 3D drawings can be constructed entirely by using the **Line** and **3Dface** tools. Apart from entering the tool name at the command line, the tool can be selected from tool icons – from the toolbox in R12 (Fig. 1.9) or from the **Surfaces** toolbar in R13 (Fig. 1.10). When constructed with 3Dfaces, the **Hide** tool will remove hidden lines

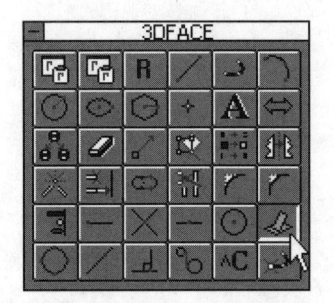

Fig. 1.9 Selecting the **3DFACE** tool icon from the toolbox in AutoCAD for Windows

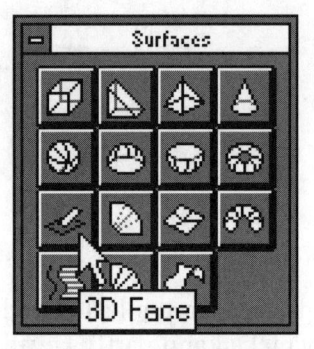

Fig. 1.10 Selecting the **3D Face** tool icon from the **Surfaces** toolbar in AutoCAD Release 13 for Windows

from behind the faces. 3Dfaces can be constructed as flat surfaces (planar) or as non-planar surfaces in 3D space. 3Dfaces are formed as triangles or as quadrilaterals – i.e. with three or four edges. There is more about **3Dface** in Chapter 2. When **3Dface** is called:

Command: 3dface *right-click*
First point: coordinates *right-click*
Second point: coordinates *right-click*
Third point: coordinates *right-click*
Fourth point: coordinates *right-click*
Third point: *right-click*
Command:

And a quadrilateral 3Dface is formed.

The tool Vpoint

When a 3D drawing has been constructed in the World Coordinate System (WCS), the result will be a plan view – i.e. as seen from above with the *x,y* plane flat on the screen surface.

An example of such a plan view drawn with the aid of the tool **3Dface** is given in Fig. 1.11.

Fig. 1.11 Plan view of a 3D drawing in the World Coordinate System (WCS)

The **Vpoint** tool allows the determining of new viewing positions in 3D space from which the user will be able to see a pictorial view of a 3D drawing. Apart from entering the tool name at the command line, the tool can be called either from the **View** pull-down menu as shown in Figures 1.12 and 1.13 when working in R12, or from the **View** toolbar as shown in Fig. 1.14 when working in R13. When **Vpoint** is called, the command line shows:

12 An Introduction to 3D AutoCAD

Fig. 1.12 Selecting **Set Vpoint** from the **View** pull-down menu in AutoCAD for Windows

Fig. 1.13 The **Viewpoints Presets** dialogue box seen when **Presets...** is selected from the **View** pull-down menu

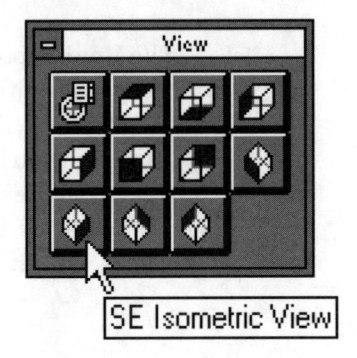

Fig. 1.14 Selecting a **Viewpoint Preset** from the **View** toolbar in R13

Command: vpoint *right-click*
VPOINT Rotate/<View point><0,0,1>:

There are three ways of responding to these prompts:

Keying x,y,z coordinates

Command: vpoint *right-click*
VPOINT Rotate/<Viewpoint><0,0,1>: -1,-1,1 *right-click*
Regenerating drawing.
Command:

This results in a pictorial parallel projection view of the 3D drawing appearing on screen as in Fig. 1.15. The keyed *x,y,z* coordinates determine the position as seen looking towards the origin 0,0,0. Thus with *x,y,z* at −1,−1,1, the viewing is looking towards the origin from *x* = −1 (i.e. from the left), with *y* = −1 (i.e. from the front) and with *z* = 1 (i.e. from above). The view is therefore looking from the left front from above. Such coordinate figures do not indicate any distance from the origin. The new view will appear occupying its full extent on screen. In order to bring the view back to its normal scale size it is necessary to **Zoom** the drawing to scale 1:1 by:

Command: z (Zoom) *right-click*
All/Center/Dynamic/Extents/Left/Previous/Vmax/Window/
    <Scale(X/XP): 1 *right-click*
Regenerating drawing.
Command:

The results of these two sets of prompts is shown in Fig. 1.15. Fig. 1.16 shows the results of a variety of *x,y,z* coordinate numbers in response to the **<View point>** prompt or to the selection of an Isometric View.

Keying r (Rotate)

This is followed by keying in two angles to obtain the required viewing position. The first is the angle made to the *x* axis **in** the *x-y* plane; the second is the angle made **to** the *x-y* plane.

Command: vpoint *right-click*
VPOINT Rotate/<View point><0,0,1>: r (Rotate) *right-click*
Enter angle in *x-y* plane from *x* axis<270>: 240 *right-click*
Enter angle from *x-y* plane<90>: 30 *right-click*
Regenerating drawing.
Command: z (Zoom) *right-click*

14 An Introduction to 3D AutoCAD

```
Command: vp (VPOINT) ↵
VPOINT Rotate/<View point> <0,0,1>: -1,-1,1 ↵
Regenerating drawing.
Command: z (ZOOM) ↵
All/Center/Dynamic/Extents/Left/Previous/
        Vmax/Window/<Scale(X/XP)>: 1 ↵
Regenerating drawing.
Command:
```

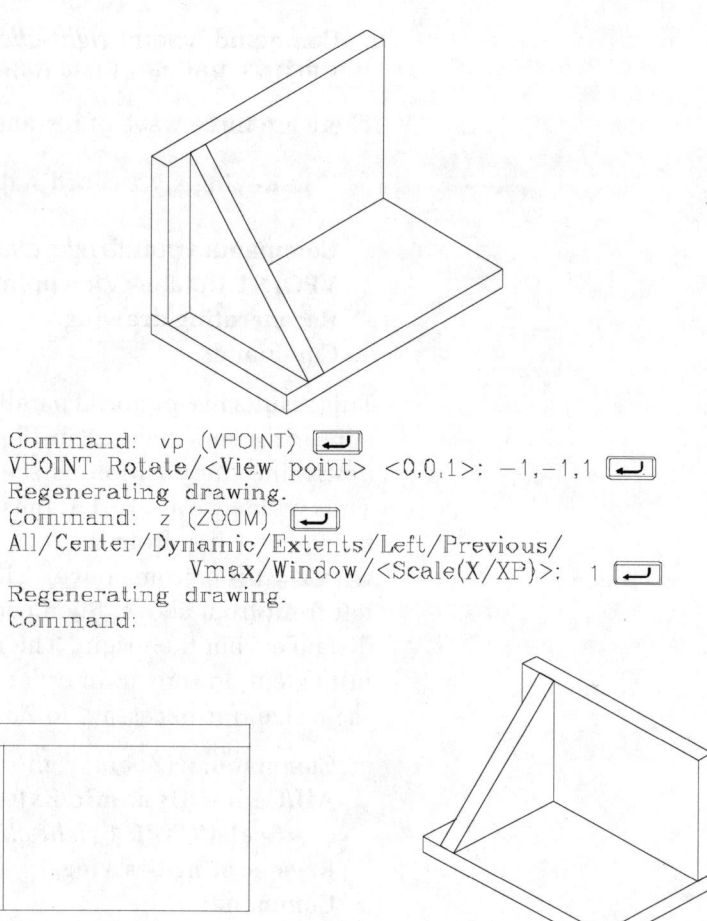

Fig. 1.15 The 3D model (Fig. 1.11) from **VPOINT** −1,−1,1

VP 0,0,1 (PLAN)

VP 1,-1,1 (Iso View SE)

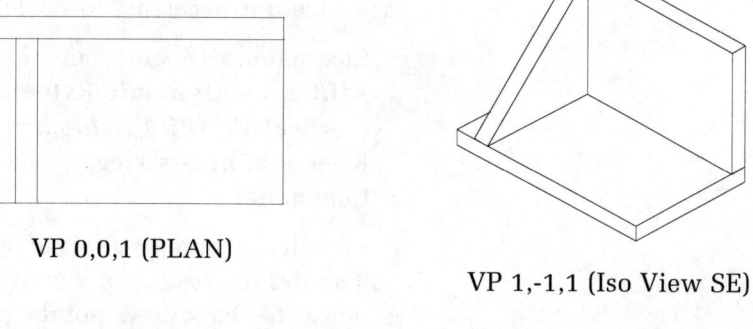

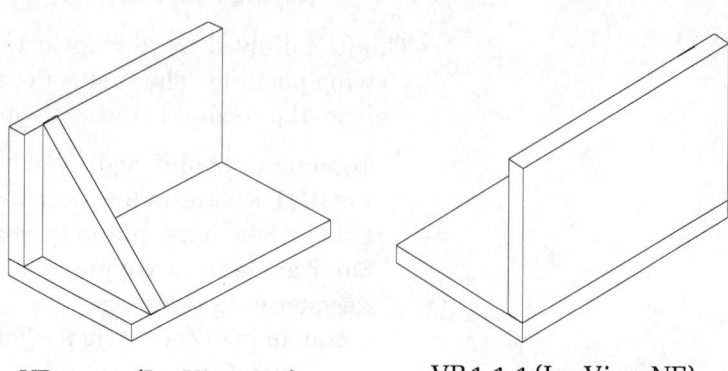

Fig. 1.16 The 3D model (Fig. 1.11) from various view points

VP -1,-1,1 (Iso View SW)

VP 1,1,1 (Iso View NE)

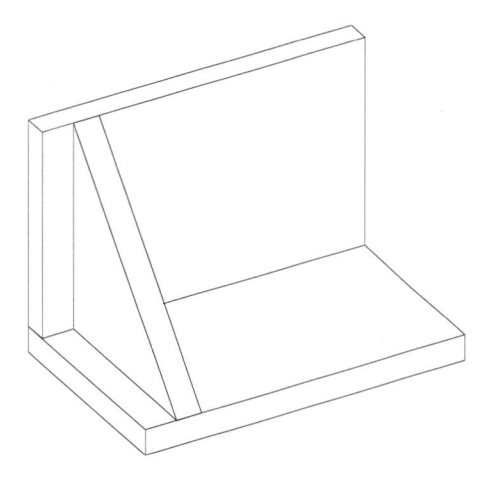

Fig. 1.17 The 3D model (Fig. 1.11) at angles to the *x* axis in the *x-y* plane and from the *x-y* plane

```
Command: vp (VPOINT)
VPOINT Rotate/<View point> <0,0,1>: r (Rotate)
Enter angle in X-Y plane from X axis <270>: 240
Enter angle from X-Y plane <90>: 30
Regenerating drawing.
Command: z (ZOOM)
All/Center/Dynamic/Extents/Left/Previous/
         Vmax/Window/<Scale(X/XP)>: 1
Regenerating drawing.
Command:
```

All/Center/Dynamic/Extents/Left/Previous/Vmax/Window/<Scale X/XP>: 1 *right-click*
Command:

The resulting pictorial view is shown in Fig. 1.17.

Pressing Return twice

While in the **Vpoint** tool prompts, either press the *Return* key twice or *right-click* twice. The screen changes and two icons appear (the compass and tripod icons of **Vpoint**) as shown in Fig. 1.18. The first is a double circle with crossing vertical and horizontal lines. This represents a world view of the screen. In this world view:

1. The centre represents the north pole (0,0,1).
2. The inner circle represents an equator (n,n,0).
3. The outer circle represents the south pole (0,0,-1).

A tiny cursor cross, which can be manipulated by moving the pointing device, can be moved to any position on, around or in this world icon. The second icon is a tripod showing the relative positions of the *x,y* and *z* axes as the cursor is moved around the world view icon with the aid of the mouse.

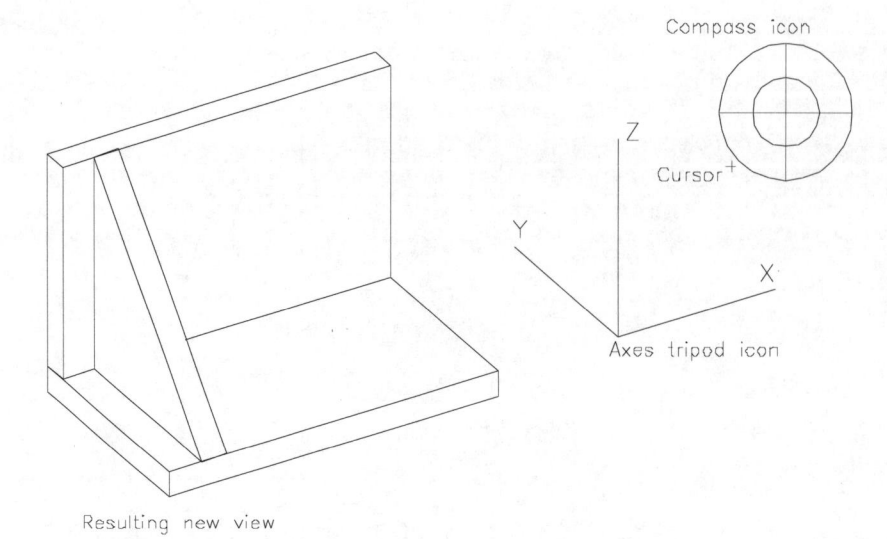

Fig. 1.18 The **VPOINT** compasses and axes tripod display

A required viewing position is determined by moving the cursor around the world icon with the aid of the mouse, noting the relative positions of the three coordinate axes, then doing a *right-click* when the required position has been selected. The screen then reverts to show a pictorial view of the 3D drawing as seen from the new selected viewing position.

Notes

1. **Vpoint** is only effective when working in Model Space (MSPACE). See Chapter 4.
2. **Vpoint** can only be used in the current Viewport. See Chapter 4.
3. **Vpoint** pictorial views are in parallel projections – i.e. perspective is not applied.
4. It is necessary to zoom the drawing to scale 1:1 after a new **Vpoint** has been chosen. This is because when a new **Vpoint** is called, the resulting new view on the screen is scaled to its current extents in relation to the graphics area of the AutoCAD editor.
5. When deciding x,y,z coordinates for view points, the direction of viewing is always towards the origin (0,0,0). The distance of the view point from the origin is not included.

The tool Hide

In certain circumstances the hidden lines of a 3D drawing can be hidden by calling the tool **Hide**. These circumstances are as follows:

1. The drawing has been constructed by using **3Dface**, **Edgesurf**, **Revsurf**, **Rulesurf**, **Tabsurf**, or with **3Dmesh** or **Pface** (see Chapter 2).

2. The drawing has been constructed as a 3D model with the aid of the Advanced Modelling Extension (AME) in AutoCAD Release 12.
3. The drawing has been created with the **Solids** tools in AutoCAD Release 13.

Command: hide *right-click*
HIDE Regenerating drawing.
Hiding lines: done 100%
Command:

Once a *right-click* has been executed, after calling the tool, no further action is necessary. When the tool is called, the drawing disappears from the screen. After all hidden lines have been removed, the 3D drawing with hidden lines removed reappears on screen. The process of removing hidden lines can take a considerable time if a large number of lines have to be hidden. The time taken also depends upon the speed of the computer in use.

The tool Elev

When this tool (**Elev**ation) is called the command line shows:

Command: elev *right-click*
New current elevation <0>: *right-click*
New current thickness <0>: 50 *right-click*
Command:

The current elevation is, initially, the position of the *x,y* plane with *z* at 0. If a new current elevation of say 50 is keyed in, the *x,y* plane will be positioned 50 coordinate units in the *z* direction above its original elevation. Figure 1.19 shows a screen view of a number of AutoCAD objects drawn in plan view in the World Coordinate System (WCS).

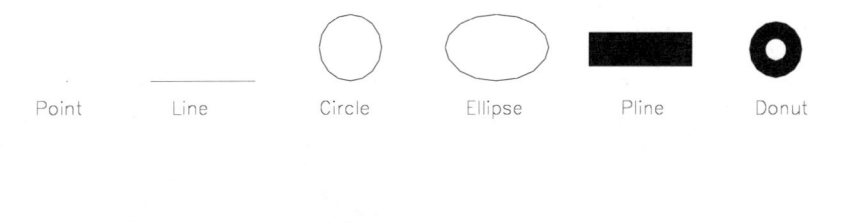

Fig. 1.19 Objects (entities) drawn in the WCS with the aid of **Draw** tools at elevation 0 and thickness 50

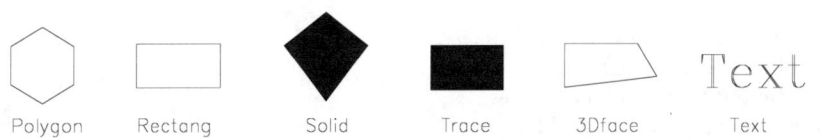

18 An Introduction to 3D AutoCAD

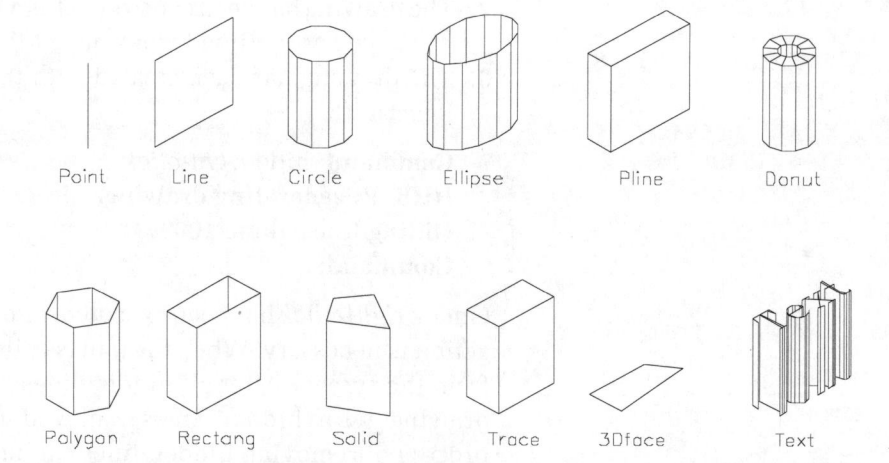

Fig. 1.20 **VPOINT** view of the objects in Fig. 1.19

The current thickness is the elevation extrusion thickness for any 2D object which is drawn when an elevation thickness is current. Figure 1.20 shows how the 2D objects of Fig. 1.19 are extruded with the current elevation at 0 and the current thickness at 50. The vertical faces of extruded objects are 3D faces, but only in the case of extruded circles, plines, solids and traces do the top faces of the extrusions become 3D faces. Thus when **Hide** is called, the resulting hidden lines views are as shown in Fig. 1.20.

3D faces, 3D polylines, 3D polygon meshes and dimensions are ignored by the **Elev**ation tool. These features cannot be extruded.

Note that even if **Solid fill** is **ON** when **Vpoint** is called to view extrusions in 3D, those areas which are solid filled in 2D are not solid filled in 3D.

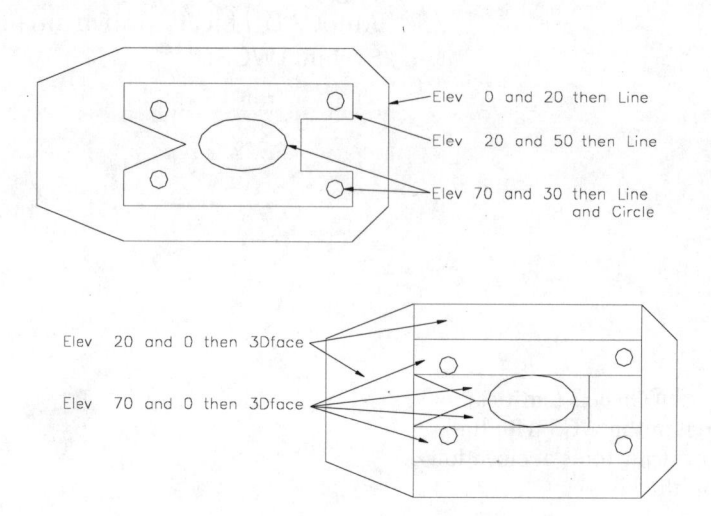

Fig. 1.21 A 3D model on different elevations and different thickness. The lower drawing has 2D faces added

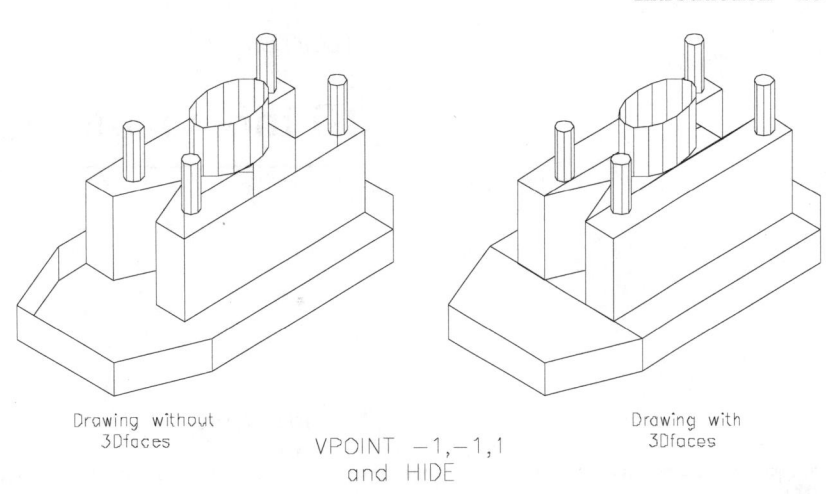

Fig. 1.22 **VPOINT** view of the 3D drawing Fig. 1.21

Drawing without 3Dfaces

VPOINT −1,−1,1 and HIDE

Drawing with 3Dfaces

It is particularly important to realise when working in 3D in Model Space, that the setting of the current elevation will affect the position of drawings relative to the initial setting of the *x,y* plane.

Figure 1.21 shows two plan views (in the WCS) of a 3D drawing constructed on three current elevation and thickness settings. The drawings therefore consist of three extrusions. The lower drawing of the two in Fig. 1.21 has had 3D faces added with the **ELEV**ation set to two different current elevations, but with the current thickness at 0 for each elevation.

Figure 1.22 is a pictorial view of the two 3D drawings of Fig. 1.21 after calling **Vpoint** at −1,−1,1. **Hide** has been called after **Vpoint** to hide hidden lines behind the 3D faces of the right-hand pictorial drawing.

CHAPTER 2

3D tools from Surfaces

Introduction

There are a number of tools available in AutoCAD Releases 12 and 13 for the construction of 3D drawings. In addition, the User Coordinate System (UCS) allows 3D drawings to be constructed on coordinate systems of the operator's own choice. More about the UCS is given in Chapter 3. This chapter is devoted to the use of the command **3Dline** and the **3D Surfaces** tools. The **Surfaces** tools are found in the **Draw** pull-down menu and sub-menus or from on-screen menus in R12 and in the **Surfaces** toolbar of R13. However, for the purpose of describing the methods of construction throughout this chapter, we will continue *entering* tool names at the command line.

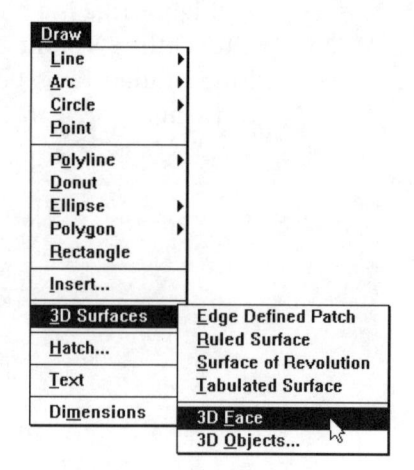

Fig. 2.1 Selecting **3D Face** from the **Surfaces** toolbar in R13

Fig. 2.2 The sub-menu of the **Draw** menu of R12 from which **3D Surfaces** commands can be selected. Selecting **3D Face**

The tools 3Dline and 3Dface

These two tools are very likely to be used in the construction of many 3D drawings. The two tools have already been touched upon in Chapter 1. Further examples of constructions involving **3Dface** will

3D tools from Surfaces 21

be given in this chapter. Two 3D drawings of a simple block, one drawn with **3Dline** and the other with **3Dface** are compared in Fig. 2.3, which shows that hidden lines of drawing constructed with **3Dline** cannot have hidden lines removed. Lines behind the surfaces of drawings constructed with the aid of **3Dface** can be removed by calling **Hide**.

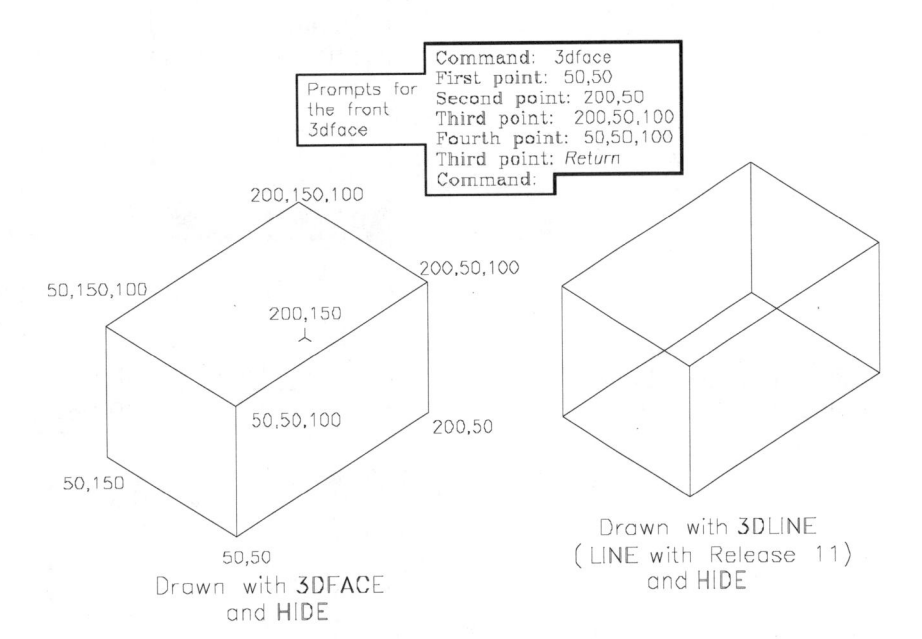

Fig. 2.3 The tool **3Dface** compared with **3Dline**

```
Command: 3dface
First point: 50,50
Second point: 200,50
Third point: 200,50,100
Fourth point: 50,50,100
Third point: Return
Command:
```
Prompts for the front 3dface

Drawn with 3DFACE and HIDE

Drawn with 3DLINE (LINE with Release 11) and HIDE

3Dfaces are constructed as three-dimensional polygonal surface meshes. The meshes may be planar or nonplanar. Each 3D face is either a triangle or a quadrilateral. The lines between adjacent triangles or quadrilaterals in surfaces constructed from a number of 3D faces can be removed by the use of the invisible prompt of the **3Dface** tool. Otherwise all edges of the triangles or quadrilaterals will appear in a 3D drawing constructed with the aid of **3Dface**.

The Surfaces tools

Select **3D Surfaces** from the **Draw** pull-down menu of R12 as shown in Fig. 2.4 and the sub-menu which appears lists the names of the **3D Surfaces** tools – **Edge Defined Patch** (Edgesurf), **Ruled Surface** (Rulesurf), **Surface of Revolution** (Revsurf), **Tabulated Surface** (Tabsurf), **3D Face** and **3D Objects**.... The same tools can be selected from the on-screen menus and sub-menus of R12 as shown in Fig. 2.5. Note that the three fullstops following the name **3D Objects...**

22 An Introduction to 3D AutoCAD

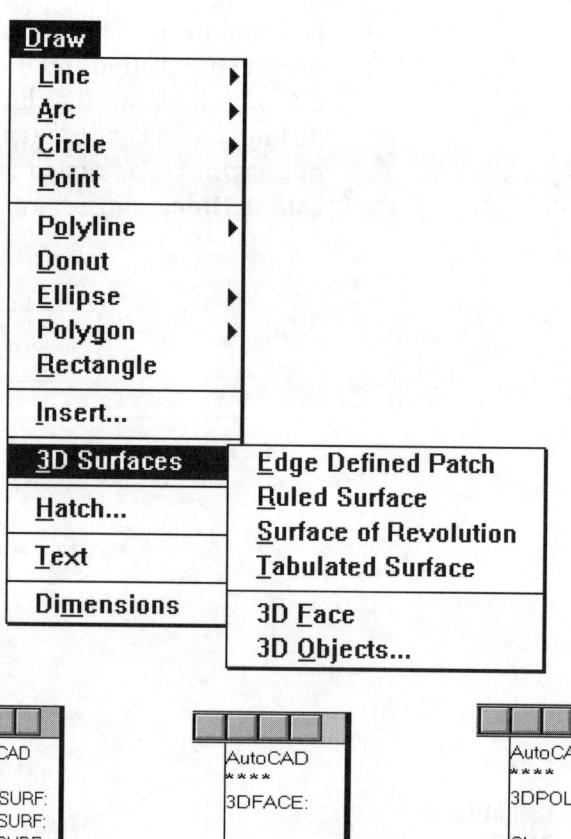

Fig. 2.4 The **3D Surfaces** sub-menu of the **Draw** pull-down menu in R12

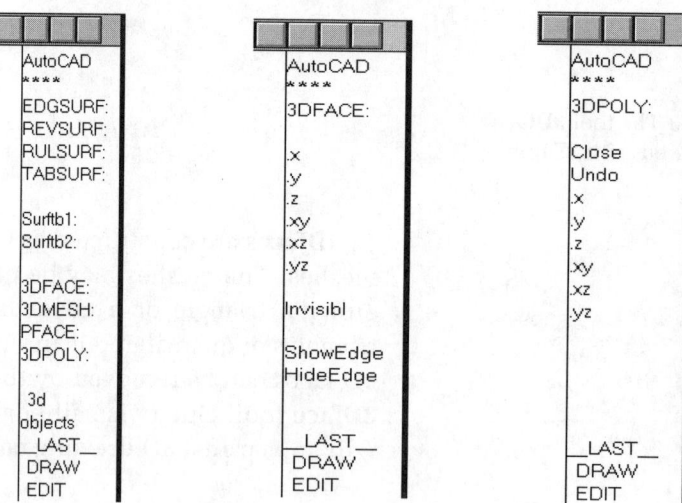

Fig. 2.5. The on-screen menus of R12 associated with the **Surfaces** tools

shows that, when this name is selected, a dialogue box will appear on screen. Examples of drawings constructed with the aid of the **Surfaces** tools are included in this chapter.

The **Surfaces** tools are given different names when called from the **Surfaces** toolbar of R13. (Fig. 2.6). In these examples **Edge Surface** is edgesurf, **Ruled Surface** is rulesurf, **Revolved Surface** is revsurf and **Extruded Surface** is tabsurf.

3D tools from Surfaces   23

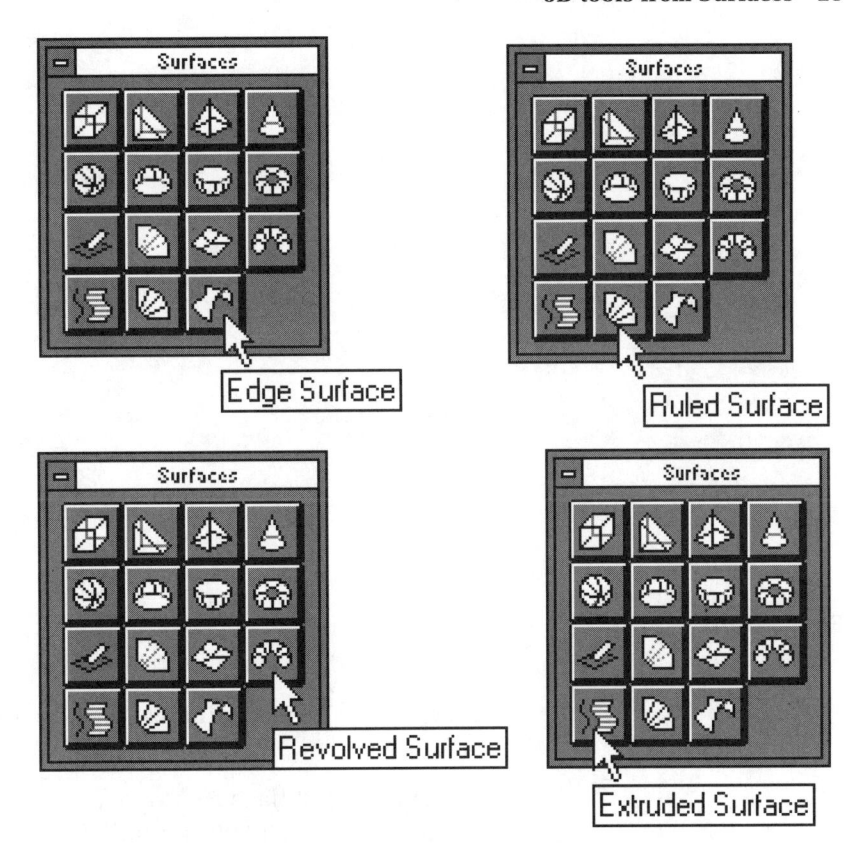

Fig. 2.6 Some **Surfaces** tool icons, with their tool tips from R13

As when constructing with the aid of the **3Dface** tool all the surfaces constructed with the aid of these other **Surfaces** tools are surface meshes made up of adjoining triangles and/or quadrilaterals. Lines behind these surface meshes can be hidden with the **Hide** tool.

The tool 3Dface

Three examples of simple drawings of blocks constructed with the aid of the **3Dface** tool are given in Figs. 2.7, 2.8 and 2.9. The reader is recommended to draw these three blocks from the instructions given below and included with the illustrations. In each of the given examples, the 3D drawings have been viewed by calling **Vpoint**, keying −1,−1,1 and then removing hidden edges by calling **Hide**.

First example (Fig. 2.7)

Figure 2.7 is a 3D drawing of a block constructed with the aid of **3Dface**. It is made up of 10 3D faces. No attempt has been made to make any of the edges of the 3D faces invisible. The 3D coordinates of the corners of all the faces are included in Fig. 2.7. Using only two-

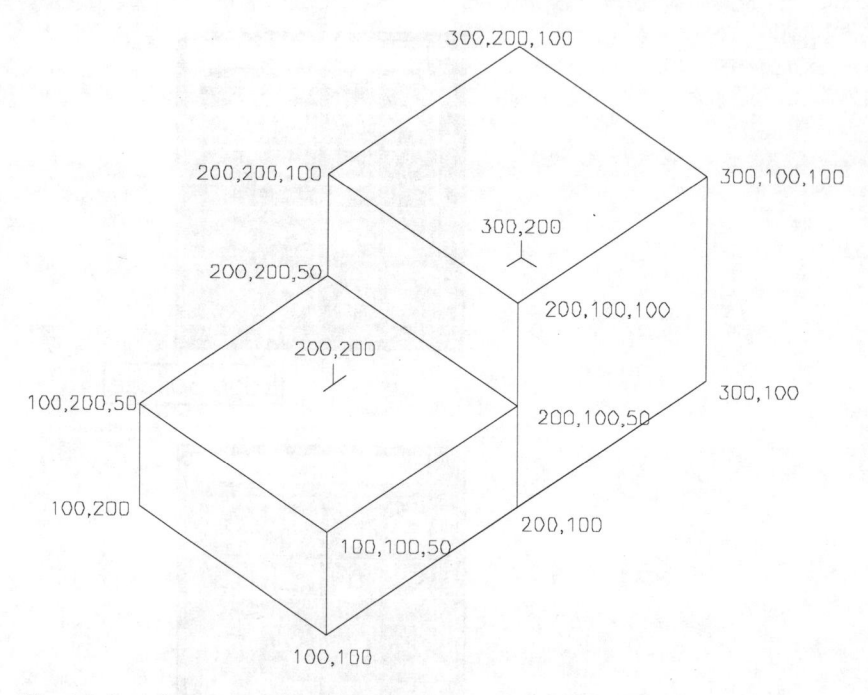

Fig. 2.7 **3Dface** – First example

dimensional *x,y* coordinates, the base of the block would be drawn as follows:

Command: 3dface *right-click*
First point: 100,100 *right-click*
Second point: 300,100 *right-click*
Third point: 300,200 *right-click*
Fourth point: 100,200 *right-click*
Third point: *right-click*
Command:

Note the second appearance of **Third point:** to which the response is either a *right-click* or press the *Return* key if one wishes to complete a single 3D face. Continuing keying or selecting coordinates at a second appearance of **Third point:** is explained in Figures 2.8 and 2.9.

Using three-dimensional *x,y,z* coordinates, the uppermost face of the block was drawn as follows:

Command: 3dface *right-click*
First point: 200,100,100 *right-click*
Second point: 300,100,100 *right-click*
Third point: 300,200,100 *right-click*
Fourth point: 200,200,200 *right-click*
Third point: *right-click*
Command:

Second example (Fig. 2.8)

Figure 2.8 is a 3D drawing of a block, parts of which have been drawn by copying or mirroring faces already drawn, in order to speed up the construction. Those parts which were copied and mirrored are shown in Fig. 2.8.

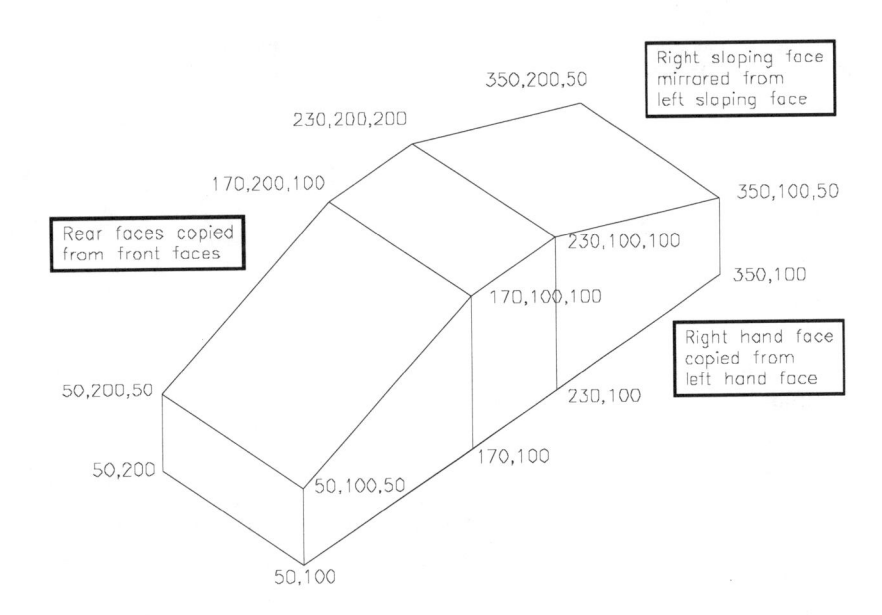

Fig. 2.8 **3Dface** – Second example

Third example (Fig. 2.9)

Another example where some 3D faces have been mirrored is shown in Fig. 2.9.

The tool 3Dface with the Invisible prompt

Fig. 2.10 includes an example of a 3D surface constructed from five faces, with some edges made invisible by involving the Invisible prompt. The sequence of constructing 3D face number 1 was:

Command: 3dface *right-click*
First point: 100,200,50 *right-click*
Second point: i (Invisible) *right-click*
      200,200,50 *right-click*
Third point: 200,100,50 *right-click*
Fourth point: 100,100,50 *right-click*
Third point: *right-click*
Command:

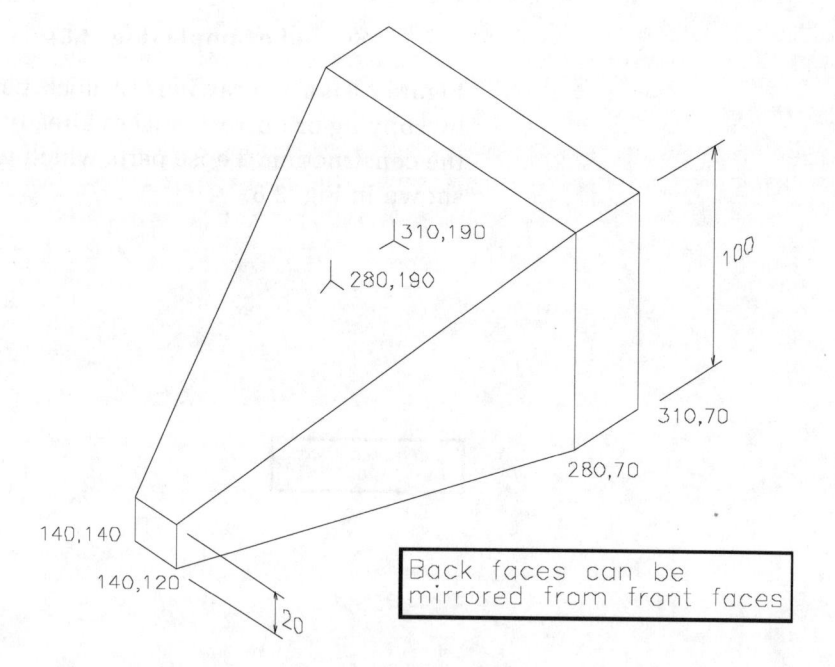

Fig. 2.9 **3Dface** – Third example

The sequence for 3D face number 5 was:

> **Command:** 3dface *right-click*
> **First point:** i (Invisible) *right-click*
> 200,200,50 *right-click*
> **Second point:** i (Invisible) *right-click*
> 300,200,50 *right-click*
> **Third point:** i (Invisible) *right-click*
> 300,100,50 *right-click*
> **Fourth point:** i (Invisible) *right-click*
> 200,100,50 *right-click*

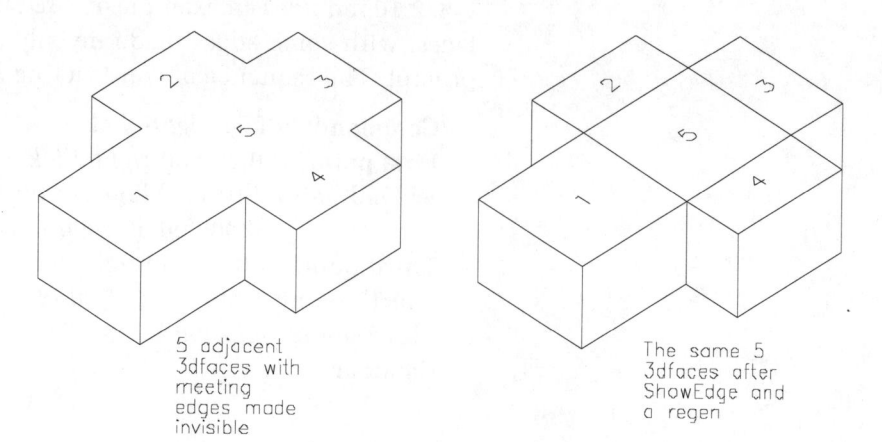

Fig. 2.10 Making **3Dface** edges invisible

Third point: *right-click*
Command:

This makes all edges of 3D face number 5 invisible.

Note that the i (Invisible) must be keyed before the coordinates of the first point of the edge to be made invisible are given. If osnaps are to be used, being associated with the coordinates they come after the i (Invisible) response.

In the on-screen **3Dface** sub-menu (Fig. 2.5), three prompts are included below the *x,y,z* filters. These are **Invisibl**, **ShowEdge** and **HideEdge**. These have the following effects:

The **Invisbl** prompt can be selected from this menu instead of entering i for Invisible.

When **ShowEdge** is selected (Fig. 2.10), the following appears at the command line:

Command: Invisible edges will be shown after next Regeneration.
Command:

If a **Regen**eration is called by:

Command: regen *right-click*
Regenerating drawing.
Command:

The hidden lines made invisible by using the Invisible prompt reappear from the drawing.

If now **HideEdge** is selected from the **3DFACE** on-screen sub-menu:

Command: Invisible edges will be HIDDEN after the next Regeneration.
Command:

If now a **Regen**eration is called:

Command: regen *right-click*
Regenerating drawing.
Command:

Hidden lines disappear from the drawing.

The tool 3Dface and the prompt Third point:

Figures 2.11 and 2.12 show how **Third point:** from the **3Dface** prompts be used to draw extra faces adjacent to previously drawn faces. All necessary prompts and responses are included with the two illustrations.

28 An Introduction to 3D AutoCAD

Fig. 2.11 Using **3Dface** to construct multiple faces

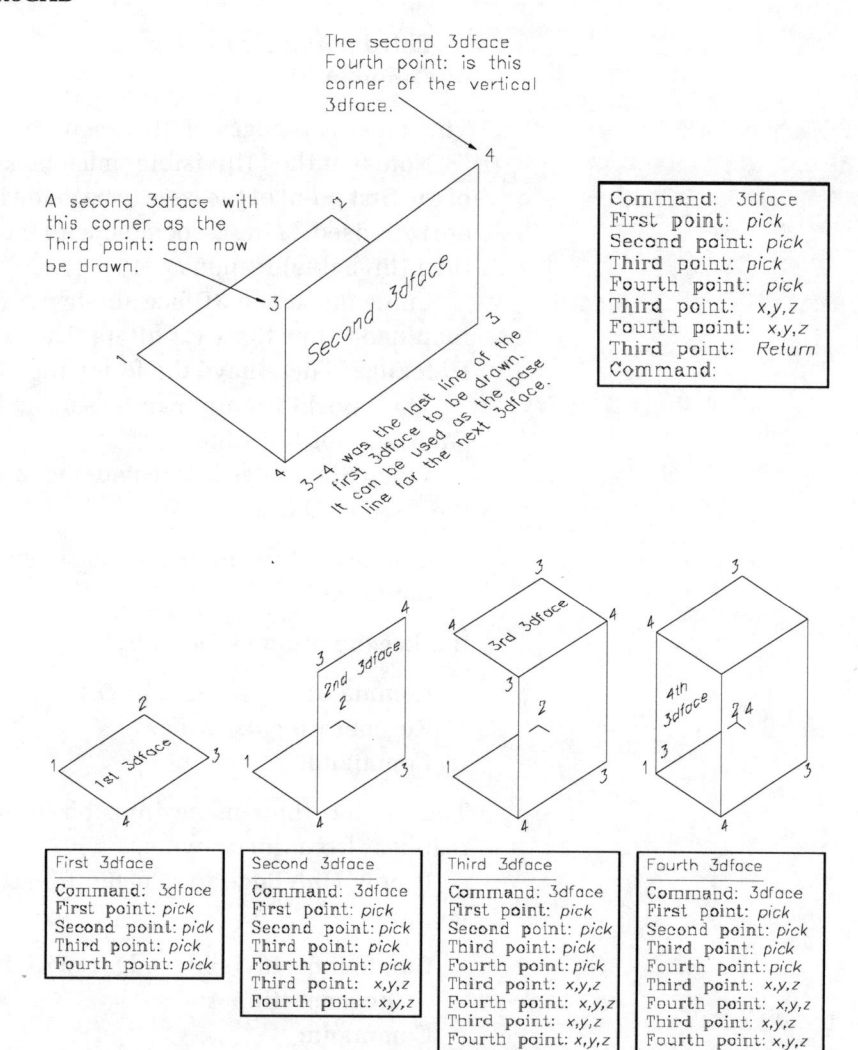

Fig. 2.12 Further multiple face construction with **3DFACE**

The Surfaces tools

The **Surfaces** tools, **Edgesurf**, **Revsurf**, **Rulesurf** and **Tabsurf** automatically form polygon surface meshes, the densities of which are controlled by the settings of two variable **Surftab1** and **Surftab2**. These two variables are set by:

    Command: surftab1 *right-click*
    New value for SURFTAB1<6>: 16 *right-click*
    Command: surftab2 *right-click*
    New value for SURFTAB2<6> 2 *right-click*
    Command:

In all cases both variables must be set to at least 2.

> **Rulesurf** depends upon settings of both **Surftab1** and **Surftab2**.
> **Revsurf** depends on settings of both **Surftab1** and **Surftab2**.
> **Rulesurf** depends upon setting of **Surftab1** with **Surftab2** set to at least 2.
> **Tabsurf** depends on setting of **Surftab1** with **Surftab2** set to at least 2.

Note that although **EDGSURF** and **RULSURF** show on the on-screen **Surfaces** sub-menu, the full names **Edgesurf** and **Rulesurf** must be keyed when entering the tool names at the keyboard.

The reader is advised to construct the examples of using the **Surfaces** tools which follow in order to familiarise him/herself with these methods of constructing surface meshes.

The tool Edgesurf

Edgesurf will fill a closed quadrilateral with a surface mesh, the mesh sizes depending upon the settings of **Surftab1** and **Surftab2**. The quadrilateral can be planar or nonplanar and its sides may be lines, arcs or curves. The tool will not function if any of the corners of the quadrilateral do not meet exactly. If edges do not join up the following message will appear at the command line:

Edge 1 does not touch another edge

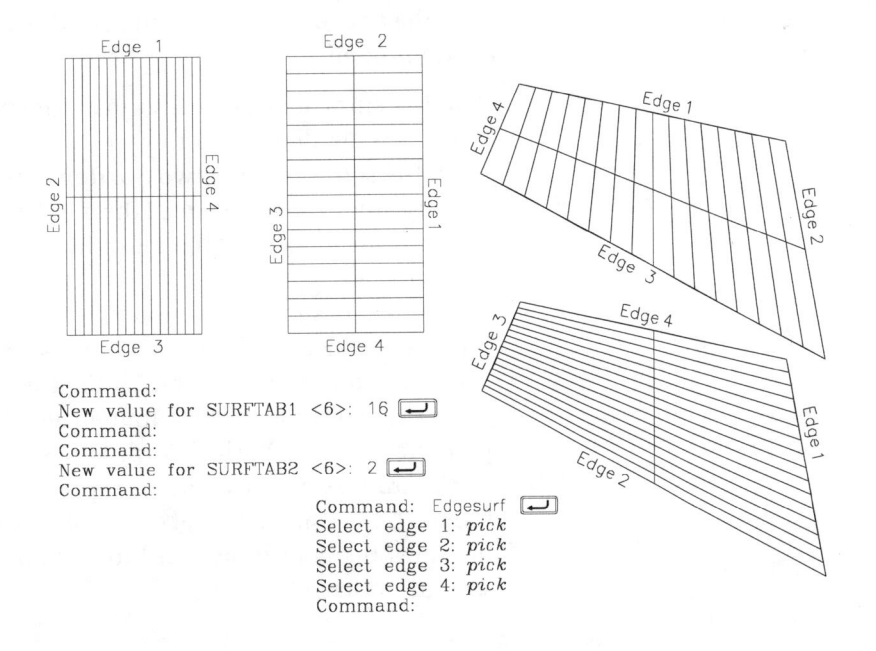

Fig. 2.13 Directions of **Surftab** settings with **Edgesurf**

30 An Introduction to 3D AutoCAD

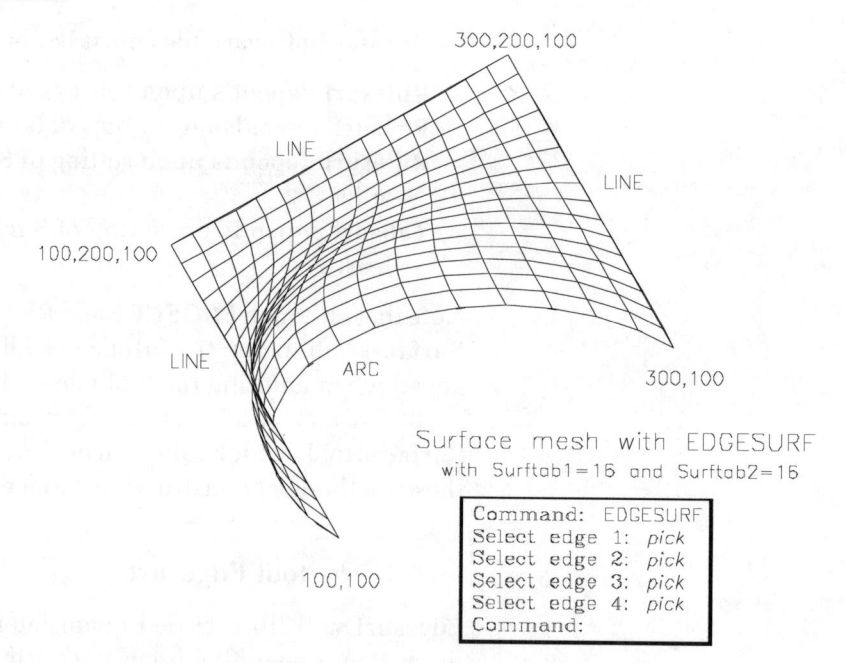

Fig. 2.14 Surface mesh constructed with **Edgesurf**

And the mesh will not appear.

The sequence of prompts when **Edgesurf** is called is:

Command: edgesurf *right-click*
Select edge 1: *pick* and edge of the quadrilateral
Select edge 2: *pick* and edge of the quadrilateral
Select edge 3: *pick* and edge of the quadrilateral
Select edge 4: *pick* and edge of the quadrilateral
Command:

And the surface mesh will form automatically. As can be seen from Fig. 2.13, the density of the mesh in both directions is dependent upon the settings of the two **Surftab** variables. **Surftab1** controls the density along the first edge of the quadrilateral to be picked. **Surftab2** controls the density of the mesh in the direction of the second edge to be picked.

Figure 2.14 shows an **Edgesurf** mesh formed within a 3D quadrilateral formed constructed from three lines and an arc. The drawing in Fig. 2.14 is a **Vpoint** view of the 3D **Edgesurf** surface mesh. Figure 2.15 gives the coordinates of the four edges of the quadrilateral as seen in plan view in the World Coordinate System (WCS).

Figure 2.16 is a second example of a 3D **Edgesurf** surface mesh formed from a quadrilateral of two lines and two arcs. This illustration includes the coordinates of the ends of the lines and arcs and the second point of the arcs.

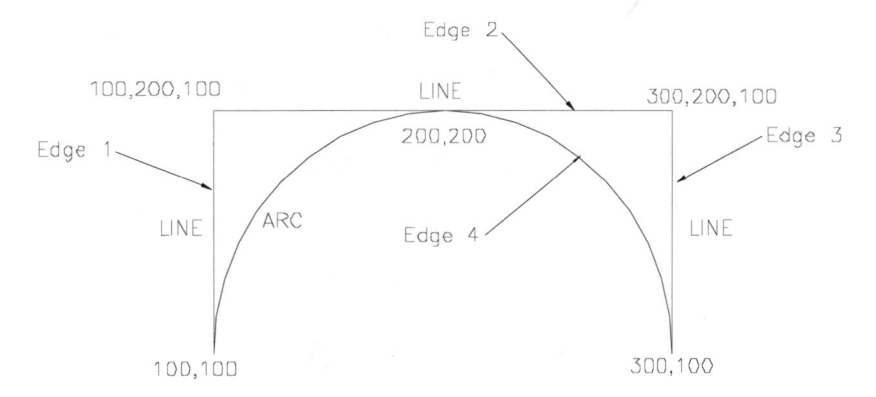

Fig. 2.15 Coordinates of the 3D outlines of Fig. 2.15

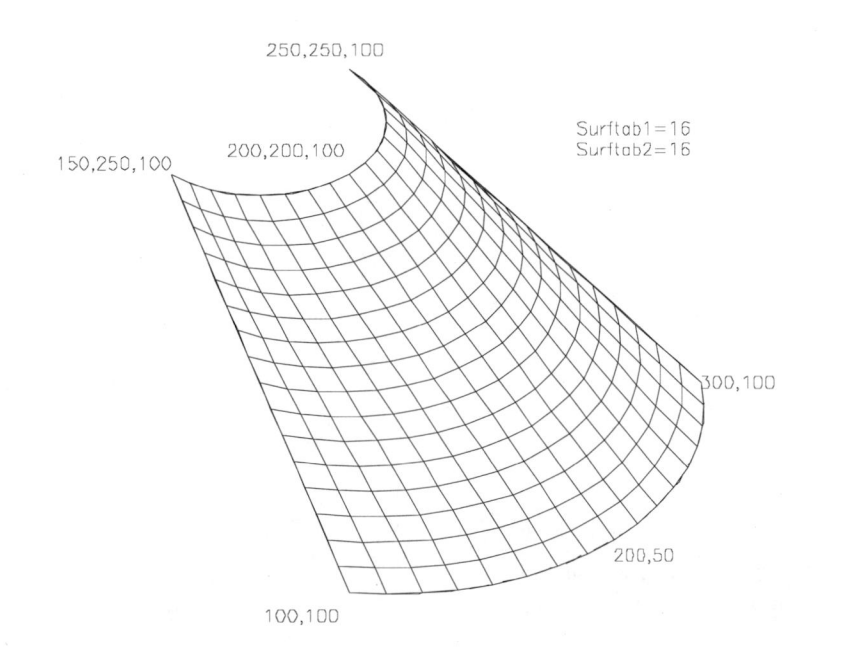

Fig. 2.16 **Edgesurf** – First example

The set of four illustrations, Figures 2.17 to 2.20, shows the stages in the construction of a 3D drawing with each face involving an **Edgesurf** surface mesh.

1. Figure 2.17 is a plan view in the WCS and includes all the coordinates for constructing the quadrilaterals for the surfaces of the block.
2. Figure 2.18 is a **Vpoint** view of the quadrilaterals showing their repositioning to enable edges to be easily picked as prompted when the **Edgesurf** tool is called.
3. Figure 2.19 shows the surface meshes added with the aid of the **Edgesurf** tool. Note the different settings of the **Surftab** variables.

32 An Introduction to 3D AutoCAD

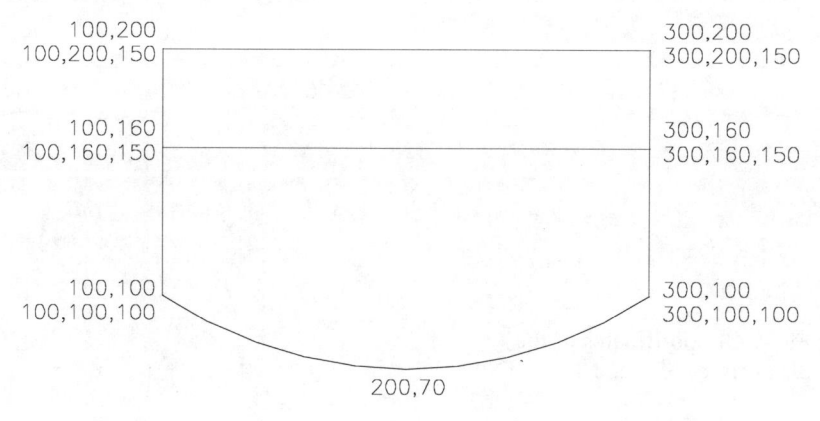

Fig. 2.17 **Edgesurf** – Second example – 3D outlines

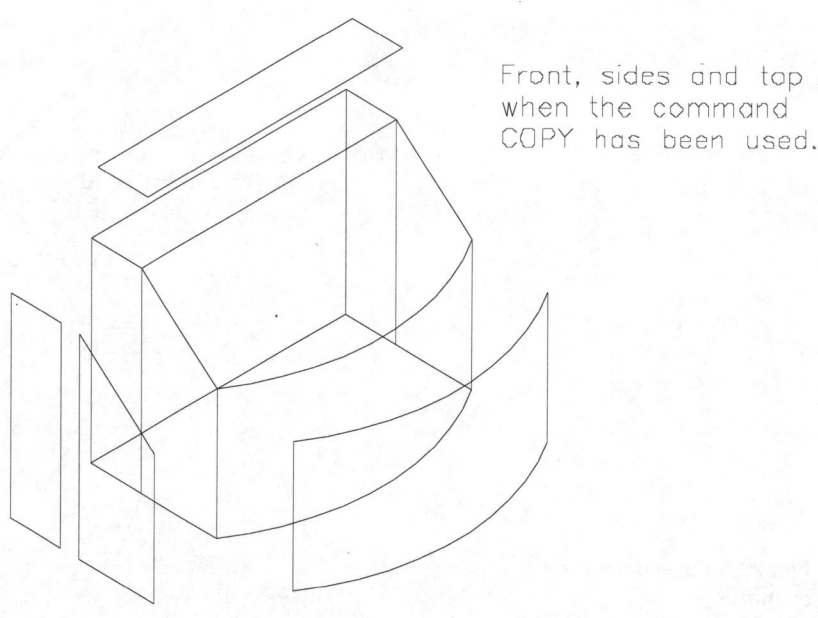

Fig. 2.18 **Edgesurf** – Second example. Stage 2 – copying sides

4. Figure 2.20 shows the completed block after the surface meshes have been move back to their original positions.

The tool Revsurf

The tool **Revsurf** can be used to construct surface meshes in the form of surfaces of revolution. The resulting 3D drawings depend upon path curves, axes of revolution and included angles of revolution. The settings of the **Surftab** variables determine the density of the surface meshes. The setting of **Surftab1** controls the density of the mesh around its circular path. The setting of **Surftab2** determines the density of the mesh in the direction of the axis of revolution. Note that the mesh density around the circular path is the same as the

3D tools from Surfaces 33

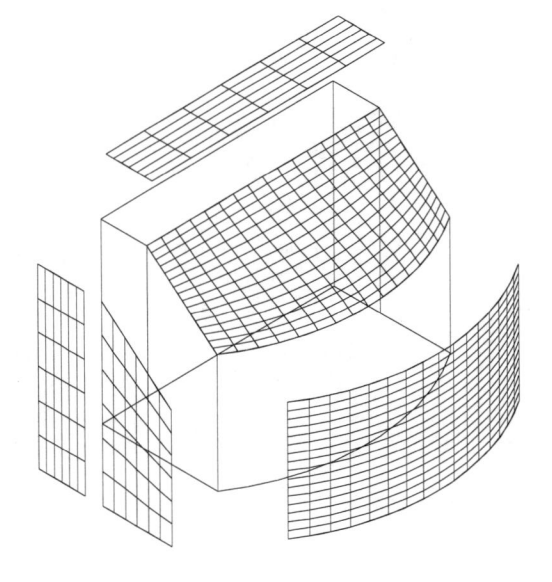

Top and sides:
    Surftab1=6;
    Surftab2=6

Slope and front:
    Surftab1=16;
    Surftab2=16.

Fig. 2.19 **Edgesurf** – Second example – Stage 3 – applying surface meshes

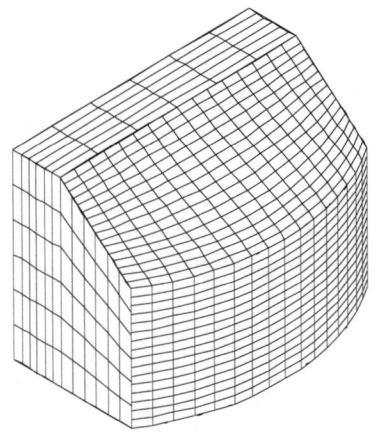

Top, slope, front and sides after using the MOVE command.

Note: Outlines of the parts have been erased.

Fig. 2.20 **Edgesurf** – Second example – Stage 4 – moving the surface meshes into their final position

Surftab1 setting regardless of the included angle. Thus, as can be seen in Fig. 2.21, when the included angle is 180° and the **Surftab1** setting is 24, the mesh density around the half circle of revolution is 24. With the included angle as a full circle, the mesh density would still be 24.

When **Revsurf** is called, the prompts at the command line follow the pattern:

Command: revsurf *right-click*
Select path curve: *pick*
Select axis of revolution: *pick*
Start angle <0>: *right-click*
Included angle (+ = cw, – = cw): *right-click*
Command:

34   An Introduction to 3D AutoCAD

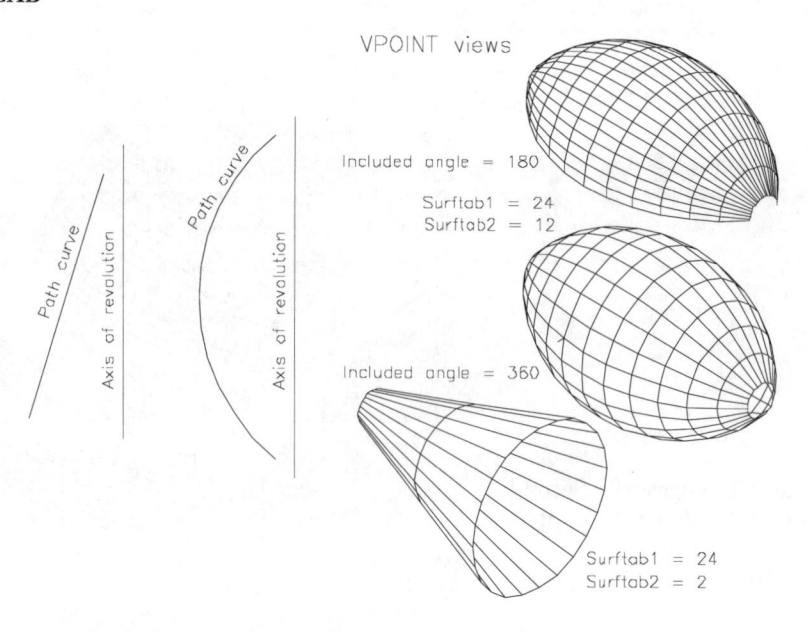

Fig. 2.21 **Revsurf** and associated **Surftab** settings

And the surface of revolution forms.

Figure 2.22 is an example of a **Revsurf** surface mesh, showing its construction. Figure 2.23 is a **Vpoint** view of the surface mesh after **Hide** has been called. Note the erasure of the axis of revolution once the surface mesh appears on screen.

Figures 2.24 and 2.25 show the construction details and a **Vpoint** view of an axle and pulley drawn as surface meshes with the aid of

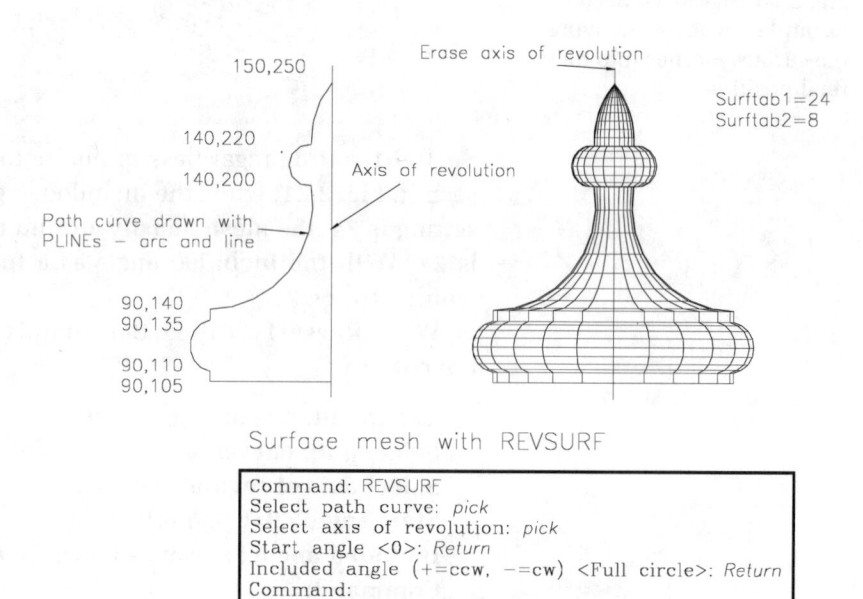

Fig. 2.22 Coordinates for a surface mesh constructed with **Revsurf**

3D tools from Surfaces 35

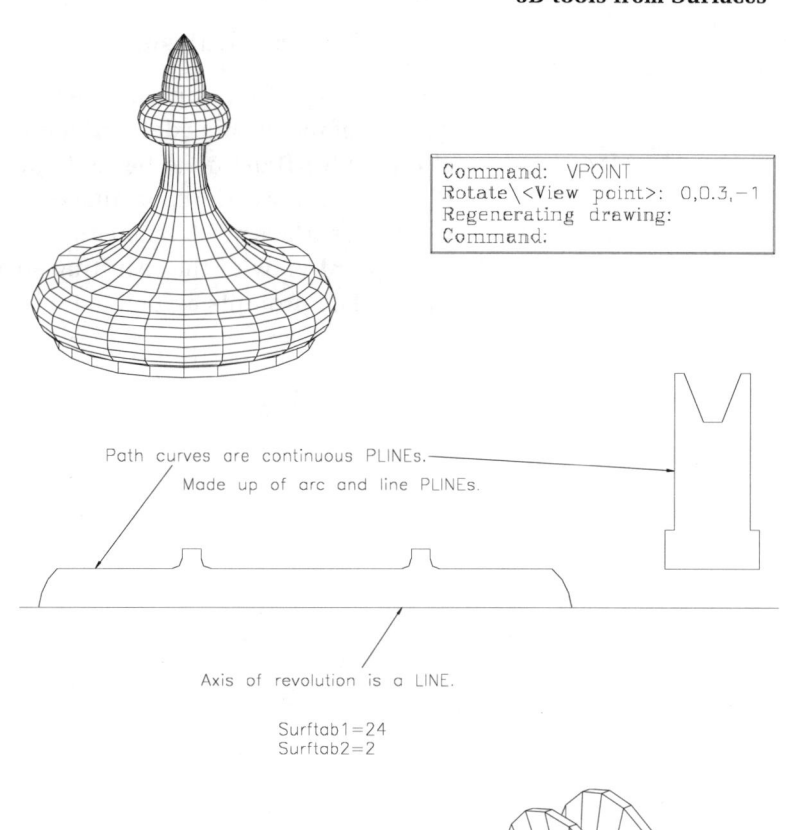

```
Command: VPOINT
Rotate\<View point>: 0,0.3,-1
Regenerating drawing:
Command:
```

Fig. 2.23 **Vpoint** of the surface mesh of Fig. 2.22

Path curves are continuous PLINEs.
Made up of arc and line PLINEs.
Axis of revolution is a LINE.
Surftab1=24
Surftab2=2

Fig. 2.24 **Revsurf** – Example. Stage 1 – **Pline** path curves and axis of revolution

VPOINT = -0.5,-1,1

Fig. 2.25 **Revsurf** – Example. Stage 2 – **Vpoint** of surface of revolution

Revsurf. Note that the path curves in this example are continuous plines. This is necessary to enable a single curve to be *picked* in response to the prompts. If the path curve had been constructed from lines and arcs, each separate line and arc would have to be picked to form the surface mesh.

The tool Rulesurf

Rulesurf will form surface meshes between lines or curves. The density of the mesh is determined solely by the setting of **Surftab1**, although **Surftab2** must be set to at least 2 for the tool to function. Figure 2.26 shows the coordinates of the 3D arcs, the prompts and the resulting surface mesh when the arcs have been selected. Figure 2.26 is a **Vpoint** view of the resulting surface mesh after **Hide** has been called. The prompts associated with the tool are:

```
Command: RULESURF
Select first defining curve: pick
Select second defining curve: pick
Command:
```

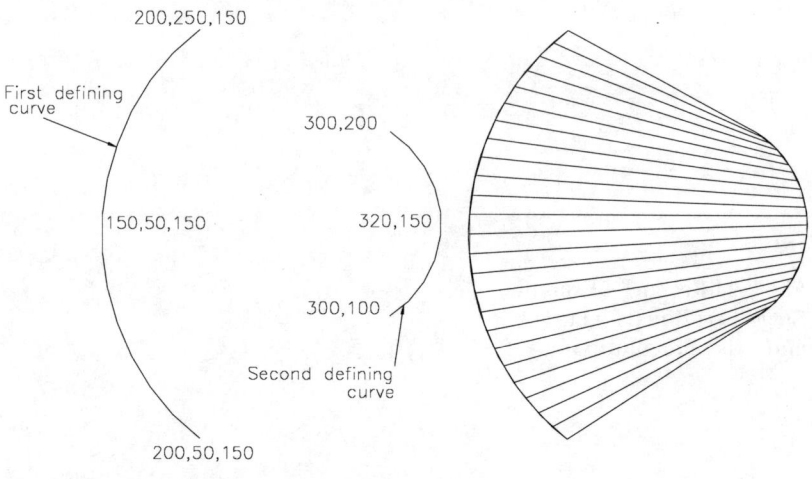

Surface mesh with RULESURF with Surftab1=24 and Surftab2=2

Fig. 2.26 **Rulesurf** – First example – defining curves of surface mesh

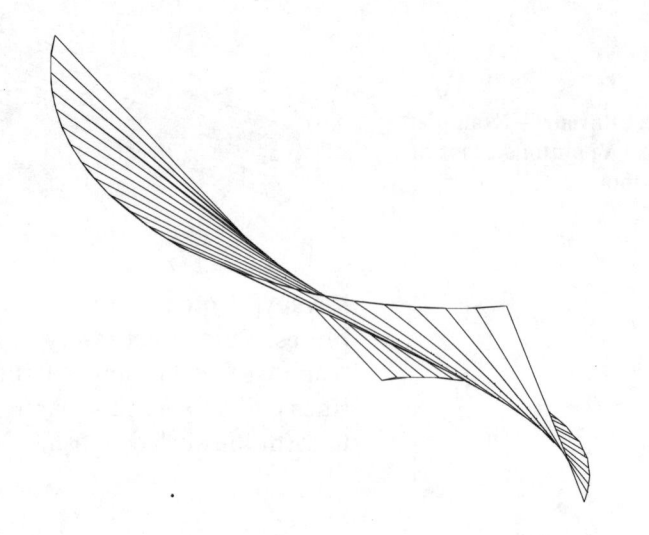

Fig. 2.27 **Rulesurf Vpoint** of Fig 2.26

3D tools from Surfaces 37

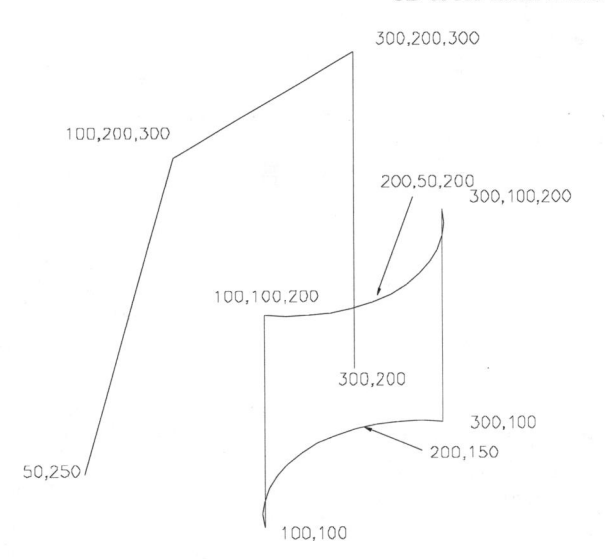

Fig. 2.28 **Rulesurf** Second example. Stage 1 – **Pline** path lines and arcs.

Command: rulesurf *right-click*
Select first defining curve: pick
Select second defining curve: *pick*
Command:

And the surface mesh forms.

Figures 2.28 to 2.30 show stages in producing a block made up from **Rulesurf** surface meshes:

1. Figure 2.28: draw the necessary defining curves;
2. Figure 2.29: copy the front arcs to make their selection as defining curves easier. Complete the **Rulesurf** meshes;

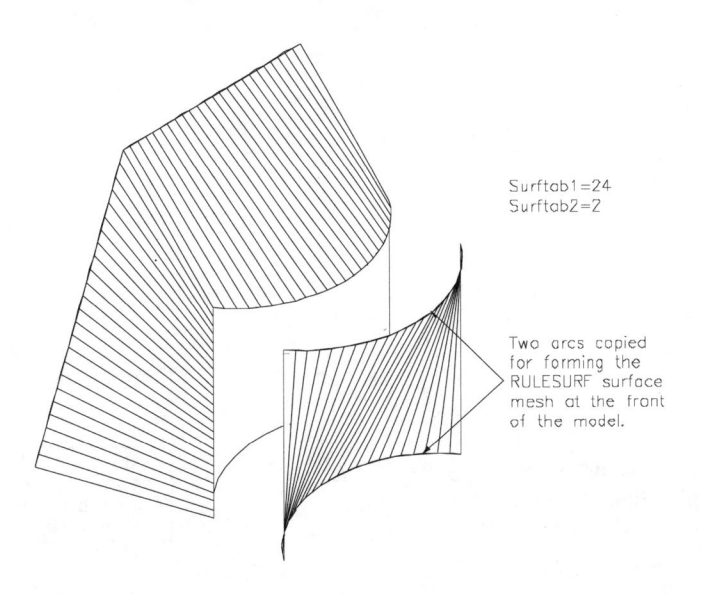

Fig. 2.29 **Rulesurf** – Second example. Stage 2 – **Vpoint** of surface mesh of Fig. 2.28 showing how front mesh is formed

38　An Introduction to 3D AutoCAD

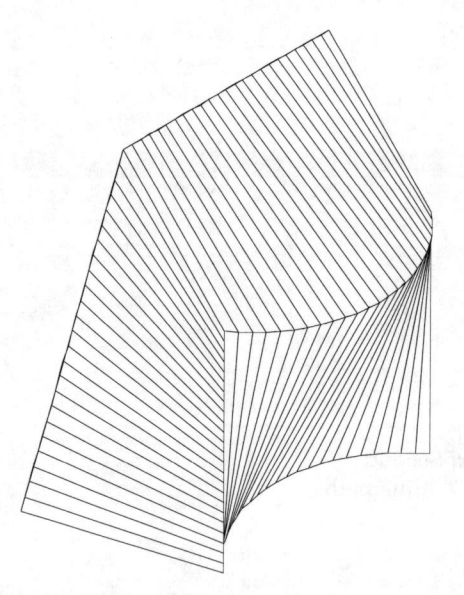

Fig. 2.30 **Rulesurf** – Second example. Stage 3 – **Vpoint** of surface mesh of Fig. 2.29 with front mesh moved to its required position

3. Figure 2.30: move the front surface mesh back into position. Use **Osnaps** to ensure exact positioning of the mesh.

The tool Tabsurf

2D **Pline** outlines can be extruded with the aid of **Tabsurf** to form surface meshes. The extrusions so produced can be compared with those formed with the aid of the **Elev**ation tool. However, whereas **Elev**ation extrusions can only occur perpendicularly to the plane on which the 2D outline is drawn, **Tabsurf** extrusions can be taken at

Outline of model drawn with PLINE.
This outline is the TABSURF path curve.

LINE drawn from 280,185 to 350,230,300
This line is the TABSURF direction vector.

Surface mesh with TABSURF
With Surftab1=4 and Surftab2=2

```
Command: TABSURF
Select path curve: pick
Select direction vector: pick
Command:
```

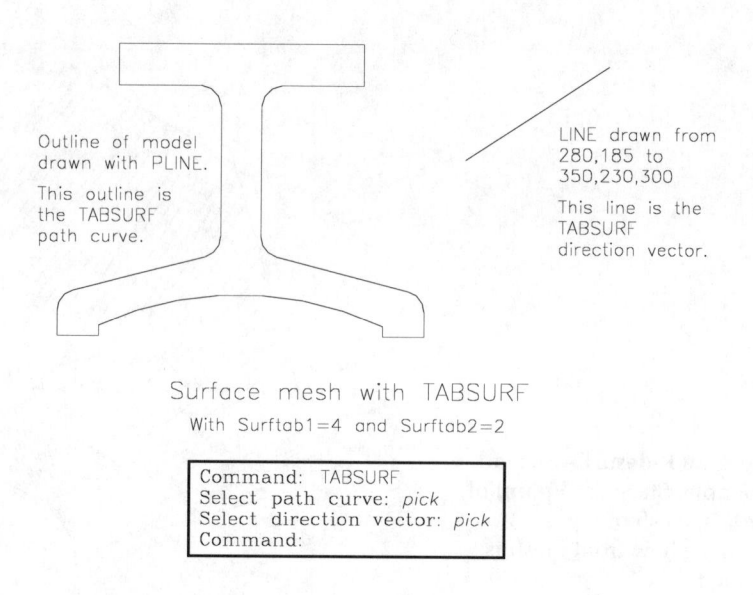

Fig. 2.31 **Tabsurf** – First example. Stage 1 – **Pline** outline and direction vector

3D tools from Surfaces

any angle to the plane. Figure 2.31 shows a pline outline of arcs and lines, together with a direction vector drawn at an angle, not perpendicular to the *x-y* plane. Figure 2.32 shows the resulting **Tabsurf** extrusion of the outline along the route indicated by the direction vector. The sequence of prompts in response to the tool being called is:

Command: tabsurf *right-click*
Select path curve: *pick*
Select direction vector: *pick*
Command:

And the extrusion is formed.

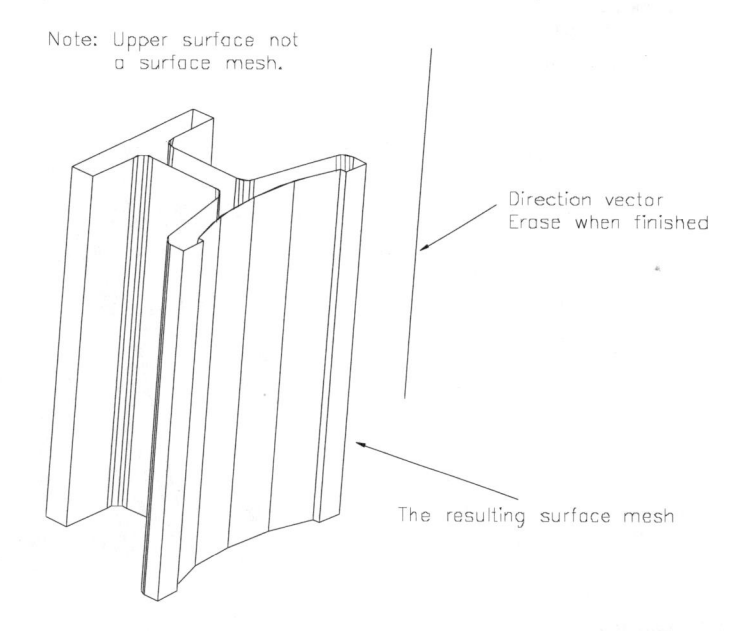

Fig. 2.32 **Tabsurf** – First example. Stage 2 – **Vpoint** of surface mesh of Fig. 2.31

Notes

1. The direction vector must not be inside or at all close to the pline outline to be extruded.
2. The length of the extrusion is governed by the length of the direction vector.
3. Only the **Surftab1** setting affects the density of the resulting surface mesh, although **Surftab2** must be set to at least 2.
4. The top surface of a **Tabsurf** extrusion does not contain a surface mesh. Thus **Hide** has no effect on hiding lines behind the upper surface of the mesh.

Figures 2.33 and 2.34 show further examples of **Tabsurf** extrusions from pline outlines and direction vectors.

40 An Introduction to 3D AutoCAD

Fig. 2.33 **Tabsurf** – Second example. Stage 1 – **Pline** outlines of three shapes

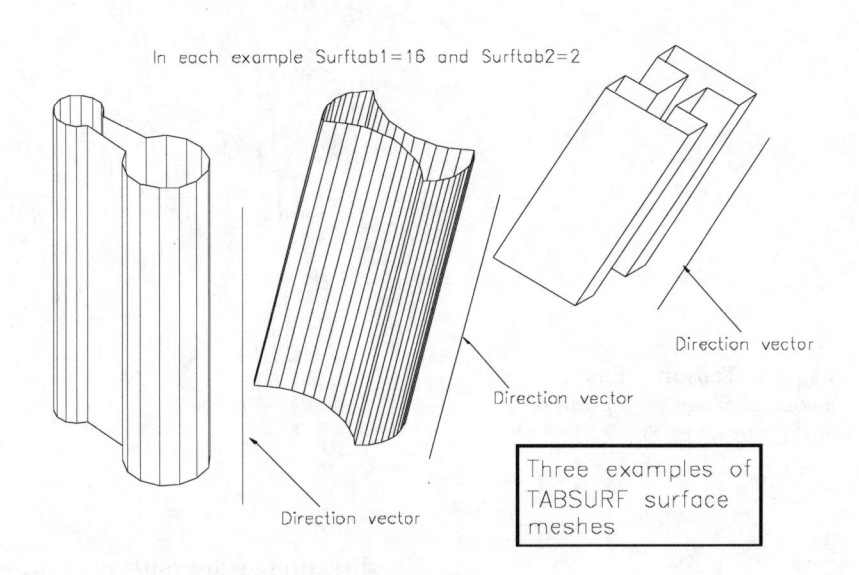

Fig. 2.34 **Tabsurf** – Second example. Stage 2 – the three surface meshes of Fig. 2.33.

The tools 3Dmesh and 3Dpoly

Surface meshes can be constructed most easily with the **Surfaces** tools mentioned previously. The two tools **3Dmesh** and **3Dpoly** are included in the AutoCAD system mainly for those operators who wish to produce AutoLisp applications or other forms of macro. Thus only a limited description of methods of constructions involving these two tools is included here.

The tool 3Dmesh

To produce the 3D mesh shown in Figures 2.35 and 2.36, the sequence of prompts and responses at the command line was:

Command: 3dmesh *right-click*
Mesh M size: 4 *right-click*
Mesh N size: 4 *right-click*
Vertex (0,0): 50,50,0 *right-click*
Vertex (0,1): 50,100,50 *right-click*
Vertex (0,2): 50,150,0 *right-click*
Vertex (0,3): 50,200,50 *right-click*
Vertex (1,0): 100,50,50 *right-click*
Vertex (1,1): 100,100,0 *right-click*
Vertex (1,2): 100,150,50 *right-click*
Vertex (1,3): 100,200,0 *right-click*
Vertex (2,0): 150,50,0 *right-click*
Vertex (2,1): 150,100,50 *right-click*
Vertex (2,2): 150,150,0 *right-click*
Vertex (2,3): 150,200,50 *right-click*
Vertex (3,0): 200,50,50 *right-click*
Vertex (3,1): 200,100,0 *right-click*
Vertex (3,2): 200,150,50 *right-click*
Vertex (3,3): 200,200,0 *right-click*
Command:

Note the order in which vertices of the M and N mesh coordinates are entered. In Fig. 2.35 the M mesh size corresponds to the vertices

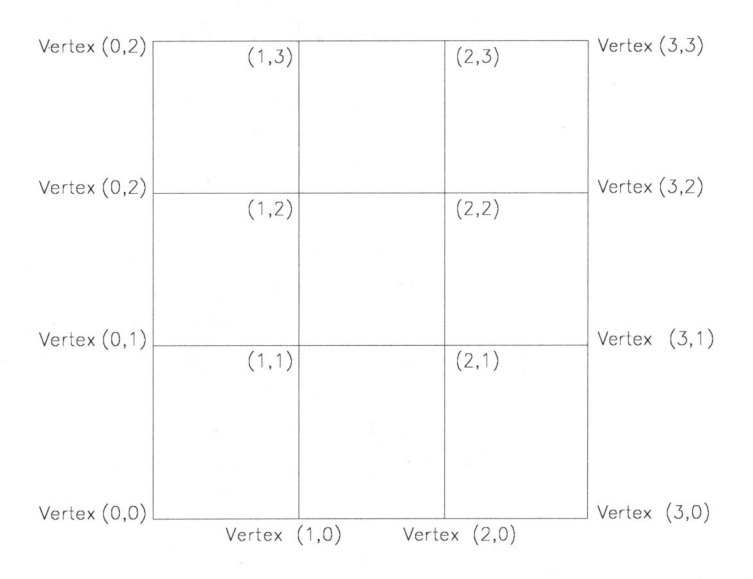

Fig. 2.35 Plan view in the WCS of a 4 × 4 surface mesh formed with **3Dmesh**

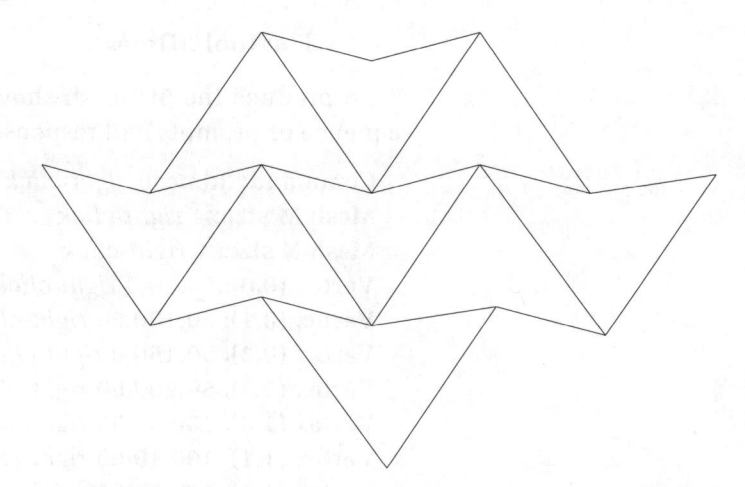

Fig. 2.36 **Vpoint** view of the surface mesh of Fig. 2.35

and the N mesh size corresponds to the horizontal vertices. Figure 2.36 is a **Vpoint** view of the resulting mesh. Note that the mesh numbers refer to the number of lines each way in the surface mesh.

The tool 3DPOLY

The tool **Pline** can only be used in one plane. It cannot therefore be called to draw a 3D polyline. 3D polylines can be drawn with the aid of the tool **3Dpoly**. When the tool is called, the command line shows:

Command: 3dpoly *right-click*
From point: *pick* or *enter* 3D coordinates *right-click*
Close/Undo/<Endpoint of line>: *pick* or *enter* 3D coordinates *right-click*
Close/Undo/<Endpoint of line>: *pick* or *enter* 3D coordinates *right-click*
Close/Undo/<Endpoint of line>: *pick* or *enter* 3D coordinates *right-click*
Close/Undo/<Endpoint of line>: *pick* or *enter* 3D coordinates *right-click*

And continue *picking* or *entering* points of coordinates until either the line is completed without closing (*right-click*) or, as a closed pline by *entering* c (Close). Keying u (Undo) will undo the last part of the pline to be drawn. Note that the width of a **3Dpoly** cannot be changed. It is always of zero thickness. Neither are arcs possible with this tool.

The tool Pface

The surface mesh of Fig., 2.38 was formed with the aid of the tool **Pface**. The sequence of prompts and responses at the command line was:

Command: pface *right-click*
Vertex 1: 100,300,0 *right-click*
Vertex 2: 100,200,50 *right-click*
Vertex 3: 100,100,0 *right-click*
Vertex 4: 200,100,50 *right-click*
Vertex 5: 300,100,0 *right-click*
Vertex 6: 300,200,50 *right-click*
Vertex 7: 300,300,0 *right-click*
Vertex 8: 200,300,50 *right-click*
Vertex 9: *right-click*
Face 1, vertex 1: 1 *right-click*
Face 1, vertex 2: 2 *right-click*
Face 1, vertex 3: 3 *right-click*
Face 1, vertex 4: 4 *right-click*
Face 1, vertex 5: 5 *right-click*
Face 1, vertex 6: 6 *right-click*
Face 1, vertex 7: 7 *right-click*
Face 1, vertex 8: 8 *right-click*
Face 1, vertex 9: 9 *right-click*
Face 1, vertex 10: *right-click*
Face 2, vertex 1: 1 *right-click*
Face 2, vertex 2: 8 *right-click*
Face 2, vertex 3: 7 *right-click*
Face 2, vertex 4: 2 *right-click*
Face 2, vertex 5: 1 *right-click*
Face 2, vertex 6: *right-click*
Face 3, vertex 1: 2 *right-click*
Face 3, vertex 2: 3 *right-click*
Face.3, vertex 3: 4 *right-click*
Face 3, vertex 4: 5 *right-click*
Face 3, vertex 5: 6 *right-click*
Face 3, vertex 6: 1 *right-click*
Face 3, vertex 7: *right-click*
Face 4, vertex 1: *right-click*
Command:

And the set of three polyfaces appears on screen – Figs. 2.37 and 2.38.

44 An Introduction to 3D AutoCAD

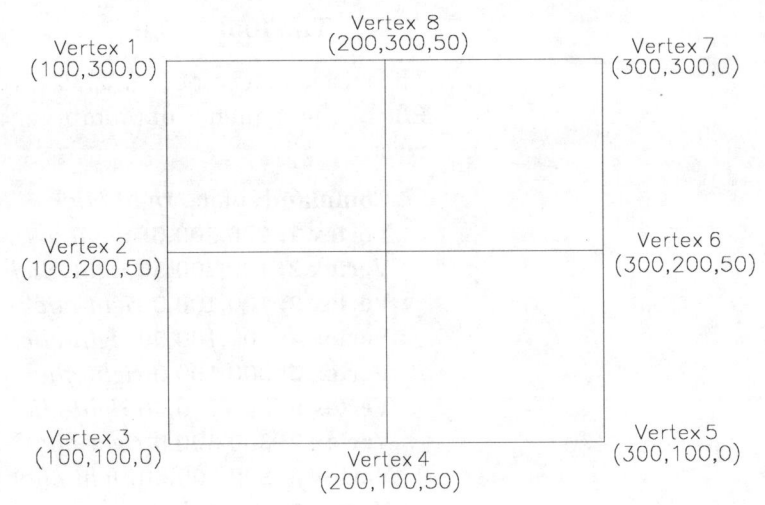

Fig. 2.37 Plan view in the WCS of a surface mesh formed with **Pface**

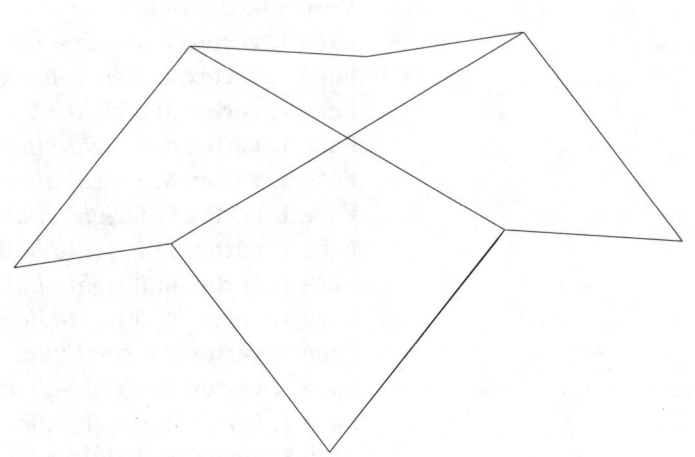

Fig. 2.38 **Vpoint** view of the mesh of Fig. 2.37

3D Objects

If working in AutoCAD Release 12 *left-click* on **Draw** in the menu bar, followed by another *left-click* on **Surfaces** in the pull-down menu which appears, followed by another *left-click* on **3D Objects** in the **Surfaces** sub-menu (Fig. 2.39) and the **3D Objects** dialogue box appears (Fig. 2.40). If working in the Windows version of Release 13, bring the **Surfaces** toolbar on screen. The tool icons for the **3D Objects** can then be selected from the **Surfaces** toolbar (Fig. 2.41). Alternatively 3dobjects can be *entered* at the command line from the keyboard. No matter which of these methods is used, the 3D Objects file (**3d.lsp**) must be loaded before the tools can be used. As an example, calling for 3D Objects results in the following at the command line:

3D tools from Surfaces

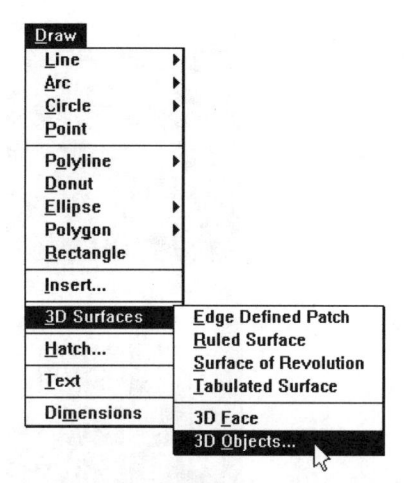

Fig. 2.39 Selecting **3D Objects** from the **3D Surfaces** sub-menu of the **Draw** pull-down menu in AutoCAD for Windows

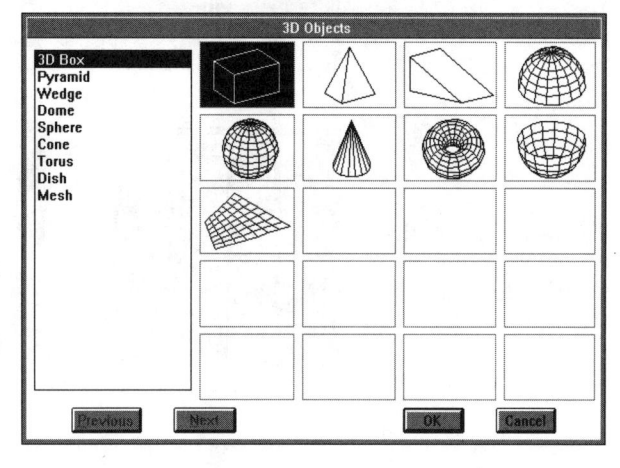

Fig. 2.40 The **3D Objects** dialogue box which appears on screen in AutoCAD for Windows when **3D Objects** is selected

Command: 3dobjects *right-click*
Initializing... 3D objects loaded.

After a short delay the **3D Objects** are loaded into memory from the **3d.lsp** file.

As an example of the use of the tool **Sphere**, one of the **3D Objects**, when it is selected either from the **3D objects** dialogue box (R12), from the **Surfaces** toolbar, or by entering the tool name, the command line shows:

Command: sphere *right-click*
Center of sphere *pick* or *enter* coordiinates
Diameter/<Radius>: *pick* or *enter* a number
Number of longitudinal segments <16>: *right-click* or *enter* another number
Number of latitudinal segments <16>: *right-click* or *enter* another number
Command:

46 An Introduction to 3D AutoCAD

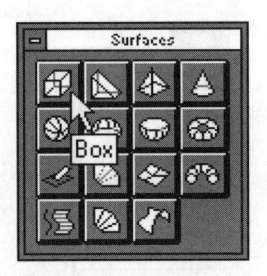

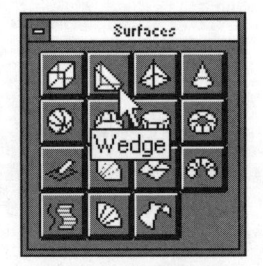

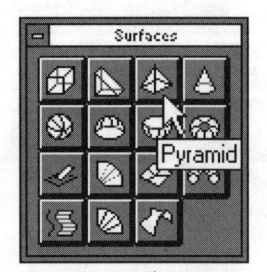

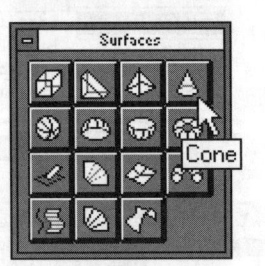

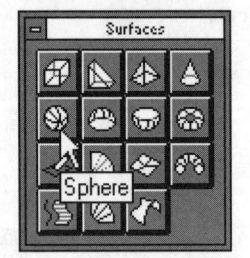

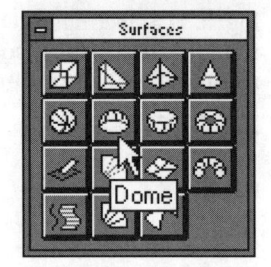

Fig. 2.41 The tool icons for the **3D Objects** with their tool tips from the **Surfaces** toolbar in AutoCAD Release 13 for Windows

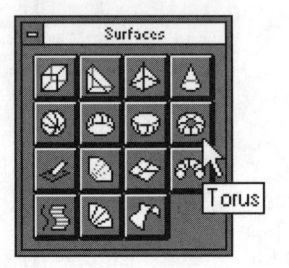

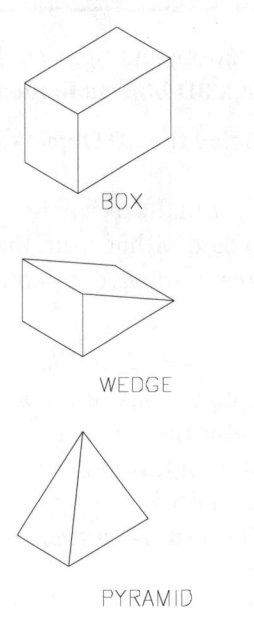

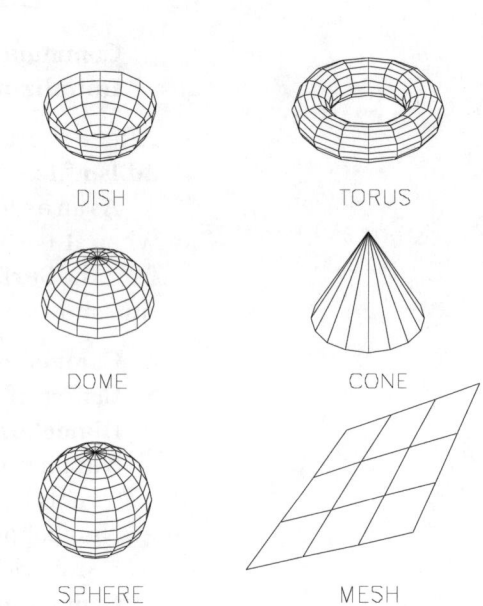

Fig. 2.42 **Vpoint** drawings of each of the **3D Objects**

3D tools from Surfaces 47

If working in Release 13, no matter which of the 3D objects is being called, the tool name must be preceded with **ai_**. Thus to call the **3D Objects tool** sphere when working in Release 13:

Command: ai_sphere *right-click*

And the 3D sphere appears on screen. Similar prompts appear for the other **3D Objects**. Figure 2.42 shows all the **3D Objects** which can be constructed. When constructing 3D drawings involving **3D Objects**, the command line prompts for each of the objects are easy to follow.

Some 3D model drawings can be constructed either wholly from, or partly from, 3D objects. Two examples are given in Fig. 2.43.

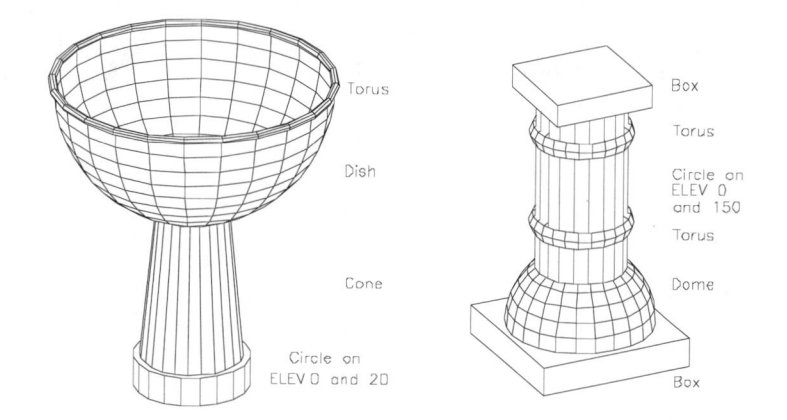

Fig. 2.43 Two 3D model drawings formed from 3D Objects and cylinders from circles in **Elev**ation

Figure 2.44 is a **Revsurf** drawing of a vase. The pline from which the 3D drawing was revolved is given in Fig. 2.45. The procedure for drawing the pline was:

1. The **Pline** was drawn to the required outline.
2. The **Pline** was offset by 0.5 units.
3. The upper ends of the **Pline** were joined by a pline arc.
4. The three plines – the two plines plus the pline arc – were joined with the aid of the **Pedit** (Edit Polyline) tool.
5. The solid of revolution was then formed with the **Revsurf** tool.

Figure 2.46 is an example of a 3D drawing constructed from **Edgesurf** and **Revsurf** surface meshes.

48   An Introduction to 3D AutoCAD

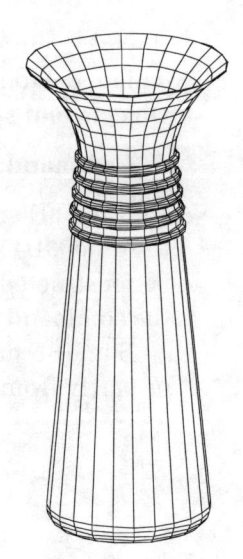

Fig. 2.44 **Vpoint** of a vase
drawn with the aid of **Revsurf**

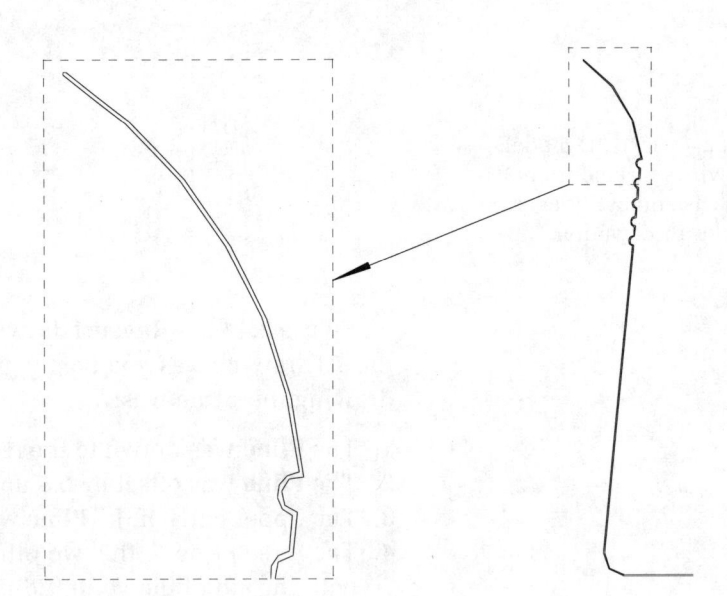

Fig. 2.45 The **Plines** on which
Fig. 2.44 are based

3D tools from Surfaces 49

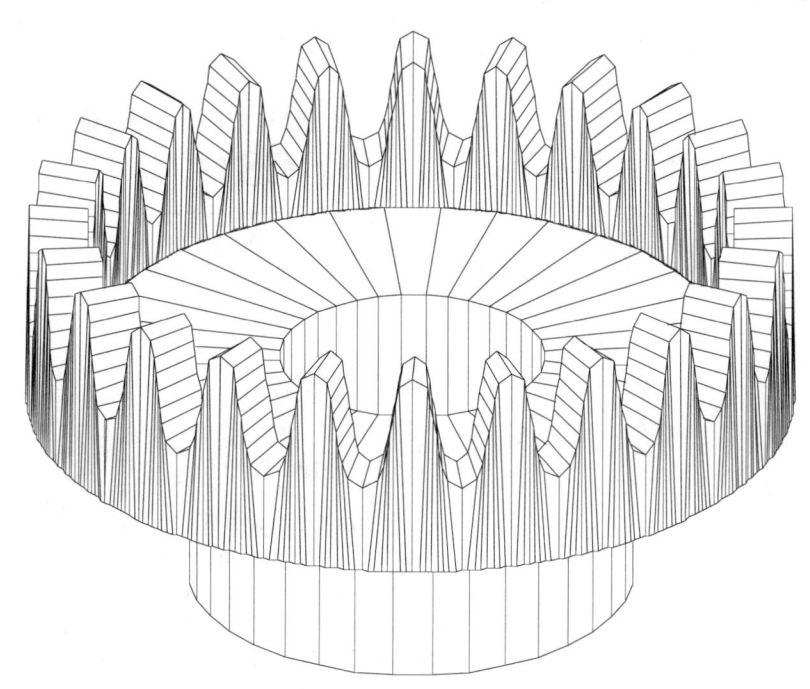

Fig. 2.46 An example of a 3D solid model drawing constructed with the aid of the tools **Edgesurf** and **Revsurf**

CHAPTER 3

The User Coordinate System (UCS)

Introduction

The User Coordinate System (UCS) enables the user to determine new positions at any angle or slope for the *x,y* plane on which to construct drawings. This allows details to be constructed on a new UCS surface as if working in the original *x,y* plane (World Coordinate System or WCS). To work freely within the UCS, the two system variables **UCSicon** and **UCSfollow** must first be set.

The variable UCSicon

Command: setvar *right-click*
Variable name or ?: ucsicon *right-click*
New value for UCSICON <0>: 3 *right-click*
Command:

If set at 1, the icon is displayed at the WCS origin or as near as is possible to the WCS origin.

If set to 3, the icon is displayed at the UCS origin, no matter where the origin is set. The UCS origin is set under the UCS tool prompts (see later in this chapter).

In fact, the two settings of the set variable **UCSicon** are either 1, or the sum of 1 and 2. If 2 is the response the icon disappears from screen.

The UCS icon can also be turned on or off as follows:

Command: ucsicon *right-click*
ON/OFF/All/Noorigin/ORigin <ON>: off *right-click*
Command:

The prompts have the following meanings:
1. **ON** – the UCS icon appears on screen.
2. **OFF** – the UCS icon disappears from the screen.

The User Coordinate System (UCS) 51

3. **A**ll – when working in viewports (see Chapter 4), the UCS icon will appear in, or disappear, from all viewports, if **a** (All) is given as a response after the icon has been turned **ON** or **OFF**.
4. **N**oorigin – when **n** is *entered* as a response, the icon goes as near to the bottom left-hand corner of the graphics area as possible.
5. **OR**igin – when **or** is entered as a response, the icon goes to the actual origin (0,0,0), no matter where the origin is on screen. Note that the origin can be changed by stating its *x,y* coordinates, or *picking* a point on a 3D drawing in response the **UCS** prompt **OR**igin.

The UCS icon

The UCS icon takes on a variety of forms (Fig. 3.1) depending upon the setting of the UCS. If the UCS is set so that it can only be viewed from edge on or nearly edge on, a broken pencil icon appears on screen. This gives a warning that the UCS may have been set wrongly, or that the system variable **UCSfollow** is not **ON** (1). Note the **PSpace** icon in Fig. 3.1, details of which will be given in Chapter 4.

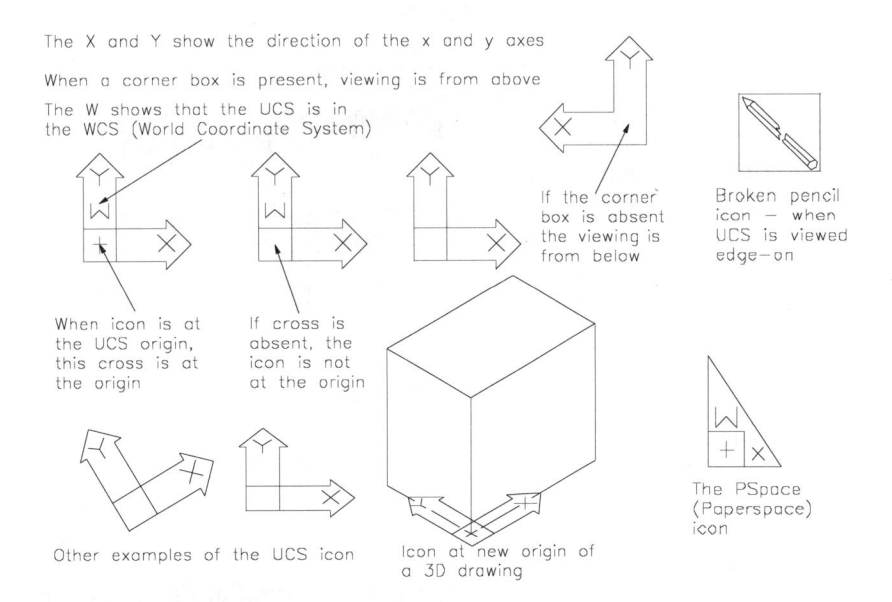

Fig. 3.1 The UCS icon in a variety of forms

The variable UCSFOLLOW

Command: ucsfollow *right-click*
New value for UCSFOLLOW <0>: 1 *right-click*
Command:

52 An Introduction to 3D AutoCAD

If set to 0 (off), the UCS remains in the World Coordinate System (WCS) position. The UCS fails to respond to responses to prompts to the UCS tool. If set to 1 (on), The UCS will be reset when a new response is made to the UCS tool prompts.

The tool UCS

In either AutoCAD R12 or R13, the UCS can be set to predetermined positions by selecting **Presets...** from the **UCS** menu of the **Settings** pull-down menu (R12), or with a *left-click* on the tool icon **Preset UCS** in the **UCS** toolbar (R13). In either case, the **UCS Orientation** dialogue box appears, from which the required preset UCS can be selected – a *left-click* in the panel holding the icon for the required setting, followed by another *left-click* on the **OK** button of the dialogue box. Figures 3.2 to 3.4 show the menu, toolbar and dialogue box.

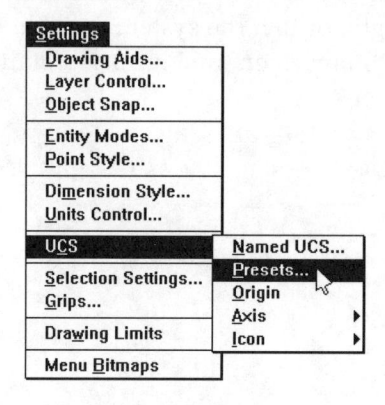

Fig. 3.2 Selecting **Presets..** from the **UCS** sub-menu of the **Settings** pull-down menu (R12)

Fig. 3.3 Selecting **UCS Presets...** from the **UCS** toolbar (R13)

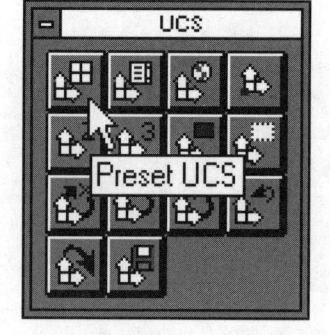

If **UCS** is *entered* at the command line, the following prompts appear:

Command: ucs *right-click*
Origin/ZAxis/3point/OBject/View/X/Y/Z/Restore/Save/Del/?/
   <World>:

The User Coordinate System (UCS) 53

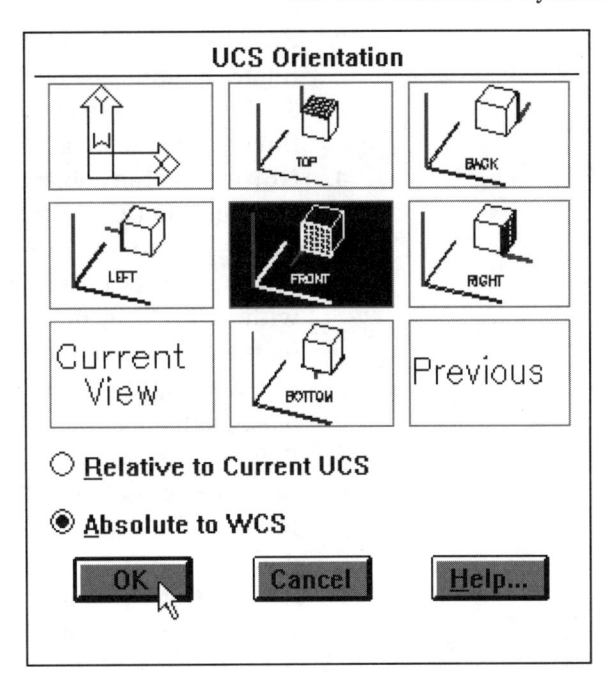

Fig. 3.4 The **UCS Orientation** dialogue box common to R12 and R13

These prompts have the following meanings:

1. **O**rigin – this resets the origin to a new *entered* or *picked* point.

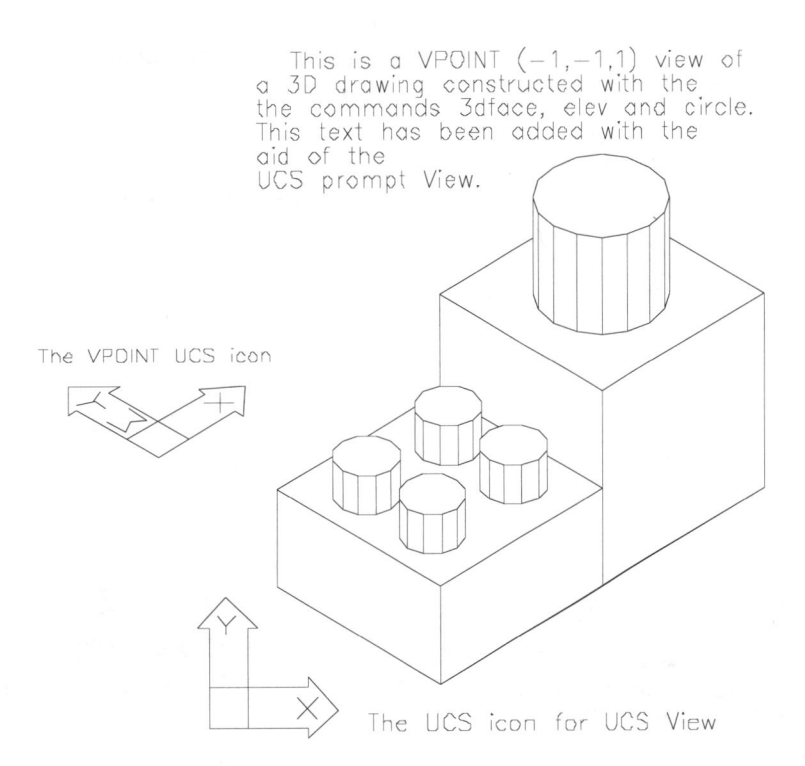

Fig. 3.5 A **Vpoint** view placed in **UCS View** so as to allow text to be added

2. **ZA**xis – *pick* two points on a new z axis and the UCS *x-y* plane rotates around this new axis to its new position.
3. **3**point – *pick* three points on screen (or *enter* the coordinates of three points) to obtain a new position for the UCS.
4. **OB**ject – pick any object (entity) on screen – line, arc, edge of plane etc., and the UCS aligns itself with the picked object.
5. **V**iew – the coordinate system reverts as if perpendicular to the screen – e.g. if the drawing editor is in a **Vpoint** viewing position, with a **UCS View** option, text can be added in a vertical position on the screen (see Fig. 3.5).
6. **X/Y/Z** – *entering* either of these, followed by *entering* the figures of an angle, places the UCS at an angle to the *x*, *y* or *z* axes.
7. **P**revious – brings on screen the last UCS to be used.
8. **R**estore – restores a named UCS which has been saved to the **S**ave prompt. Fig. 3.6 shows named saved UCS in the **UCS Control** dialogue box.
9. **S**ave – see Restore above.
10. **D**el – deletes a named UCS.
11. **?** – and pressing *Return* twice brings a list such as that shown below, of previously saved UCS planes on screen:

Current UCS: *WORLD*
Saved coordinate systems:
DOOR
  Origin = <150,100,0>, X Axis = <1,1,0>
  Y Axis = <0,0,1>, Z Axis = <1,-1,0>
FRONT
  Origin = <130,100,0>,
  Y Axis = <0,0,1>, Z Axis = 0,-1,0>
LEFT

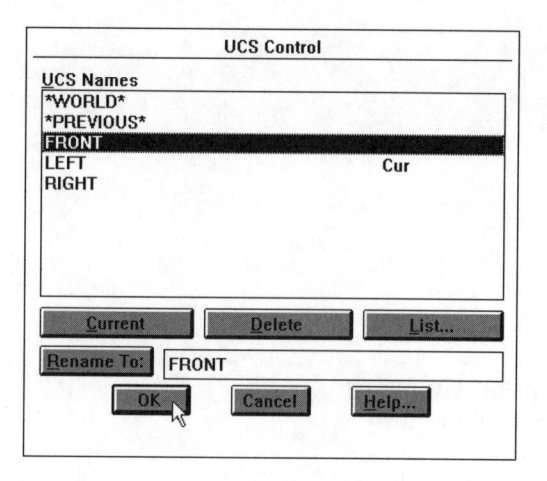

Fig. 3.6 **Save**d UCS settings showing in the **UCS Control** dialogue box

The User Coordinate System (UCS)

　　　Origin = <130,100,0>, X Axis = <0,1,0>
　　　Y Axis = <0,0,1>, Z Axis = <1,0,0>
　　RIGHT
　　　Origin = <240,100,0>, X Axis = <0,1,0>
　　　Y Axis = <0,0,1>, Z Axis = <1,0,0>
　　ROOF
　　　Origin = <240,100,0>, X Axis = <0,1,1>
　　　Y Axis = <1,0,0>, Z Axis = <0,1,-1>
　　ROOF1
　　　Origin = <240,155,125>, X Axis = <0,1,-1>
　　　Y Axis = <1,0,0>, Z Axis = <0,-1,-1>

12. **W**orld – restores the World Coordinate System (WCS)

Warning

Unless care is taken when setting a new UCS plane, the results may not be as expected. An example of problems which may arise is given in Figures 3.7 and 3.8. As can be seen from Fig. 3.7, if, while in the World Coordinate System (WCS), a UCS **3point** is required, the new UCS comes up, as expected when a positive value for the z coordinate is entered. That is – in the new UCS (really the front view of the 3D boxes) – the boxes appear above the WCS x-y plane. Note that the responses to the UCS **3point** option in this case will be:

Command: ucs *right-click*
**Origin/ZAxis/3point/OBject/View/X/Y/Z/Restore/Save/Del/?/
　<World>:** 3 (3point) *right-click*

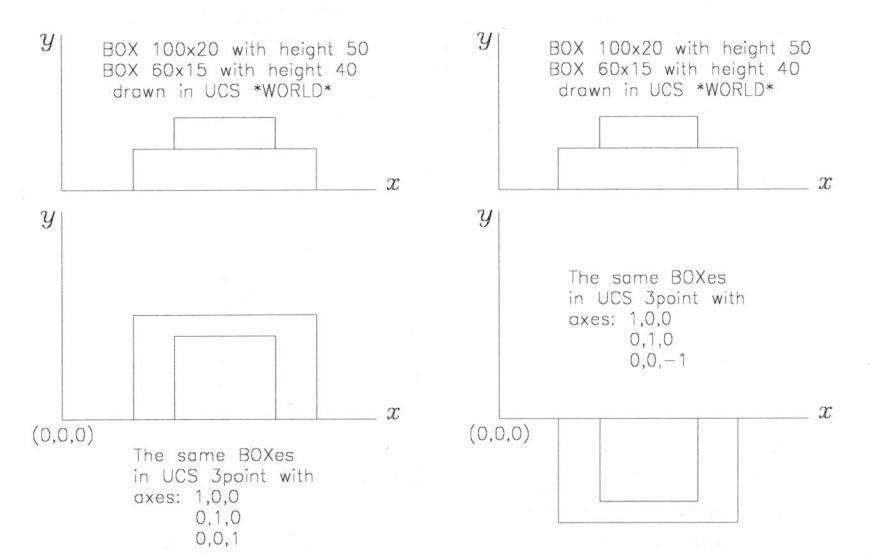

Fig. 3.7 Problems which may arise when setting a new UCS plane with **3point**

56 An Introduction to 3D AutoCAD

Origin point <0,0,0>: *right-click*
Point on positive portion of the X-Axis <1,0,0>: *right-click*
Point on positive-Y portion of the UCS X-Y plane <0,1,0>: 0,0,1
   right-click
Regenerating drawing.
Command: z (Zoom) *right-click*
All/Center/Dynamic/Extents/Left/Previous/Vmax/Window/<Scale (X/XP)>: 1 *right-click*
Command:

If a negative value for the z coordinate is *entered*, the boxes will appear below the WCS x-y plane.

If a new UCS **3point** is required when a new UCS has appeared on screen, with the same boxes as were drawn in the WCS, the boxes will appear above the x-y plane in the UCS only if a negative value for the z coordinate is *entered*. This is shown in Fig. 3.8.

The same precautions apply when rotating about x, y and z, in response to the **X/Y/Z** options of the UCS tool system. A positive angle will be necessary in most cases.

This is because a positive rotation of the x-y plane around the x, y or z axes will be in an anticlockwise direction looking towards the origin (0,0,0). The direction of rotation is covered by the **right-hand rule**;

The right-hand rule

Imagine you are gripping the axis in your right hand and the thumb of that hand is pointing towards the direction of the positive value

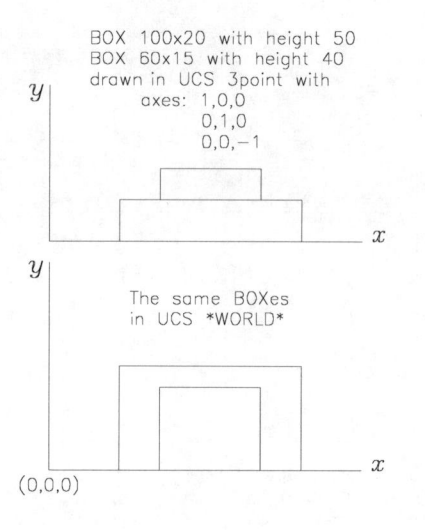

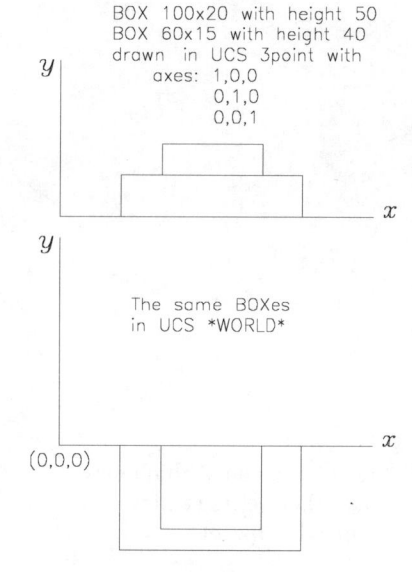

Fig. 3.8 Further problems with the UCS **3point** option

The User Coordinate System (UCS)　57

of the axis (away from the origin). The tips of your fingers are pointing in the positive direction of rotation.

Calling a new User Coordinate System

A new UCS can be set by *entering* responses to the **UCS** tool prompts as shown above. Another method is to *pick* **UCS Presets...** from the **UCS** sub-menu of the **Settings** pull-down menu (Fig. 3.2 on page 52) and select a required new UCS from the **UCS Orientation** dialogue box which appears (Fig. 3.4). However, if a new UCS plane is required which is not available from those shown in the **UCS Orientation** dialogue box, then the operator will need to resort to *entering* responses to the **UCS** prompts options.

An example of a 3D drawing with the aid of the UCS

An example of some of the various settings of the UCS is given in Figures 3.9 and 3.10 showing the stages of drawing a 3D model of a simple electronics control box.

1. Stage 1 – Fig. 3.9. Drawing 1. A **Vpoint** view of the outline of the box, including overall dimensions, has been drawn in the WCS (UCS – World) with **3Dface**s.
2. Stage 2 – Fig. 3.9. Drawing 2. By setting **Elev** at various settings, draw the three parts of the aerial.

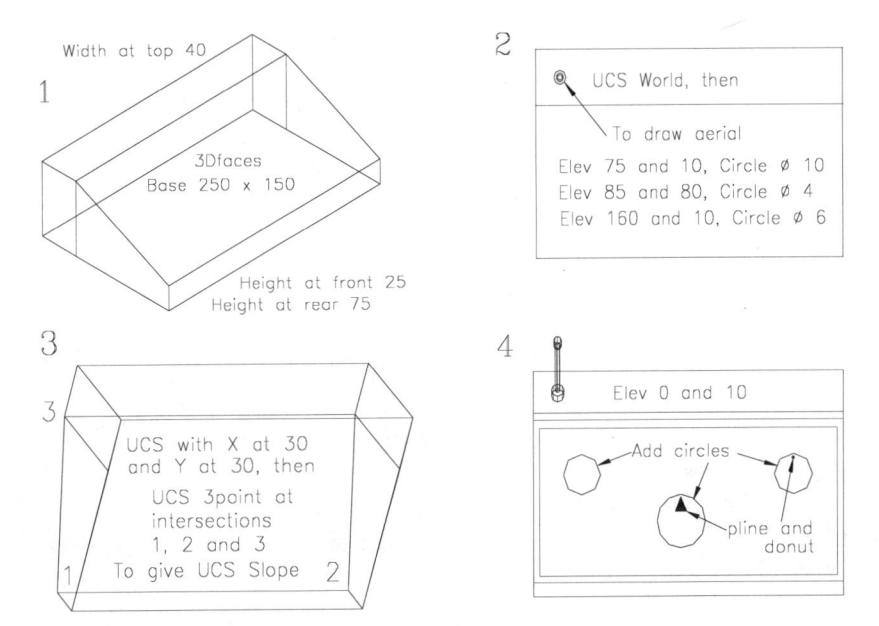

Fig. 3.9 Stages 1 to 4 in constructing a 3D model drawing with the aid of the **UCS**

58 An Introduction to 3D AutoCAD

3. Stage 3 – Fig. 3.9. Drawing 3. The procedure is as follows:
   (a) Call **UCS**, *enter* X, set at 30.
   (b) Call **UCS**, *enter* Y, set at 30.
   (c) Call **UCS**, *enter* 3, pick points 1, 2 and 3 in response to the prompts which appear at the command line. This results in the **UCS** being set with the sloping face flat on the screen surface. Use **Osnaps** if necessary (Drawing 4 of Fig. 3.9).
4. Stage 4 – Fig. 3.9. Drawing 4. Follow the steps:
   (a) In this **UCS** set **Elev** to 0 and 10 and add the circles of the controls;
   (b) Set **Elev** to 10 and 0 and add a doughnut and a pline triangle to the top of the control knob.
5. Stage 5 – Fig. 3.10. Drawing 5. Set **Elev** to 0 and 0 and add details of control settings and the pline box and text.
6. Stage 6 – Fig. 3.10. Drawing 6. Call **UCS World**. Set **Elev** to 75 and 0. Add pline box and text.
7. Stage 7 – Fig. 3.10. Drawing 7. Set **Elev** back to 0 and 0. Call **Vpoint** and *enter* -1,-1,1. Call **Hide**.

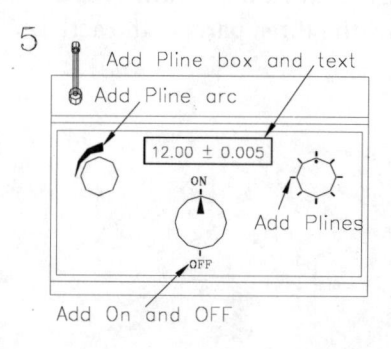

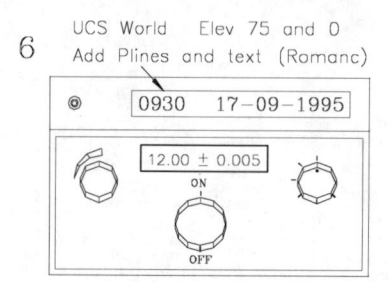

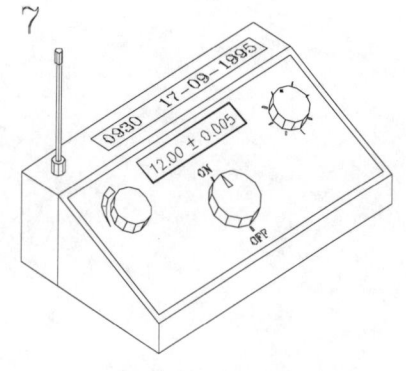

Fig. 3.10 Stages 5 to 7 in constructing a 3D model in the **UCS**

Notes on the UCS

1. The set variable **UCSfollow** must be **ON** (set at 1) in order that a new UCS can be set.
2. If the UCSicon is to indicate the Origin of a new **UCS**, the set variable **UCSicon** must be set **ON** and set to 3.
3. When a new **UCS** has been selected – by using any of the prompts – call **Zoom** and *enter* the figure 1, in order to re-scale the resulting drawing on screen.
4. No matter which prompt has been employed, the Origin (0,0,0) will rarely be in the same position on screen as when in the WCS. If determining points by means of coordinates in a new UCS check where the Origin is.
5. When rotating the UCS through 90° with the aid of the **X**, **Y** or **Z** prompts, the UCS will be rotated through 90° around the *x*, *y* or *z* screen axes, unless a new Origin is selected after answering **o** (Origin) in the UCS prompts. The result of not selecting a new Origin for an *x*-axis rotation is shown in Fig. 3.12.
6. When rotating the UCS around the *x*-axis, the UCS prompts need to be answered twice (or even three times):

    (a) Set a new origin by *entering* **o** (Origin), *right-click* and *pick* the required new origin. This sets the origin and the UCS icon appears at the selected origin (If **UCSicon** is set at 3).

    (b) *Enter* X *right-click*. Then *enter* the required angle of rotation *right-click*. The new UCS will appear (if **UCSfollow** is set to 1).

    (c) *Enter* **s** (Save) *right-click* and *enter* a suitable UCS name to save the new UCS under that name.

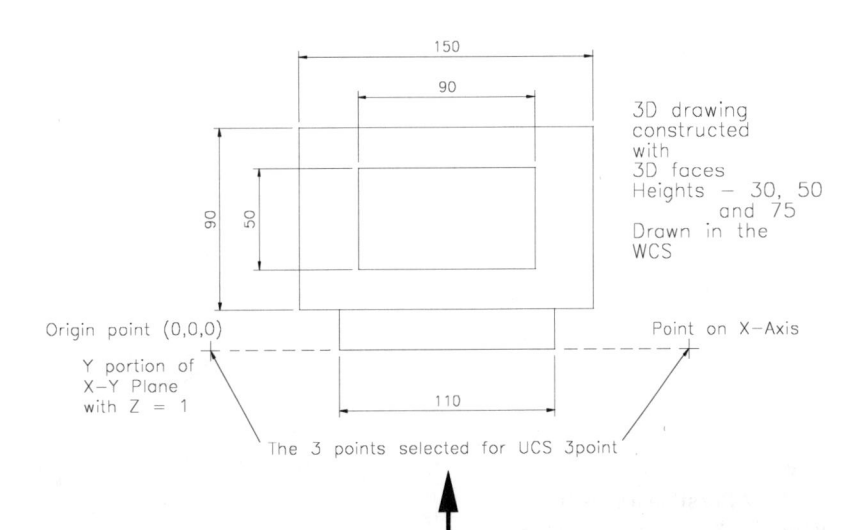

Fig. 3.11 Selection of points for a **3point** UCS

7. When rotating with the aid of the **3point** prompt, the rotation takes place around the operator's chosen axis. As an example Fig. 3.11 is a 3D model drawing constructed with the aid of **3Dface** in the WCS. If a view looking at the front of the block is required, the UCS can be changed by answering with either **X** or **3point** to the UCS prompts. Figure 3.12 compares the results of adding a cylinder with the aid of **Elev** and **Circle** while in each of the UCS planes called with the **X** prompt (without selecting a new Origin) and with the **3point** prompt.
8. When using the **3point** option:
   (a) A rubber band, connected to the first point selected, keeps the operator aware of the previous selections. It is advisable to have **Blipmode** set **ON** because the blips then show the selected points.
   (b) If selecting the three points while in the WCS, the first two points can be picked, then *enter* the filter **.xy** then, when **(need Z)** appears, *entering* any number will set the new 3point UCS. As with **Vpoint**, the coordinate number *entered* indicates only the direction of the required axis, not its length. The final prompt of the 3point series is:

   Point on the positive-Y portion of the UCS XY plane :

   This can be answered with any figure – usually 1.

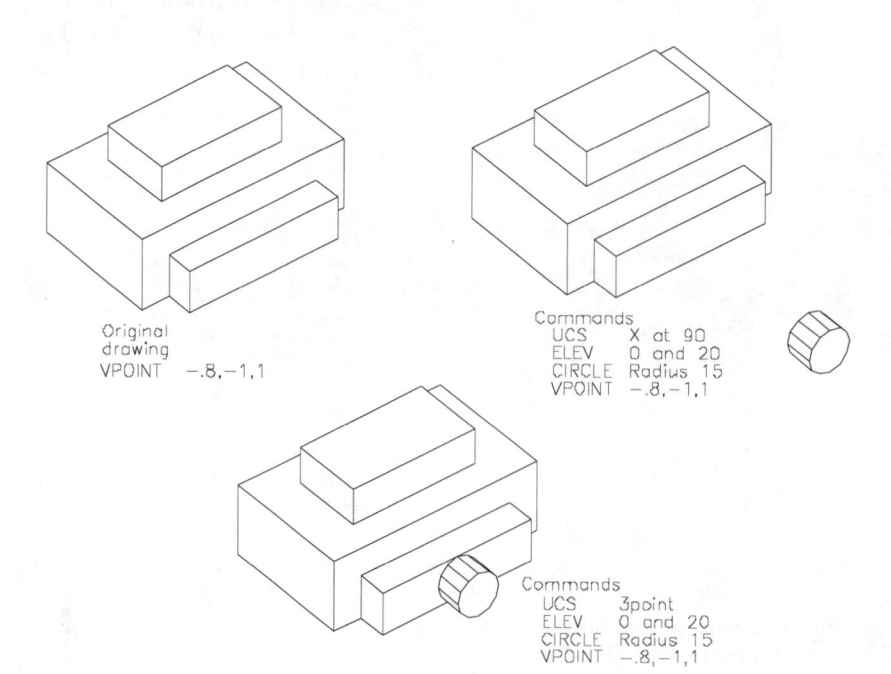

Fig. 3.12 Possible errors in using the **X** option of the UCS

The User Coordinate System (UCS)   61

Fig. 3.13 The **UCS** on-screen menus from AutoCAD R12 (DOS version)

Exercises

This group of exercises is included here to allow the reader to practise the 3D tools explained in this chapter and in Chapter 2, by constructing a number of simple 3D drawings. Short instructions are included with either the text or with the illustrations accompanying each exercise.

1. Figure 3.14 is a drawing of a tenon on the end of a block. Construct the 3D drawing Fig. 3.14 with the aid of the **3Dface** tool. Then place the drawing in a pictorial with **Vpoint**. Then **Hide** hidden lines behind the **3Dface**s.
2. Construct the 3D drawing of Fig. 3.15. Follow the details of sizes and tools included with the given drawing.

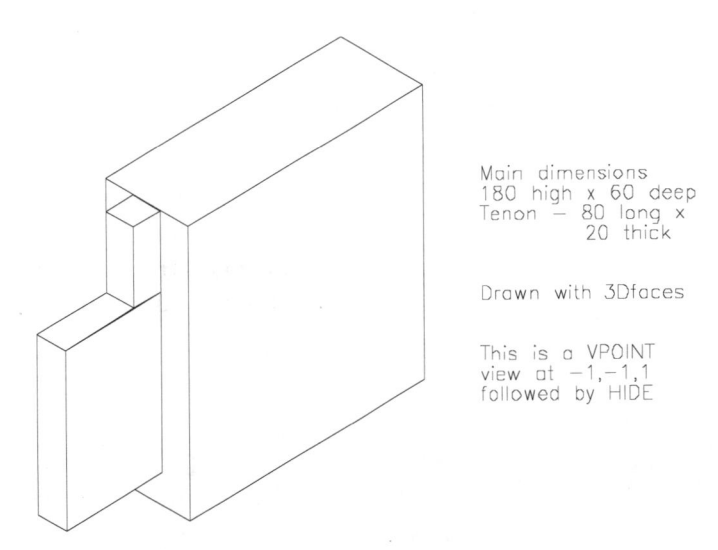

Main dimensions
180 high x 60 deep
Tenon — 80 long x
         20 thick

Drawn with 3Dfaces

This is a VPOINT view at −1,−1,1 followed by HIDE

Fig. 3.14 Exercise 1

62 An Introduction to 3D AutoCAD

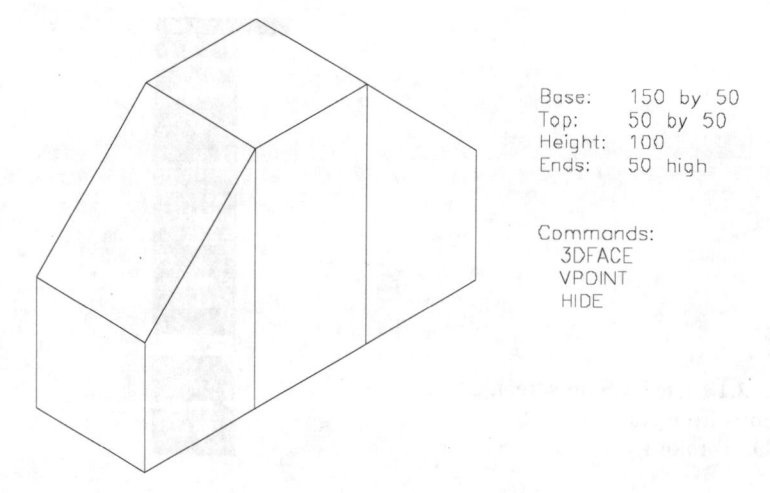

```
Base:    150 by 50
Top:     50 by 50
Height:  100
Ends:    50 high

Commands:
  3DFACE
  VPOINT
  HIDE
```

Fig. 3.15 Exercise 2

3. Construct the 3D drawing of Fig. 3.16. Follow the details of sizes and tools included with the given drawing.

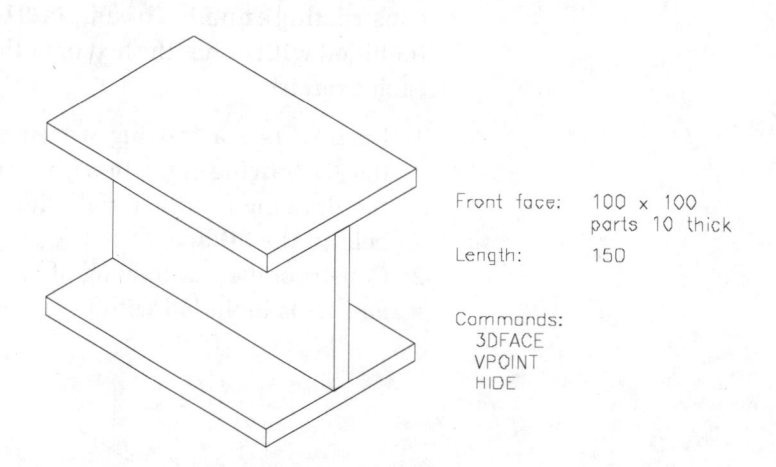

```
Front face: 100 x 100
            parts 10 thick
Length:     150

Commands:
  3DFACE
  VPOINT
  HIDE
```

Fig. 3.16 Exercise 3

4. Construct the given drawing, Fig. 3.17, with the aid of the tool **3Dface**. Use the **Invisible** option of the **3Dface** tool prompts to make lines between the 3Dfaces invisible. When the construction is complete, place the drawing in a pictorial view with **Vpoint**. **Hide** lines behind the 3Dfaces.

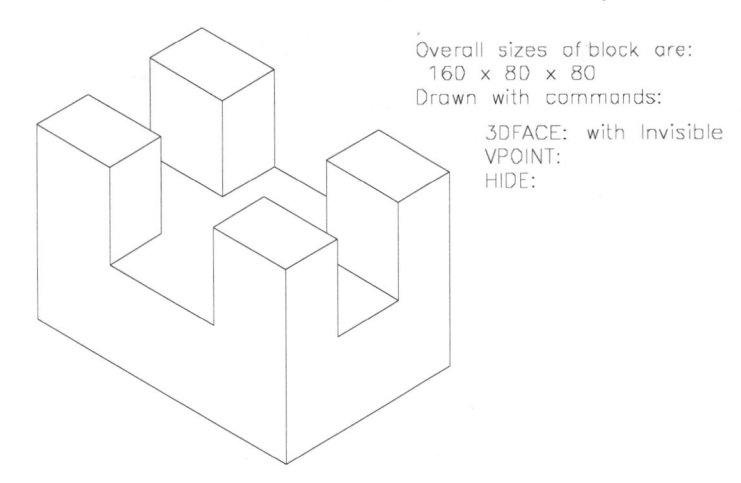

Overall sizes of block are:
160 x 80 x 80
Drawn with commands:

3DFACE: with Invisible
VPOINT:
HIDE:

Fig. 3.17 Exercise 4

5. Construct the drawing shown in Fig. 3.18 with the aid of the **3Dface** tool, including the **Invisible** option. Dimensions of the 3D drawing are:

   (a) The base is 260 by 120;
   (b) The height is 100;
   (c) The top surface faces are 120 by 40 and 120 by 20.

   To avoid having to draw the sloping and vertical faces twice, draw the left-hand and front faces, then with the aid of the **Mirror** tool, copy from left to right and from front to back. When the drawing is completed, place it in a pictorial view with **Vpoint** and **Hide** lines behind the 3Dfaces.

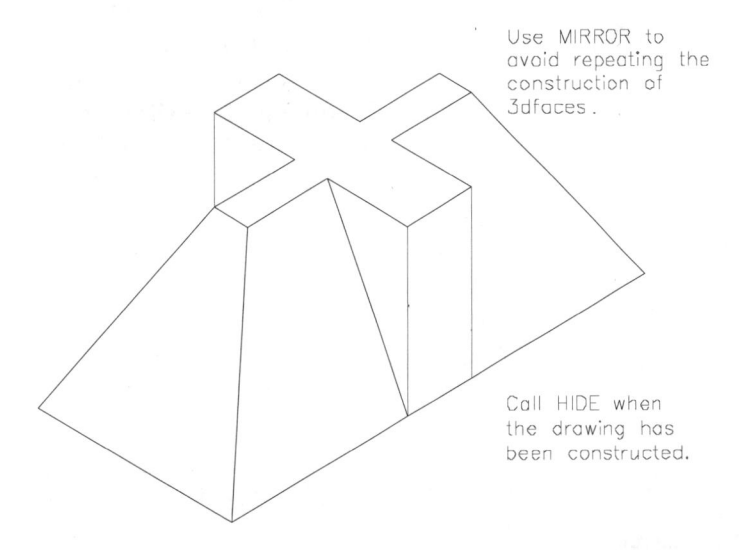

Use MIRROR to avoid repeating the construction of 3dfaces.

Call HIDE when the drawing has been constructed.

Fig. 3.18 Exercise 5

64 An Introduction to 3D AutoCAD

6. Construct the 3D drawing given in Fig. 3.19. Work to the sizes given, estimating those not included. Use the tools indicated with the drawing.

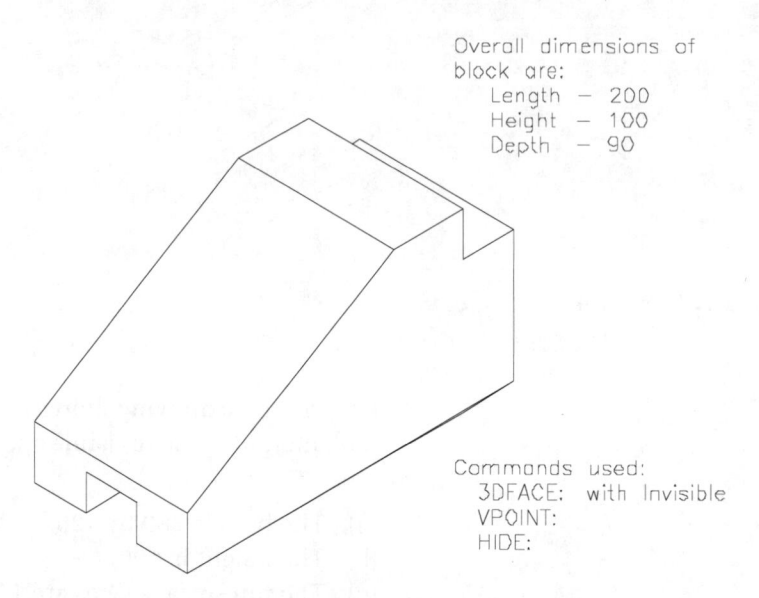

```
Overall dimensions of
block are:
    Length  -  200
    Height  -  100
    Depth   -  90
```

```
Commands used:
    3DFACE: with Invisible
    VPOINT:
    HIDE:
```

Fig. 3.19 Exercise 6

7. Construct the 3D drawing given in Fig. 3.20. The construction should proceed in four stages:
   (a) Stage 1. With **Elev** at 0 and with thickness 25, draw the back strip;
   (b) Stage 2. With **Elev** reset to 25 and with thickness 10, draw the outline of the shelf;
   (c) Stage 3. With **Elev** reset to 35 with thickness 0, draw 3Dfaces on the shelf top. Draw the left-hand half, with the **Invisible** option, then **Mirror** the right-hand half from the left-hand.
   (d) Stage 4. View the drawing with **Vpoint** at −1,−1,1 and **Hide** lines behind the 3Dfaces and the extrusions.

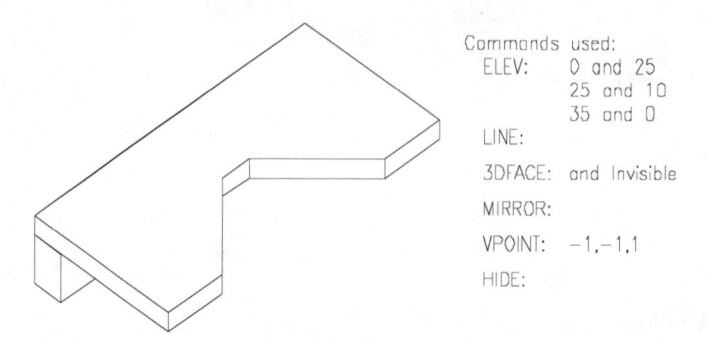

```
Commands used:
    ELEV:    0 and 25
             25 and 10
             35 and 0
    LINE:
    3DFACE:  and Invisible
    MIRROR:
    VPOINT:  -1,-1,1
    HIDE:
```

Fig. 3.20 Exercise 7

The User Coordinate System (UCS)

8. Two views of a poppet valve are given in Fig. 3.21. Construct the poppet valve drawing, following the details given with the drawing.

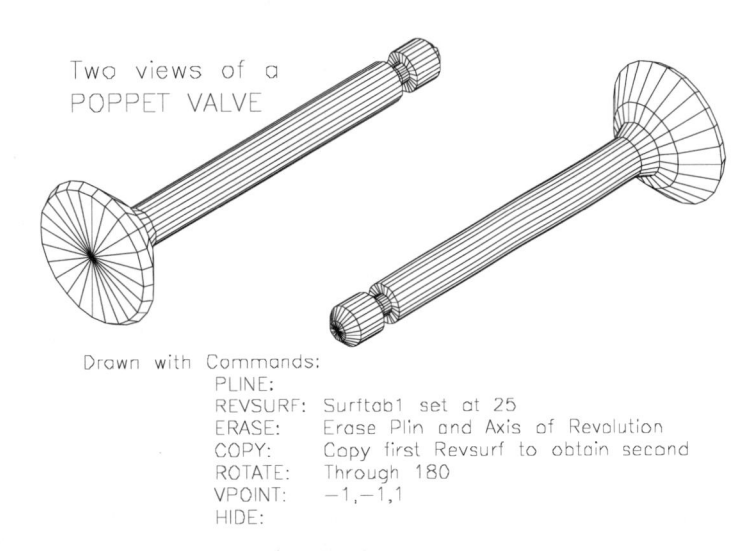

```
Two views of a
POPPET VALVE

Drawn with Commands:
    PLINE:
    REVSURF: Surftab1 set at 25
    ERASE:   Erase Plin and Axis of Revolution
    COPY:    Copy first Revsurf to obtain second
    ROTATE:  Through 180
    VPOINT:  -1,-1,1
    HIDE:
```

Fig. 3.21 Exercise 8

9. Views of three 3D objects, constructed with the aid of **Tabsurf** and **Rulesurf**, are shown in Fig. 3.22. Construct the three drawings. A problem arises when fitting **Rulesurf** surfaces to **Tabsurf** extrusions. When the pline outlines for the **Tabsurf** extrusions are drawn, they will be on the surface of the WCS *x-y* plane. When fitting the **Rulesurf** surface mesh, instead of fitting it on the top of the **Tabsurf** extrusion as might be expected, it may fit on the bottom. The reader is advised to solve this problem without further help.

```
Commands used:
    PLINE:
    LINE:
    TABSURF: Surftab1 8
    RULESURF:
    MOVE:
    VPOINT:
    HIDE:
```

Upper views without RULESURF top

Lower views with RULESURF top (Surftab1 24)

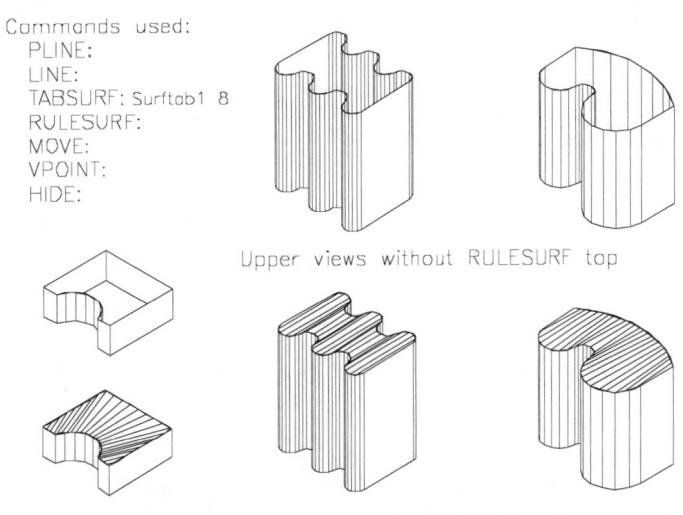

Fig. 3.22 Exercise 9

10. Figure 3.23 is a 3D drawing of a model formed with the aid of the **3D Object** box. Following the order of work given, construct the drawing.

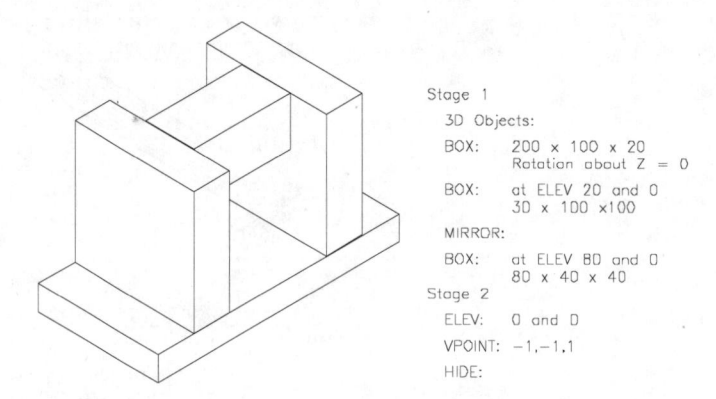

Stage 1
3D Objects:
BOX: 200 x 100 x 20
       Rotation about Z = 0
BOX: at ELEV 20 and 0
       30 x 100 x100
MIRROR:
BOX: at ELEV 80 and 0
       80 x 40 x 40
Stage 2
ELEV: 0 and 0
VPOINT: -1,-1,1
HIDE:

Fig. 3.23 Exercise 10

11. A 3D drawing of a lathe headstock fitting is given in Fig. 3.24. Construct the drawing following the details given with the drawing.

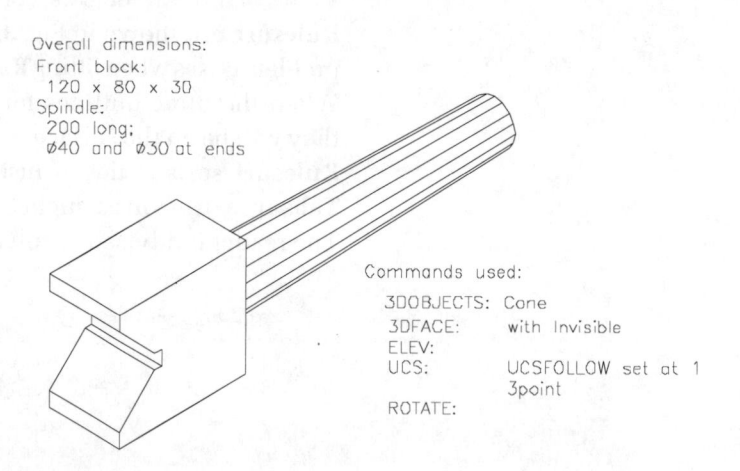

Overall dimensions:
Front block:
  120 x 80 x 30
Spindle:
  200 long;
  ⌀40 and ⌀30 at ends

Commands used:
3DOBJECTS: Cone
3DFACE: with Invisible
ELEV:
UCS: UCSFOLLOW set at 1
           3point
ROTATE:

Fig. 3.24 Exercise 11

12. Following the details of the stages given in Fig. 3.25, construct the given 3D drawing.

The User Coordinate System (UCS)

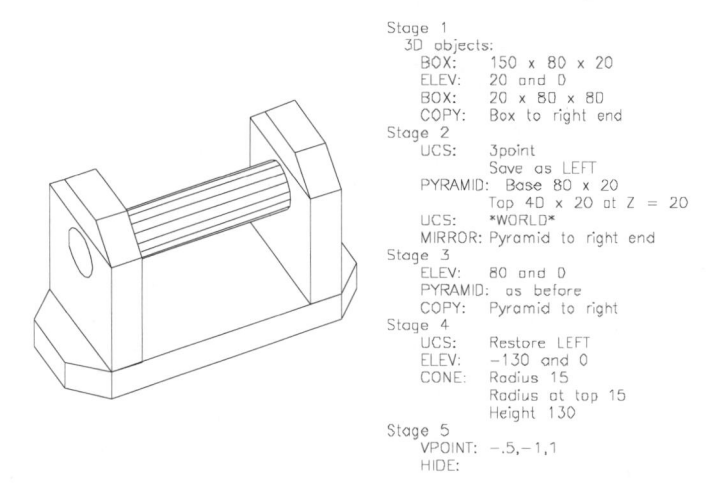

```
Stage 1
    3D objects:
        BOX:    150 x 80 x 20
        ELEV:   20 and 0
        BOX:    20 x 80 x 80
        COPY:   Box to right end
Stage 2
        UCS:    3point
                Save as LEFT
        PYRAMID: Base 80 x 20
                 Top 40 x 20 at Z = 20
        UCS:    *WORLD*
        MIRROR: Pyramid to right end
Stage 3
        ELEV:   80 and 0
        PYRAMID: as before
        COPY:   Pyramid to right
Stage 4
        UCS:    Restore LEFT
        ELEV:   -130 and 0
        CONE:   Radius 15
                Radius at top 15
                Height 130
Stage 5
        VPOINT: -.5,-1,1
        HIDE:
```

Fig. 3.25 Exercise 12

13. Figure 3.26 is a 3D drawing of a handle for fitting to a braking device. It has been constructed from surface meshes. Figure 3.27 shows the **Edgesurf** outlines for the body of the handle. These **Edgesurf** outlines were drawn on several UCS planes. The **Rulesurf** outlines were also drawn on a UCS plane with **Elev** set at 0 with a thickness of 10.
Following the details given with the two illustrations, construct the 3D drawing of the handle.

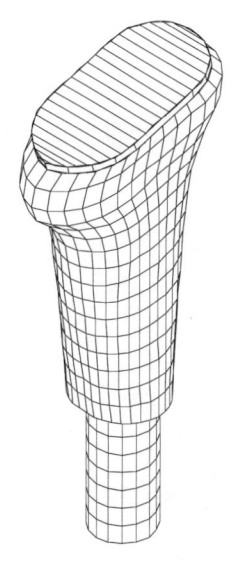

```
Commands used:
    PLINE:      Edgesurf outlines
                Rulesurf outlines
    UCS:        Several
                UCSfollow set at 1
                UCSicon set at 3
    EDGESURF:   Surftab1 set at 16
                Surftab2 set at 16
    ELEV:       0 and 10
    RULESURF:   Surftab1 set at 24
                Surftab2 set at 2
    MIRROR:     To mirror Edgesurf mesh
    VPOINT:     -1,-1,1
    HIDE:
```

Fig. 3.26 Exercise 13

68 An Introduction to 3D AutoCAD

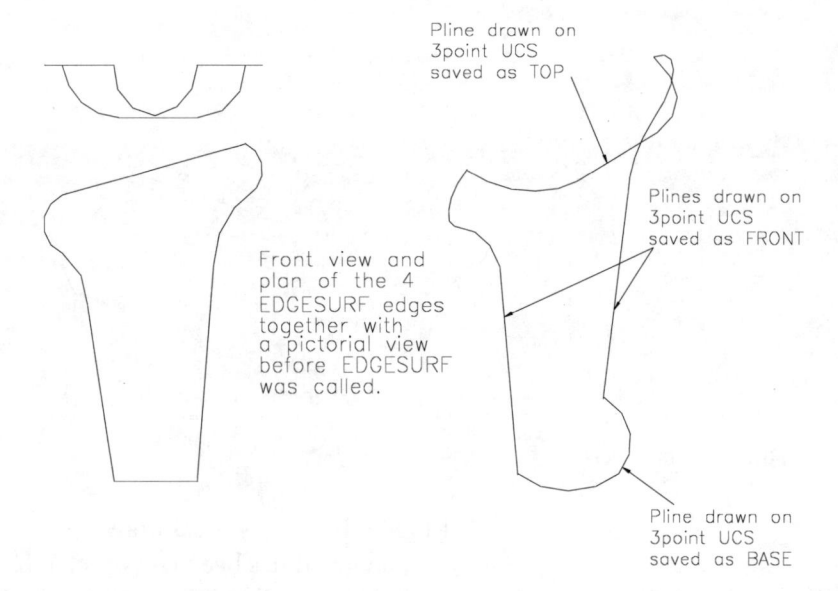

Pline drawn on 3point UCS saved as TOP

Plines drawn on 3point UCS saved as FRONT

Front view and plan of the 4 EDGESURF edges together with a pictorial view before EDGESURF was called.

Pline drawn on 3point UCS saved as BASE

Fig. 3.27 The **Pline**s for Exercise 13

14. Another braking device handle is shown in Fig. 3.28. This 3D drawing was constructed in a similar manner to the drawing given with Exercise 13.

Construct the handle, working to the details given with Fig. 3.28.

The 4 Edgesurf edges

Commands used:

PLINE:

UCS: 3point:
           FRONT
           TOP
           BASE
           WORLD

MIRROR:

EDGESURF: Surftab1 at 16
           Surftab2 at 32

RULESURF: Surftab1 at 16
           Surftab2 at 2

VPOINT: $-1.5,-1,1$

HIDE:

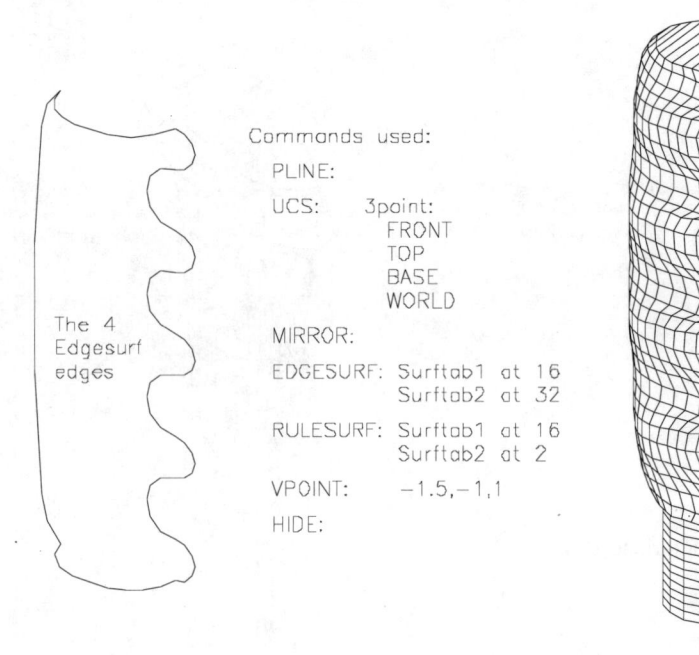

Fig. 3.28 Exercise 14

15. Figure 3.29 shows yet another 3D drawing of a braking handle. Construct the drawing working to the same principles as with the two previous Exercises.

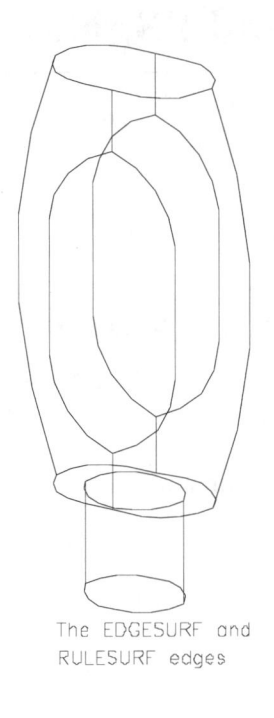

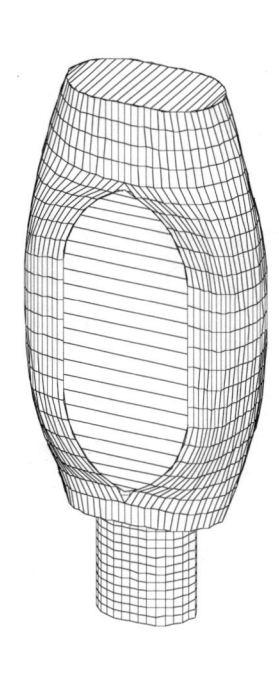

Fig. 3.29 Exercise 15

CHAPTER 4

Viewports, Tilemode, MSpace and PSpace

The tool Viewports

Either *left-click* on **Tiled Viewports** (R12) or on **Layout** (R13), both shown in Fig. 4.1, to bring the **Tiled Viewport Layout** dialogue box on screen showing the different types of viewport layouts (Fig. 4.2) or, at the command line:

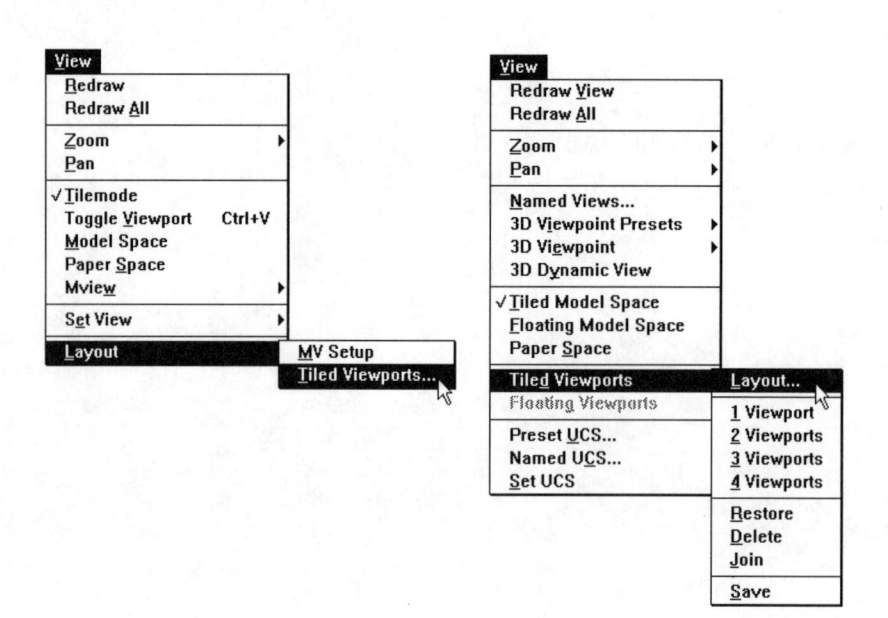

Fig. 4.1 Selecting **Viewports** form R12 (left) or R13 (right)

Command: vports *right-click*
Save/Restore/Delete/Join/Single/2/<3>/4/:

Figure 4.2 shows the different types of viewports available. No matter which option is available, clear prompts allow the operator to choose how many and in whatever relative positions the viewports can be arranged on screen. Note that the default for the viewports

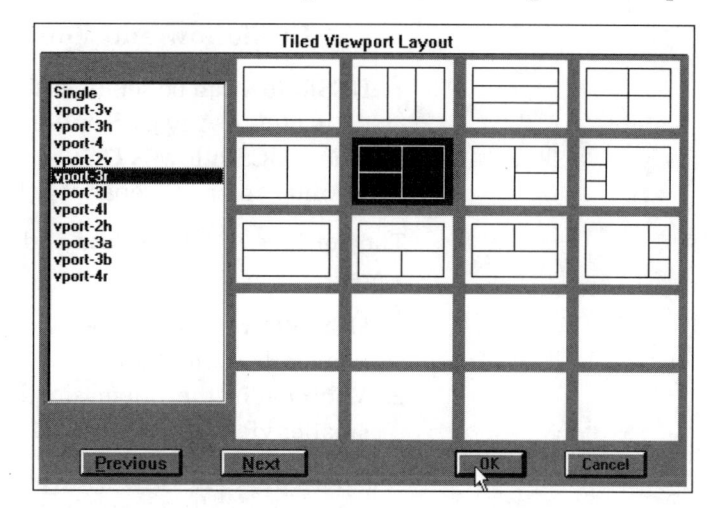

Fig. 4.2 The **Tiled Viewport Layout** dialogue box resulting from selecting **Tiled Viewports** or **Layout** from the **View** pull-down menu

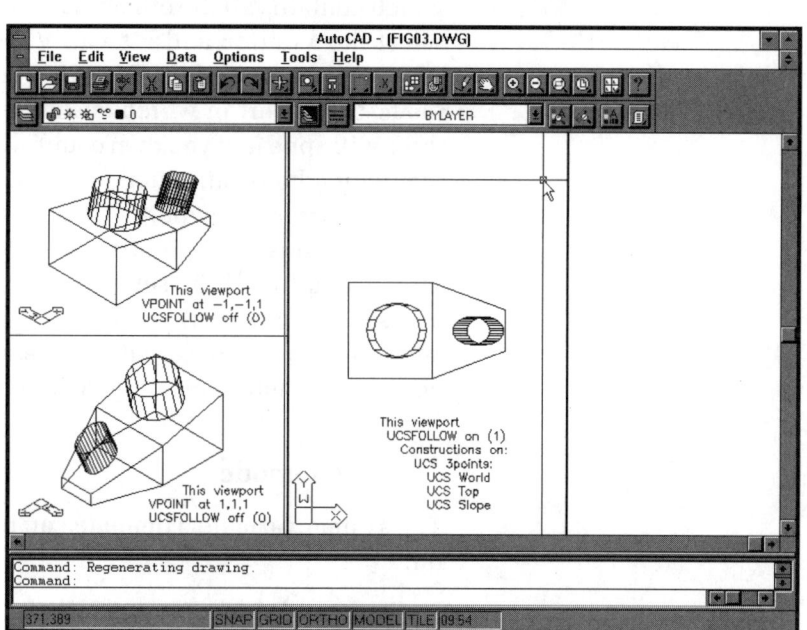

Fig. 4.3 A 3D drawing under construction in a three viewport screen in R13

option is **<3> Right**. Figure 4.3 is an example of a three-viewport screen with the right-hand viewport being the largest of the three. As a 3D model drawing is constructed in the largest of the three viewports, changes are reflected in the other two. In this example, the two smaller viewports are showing pictorial views from different viewpoints, thus any errors which may occur during construction will probably be identified in the two smaller pictorial views as the drawing is being created.

UCSfollow and Vpoint settings in Viewport

1. **UCSfollow** can be set for each viewport – **ON** (1) in some and **OFF** (0) in others. Any UCS options will be followed in those viewports where **UCSfollow** is **ON**.
2. **Vpoint** can be set separately for each viewport.

The settings of **UCSfollow** and **Vpoint** in the example of Fig. 4.3 were:

1. **UCSfollow** – in the largest viewport set to 1 (on); in the two smaller viewports set to 0 (off).
2. **Vpoint** – in the upper smaller viewport set to -1,-1,1; in lower smaller viewport set to 1,1,1.

It is possible to have 17 viewports on screen – one of which is that which contains all the others. This can be checked – call **Viewports**, select the **4** option and **Fit**, call **Viewports** again and window four viewports in each of the four viewports. The result will be that, in the last viewport in which one attempts to fit four viewports, only three will appear. If you then count all viewports on screen, including that which holds all others, you will find a total of 17.

The current viewport – that in which constructions can take place – is chosen by pointing at the selected viewport and pressing the *pick* button of the selection device – usually a *left-click* of the mouse. The cursor cross hairs then appear in the selected viewport and tools which are called are operative only in that viewport and not in the others. This only occurs in **MSpace** – see below.

Tilemode

The system variable **Tilemode** can be **ON** (1) or **OFF** (0). To turn it off:

> **Command:** tilemode *right-click*
> **New value for TILEMODE <1>:** 0 *right-click*
> **Command:**

Why the name "Tilemode"? If **Tilemode** is **ON**, viewports can only be set on the screen side by side as if set like tiles on a wall, i.e. in fixed positions side by side in such a manner that they cannot be moved from their set positions. When **Tilemode** is **OFF**, each viewport can be moved to a new position relative to the other viewports, scaled, copied or erased.

Model Space and Paper Space

With the drawing editor set to **Model Space** (**MSpace**), constructions of either 2D or 3D drawings are possible. **MSpace** is available whether **Tilemode** is **ON** or **OFF**.

With the drawing editor set to **Paper Space** (**PSpace**) 3D drawings cannot be constructed, but notes can be added to 3D drawings which have been constructed in **MSpace**. While in **PSpace**, viewports can be rearranged for position and the plotting of the contents as many viewports as are on the screen is possible. **PSpace** can only operate when **Tilemode** is **OFF**.

With **Tilemode** set **OFF**, **PSpace** can be changed to **MSpace** by:

Command: ms (MSpace) *right-click*
Command:

And the screen changes to **Model Space**.

Similarly with **Tilemode** set **OFF**, to change back to **PSpace**:

Command: ps (PSpace) *right-click*
Command:

And the screen reverts to **Paper Space**.

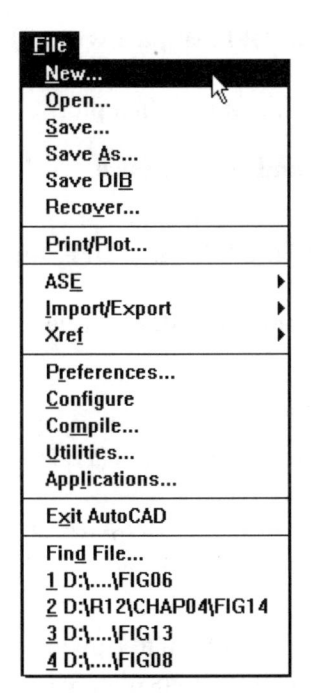

Fig. 4.4 Calling for a **New...** drawing from the **File** pull-down menu (R12)

When a **New** drawing is called from the **File** pull-down menu (Fig. 4.4), the prototype file **acad.dwg** is automatically loaded from disk, unless AutoCAD has been configured (under **7. Configure operating parameters** followed by **2. Initial drawing setup**) to load a different prototype drawing file.

The **acad.dwg** file sets a number of variables which control methods of drawing in the drawing editor. One of these variables in **Tilemode** which in **acad.dwg** is usually set **ON** (1).

A method of constructing 3D drawings in the AutoCAD drawing editor is:

1. Construct the required drawing in **MSpace**, which is immediately available because **Tilemode** is **ON**.
2. Set **Tilemode** to **OFF** (0), which changes the screen to **PSpace**.
3. Make and set a new layer **Vports** (or **VP**). Set the colour of this viewport to a colour other than that in which the 3D drawing has been constructed.
4. Set up the screen for the required number of viewports.
5. Add notes and rearrange the viewports as necessary.
6. Plot/print from **PSpace** (all viewports on screen) when ready to do so. Plotting/printing can also be carried out from **MSpace**, but only the current Viewport will plot/print.
7. If amendments are required in a 3D drawing, they can only be made after calling **MSpace**. This is because 3D drawing cannot proceed

in **PSpace**. Note that even with **Tilemode** set **OFF**, **MSpace** will still function if called from **PSpace**.
8. Note that the edges of the viewports will not appear in a plot.

Further notes about Model Space and Paper Space

1. In **PSpace**, the **PSpace** icon appears at the lower left hand corner of the graphics area only if **UCSicon** is **ON**. If **UCSicon** is **OFF**, the **PSpace** icon does not appear.
2. **Vpoint** is not available in **PSpace**. If **Vpoint** is called while in **PSpace**, a warning message appears:

Command not allowed in Paper Space

3. **UCSfollow** is not operative in **PSpace** even when set **ON** (1). This means that a new **UCS** cannot be set in **PSpace**.
4. Although new **UCS** planes cannot be constructed in **PSpace**, the **UCS** views currently in **MSpace** will remain when changing to **PSpace** from **MSpace**.

Viewports can be set up in either **MSpace** or in **PSpace**. However, when in **PSpace** the tool **Viewports** is not allowed. In its place a tool **Mview** is available in **PSpace** for the setting of the required number of viewports.

When **PSpace** is first called (usually by setting **Tilemode** to **OFF** (0), the graphics area becomes blank, except for the **PSpace** icon at the bottom left. Nothing can be added in the graphics area until one or more viewports are set with the aid of the tool **Mview** as follows:

Command: mview *right-click*
ON/OFF/Hideplot/Fit/2/3/4/Restore/<First point>: f (Fit) *right-click*
Command:

And the graphics area changes to a single viewport occupying (fitting) the whole of the graphics area. Any drawing construction from **MSpace** also appears in the graphics area. If the response to the **Mview** options is 2, 3 or 4, the screen changes to contain 2, 3 or 4 viewports. An example of a four-viewport drawing is given in Fig. 4.5

When in **PSpace** with several viewports, each viewport can be moved with the aid of the **Move** tool as shown in Fig. 4.6. This illustration also shows that a viewport can be acted upon by the **Mirror** tool.

The **Mview** prompts have the following meanings:

1. **OFF** – the contents of a viewport can be cleared by *picking* an edge of that viewport. The viewport then becomes blank. An example,

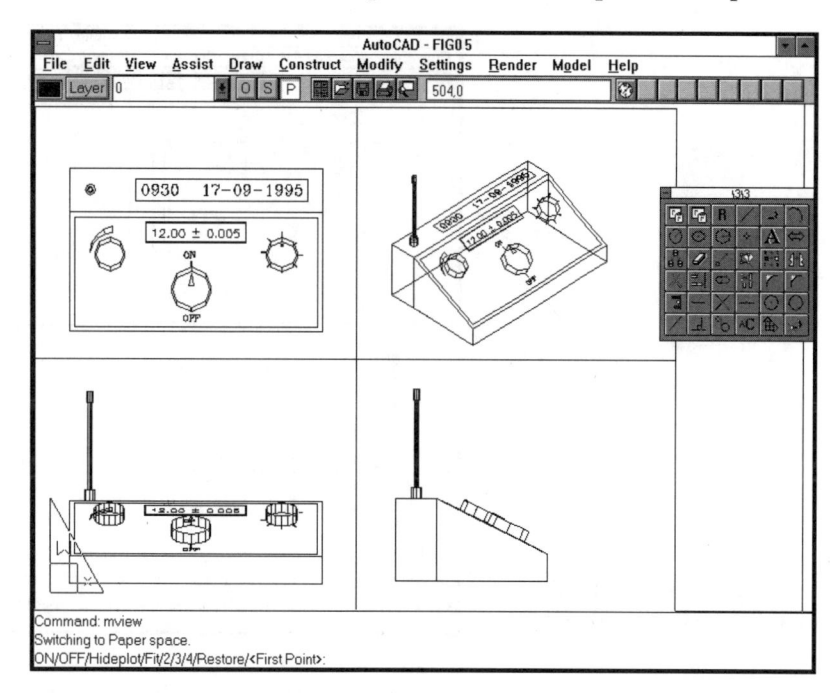

Fig. 4.5 A four-viewport drawing of a 3D model

of a viewport turned **OFF** is given in Fig. 4.7.
2. **ON** – brings back into on screen the contents of a viewport which has been turned off.

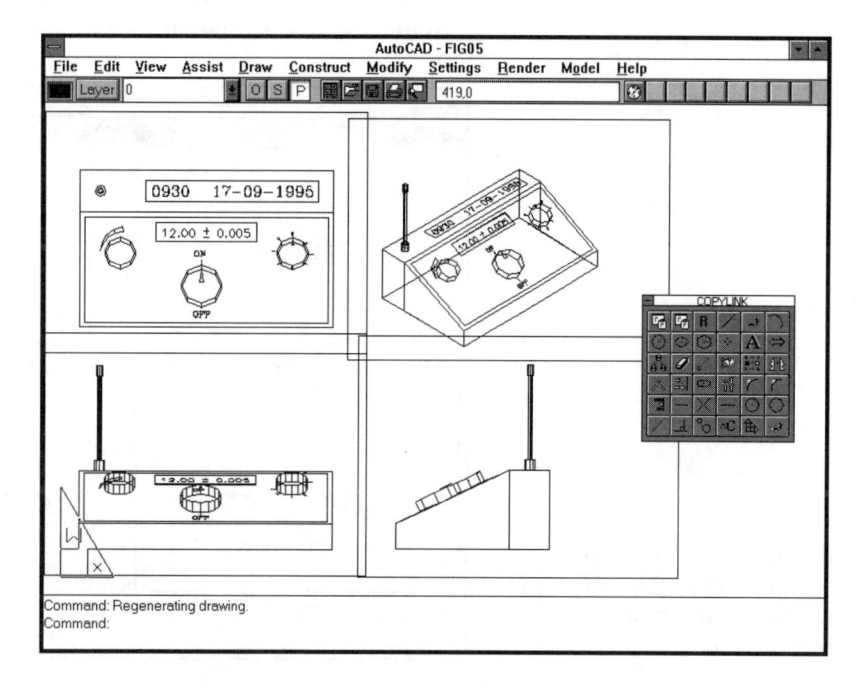

Fig. 4.6 Fig. 4.5 with viewports acted upon by **Move** to more suitable positions. Note the viewport with an end view has been acted upon with **Mirror** to obtain a sensible Third angle projection for the end view

76 An Introduction to 3D AutoCAD

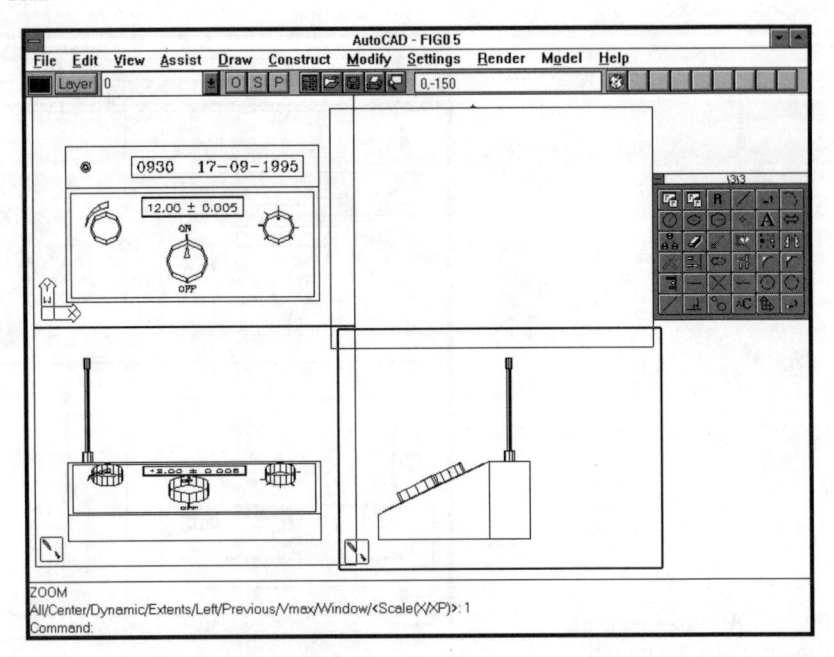

Fig. 4.7 Fig. 4.6 with one viewport turned off with the aid of the **Mview** option **OFF**

3. **H**ideplot – if an edge of a viewport is selected when **Hideplot** is **ON**, hidden lines within that viewport will be removed when plotting or printing.
4. **Fit/2/3/4** – number of viewports required. If **Fit** then only a single viewport occupying the whole of the graphics area appears.
5. **R**estore – the contents of a viewport can be restored and fitted in a window of the operator's choice, by following the **Fit/<First>**

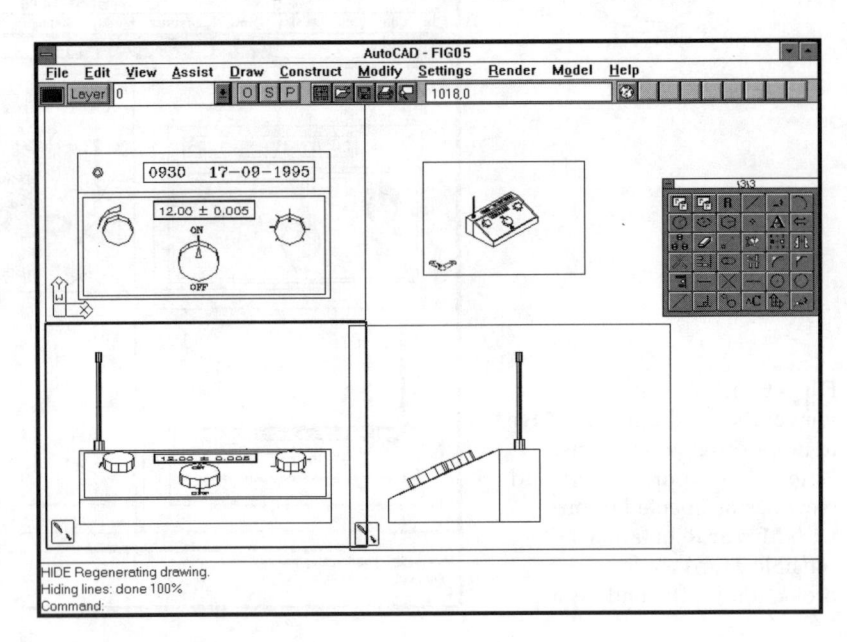

Fig. 4.8 Fig. 4.7 with the viewport retsored to screen by a **Restore** prompt of the **Mview** tool

Viewports, Tilemode, MSpace and PSpace

point: and **Second point:** prompts. In Fig. 4.8, a **R**estored viewport has been displayed into a small window by selecting the first and second points of the window corners.
6. **First point** – viewport(s) can be fitted into a window by selecting **First point:** and **Second point:**

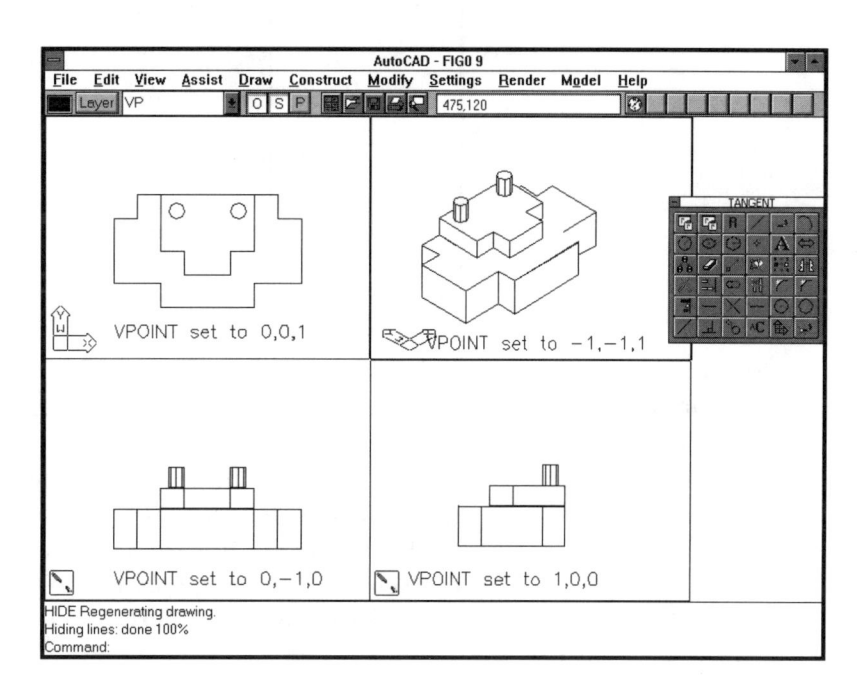

Fig. 4.9 A 3D drawing with each viewport showing a different **Vpoint** view

Viewports in PSpace and MSpace

1. When in **PSpace**, viewports can be turned off or on, moved, erased, scaled, copied or mirrored. An edge of the viewport to be acted upon by the any of such tools is *picked* for the required change to occur within the viewport. The tools are used in exactly the same manner as when constructing a drawing with their aid.
2. When in **MSpace**, the viewing position for 3D drawings can be set in each viewport independently with the aid of the tool **Vpoint** (Fig. 4.9). Remember **Vpoint** is not available in **PSpace**, but the **Vpoint** views set in **MSpace** are retained when switching back to **PSpace**.

Setting viewports in Paper Space

The following procedure for setting viewports in **PSpace** is intended to allow a plot of a 3D drawing to obtain a three-view orthographic projection, together with a pictorial view. The drawing has been constructed in a graphics area set to limits of 420,297 (for a full size plot on an A3 size sheet.

78 An Introduction to 3D AutoCAD

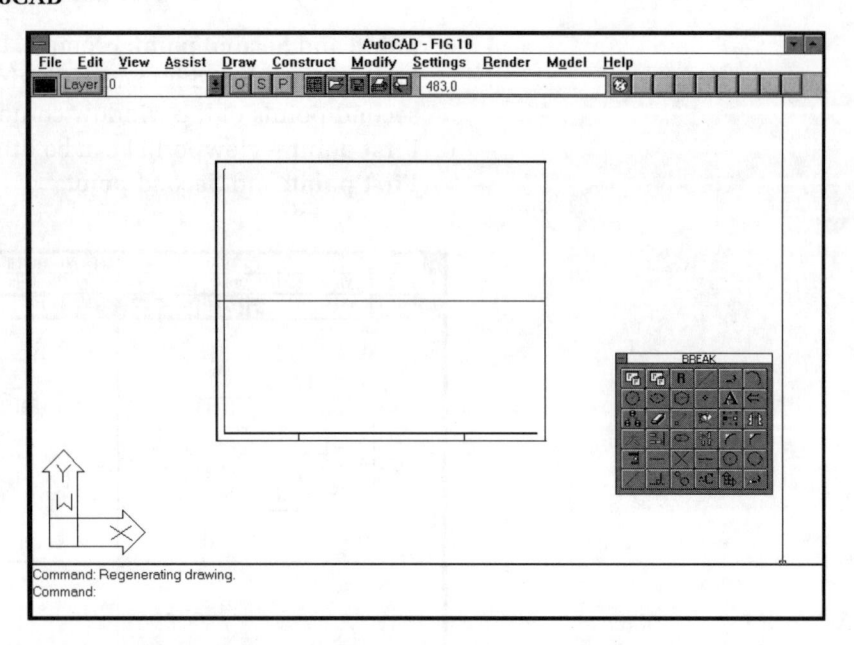

Fig. 4.10 a 3D drawing constructed in **MSpace**

1. Construct the drawing in **MSpace** (Fig. 4.10).
2. Set **Tilemode** to 0 (**OFF**). This sets up **PSpace** (Fig. 4.11).
3. Set **Limits** to 420,297 (A3 sheet size in millimetres).
4. **Zoom** all. Sets graphics area to the limits 420,297.
5. Make a new layer **Vport**, colour yellow.

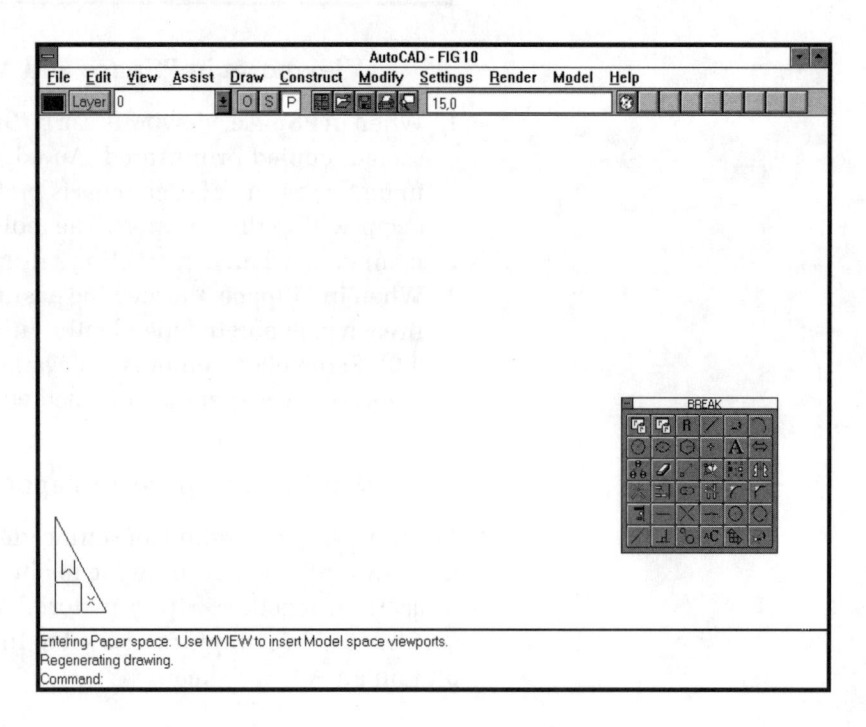

Fig. 4.11 The graphics area changed to **PS**pace. The drawing disappears

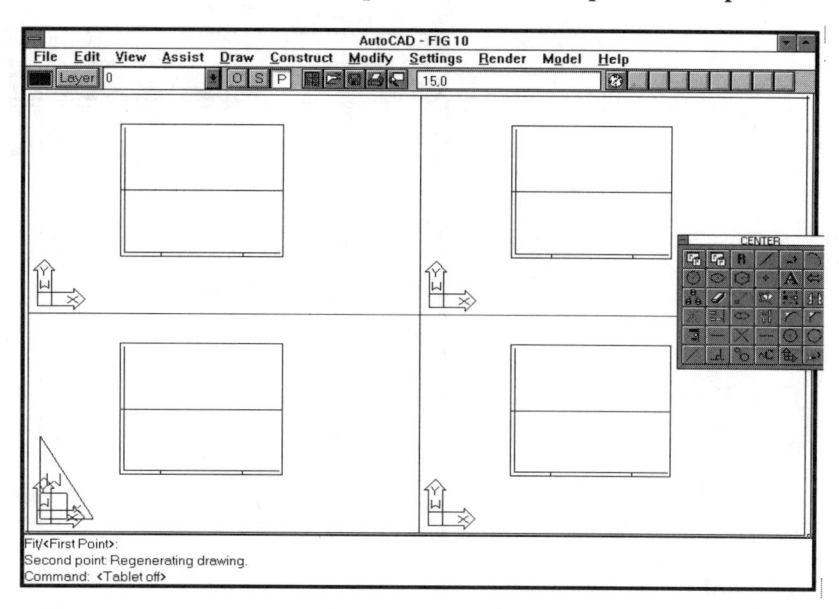

Fig. 4.12 In **Mview** – four viewports. Fitted to graphics area. The drawing reappears

6. Make the layer **Vport** current.
7. Call **Mview** to obtain four viewports, fitted to the screen (Fig. 4.12).
8. Call **MSpace**.
9. Call **Vpoint** in each viewport in turn (*left-click* in viewport) and set viewing positions:

    (a) Top left viewport 0,0,1;
    (b) Bottom left viewport 0,–1,0;
    (c) Bottom right viewport 1,0,0;
    (d) Top right viewport –1,–1,1.

    The results of these various **Vpoint** settings are shown in Fig. 4.13.
10. **Zoom** 1 in each viewport in turn.
11. Call **PSpace**. Call **Move**. Move each viewport in turn to obtain a good orthographic projection of the views (Fig. 4.14).
    Viewports can be moved by *picking* an edge of a viewport and dragging it to its required new position.
12. Call **Mview**. Choose the **Hideplot** option. Set to **ON**. Select an edge of each viewport in turn. Ensures that hidden lines are removed when plotting or printing.
13. Turn layer **Vport** off. Removes viewport lines.
14. Add border lines and title as required. Dimensions can also be added at this stage (Fig. 4.15)
15. Plot/print the drawing with hidden lines removed.

Note that when more than a single viewport is displayed in the graphics area, only the active viewport will be plotted if in **MSpace**. The contents of all viewports will be plotted if in **PSpace**.

80 An Introduction to 3D AutoCAD

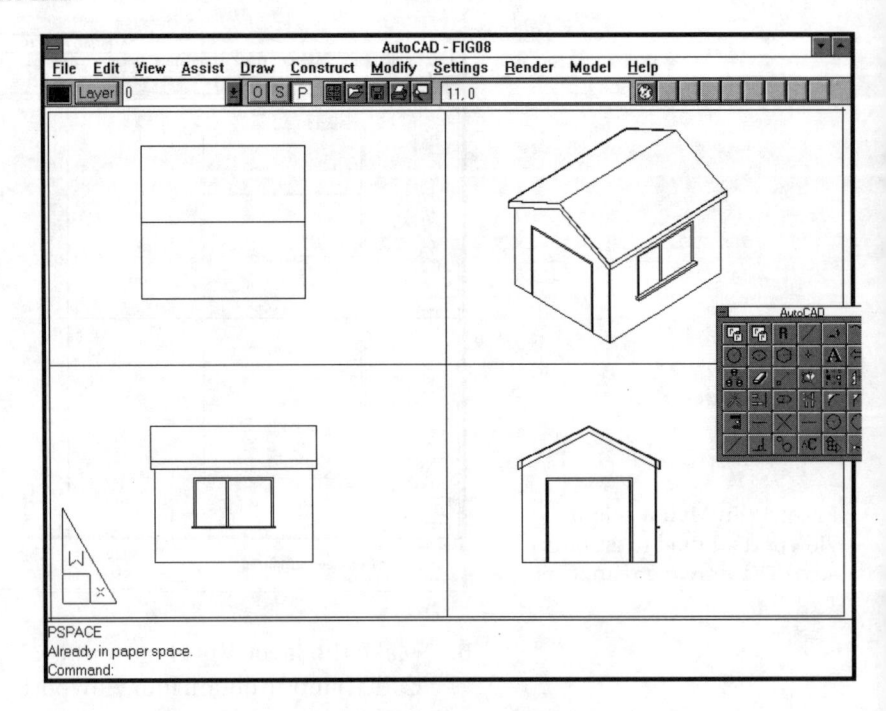

Fig. 4.13 Four viewports rearranged with **Vpoint** to obtain orthographic views and a pictorial view

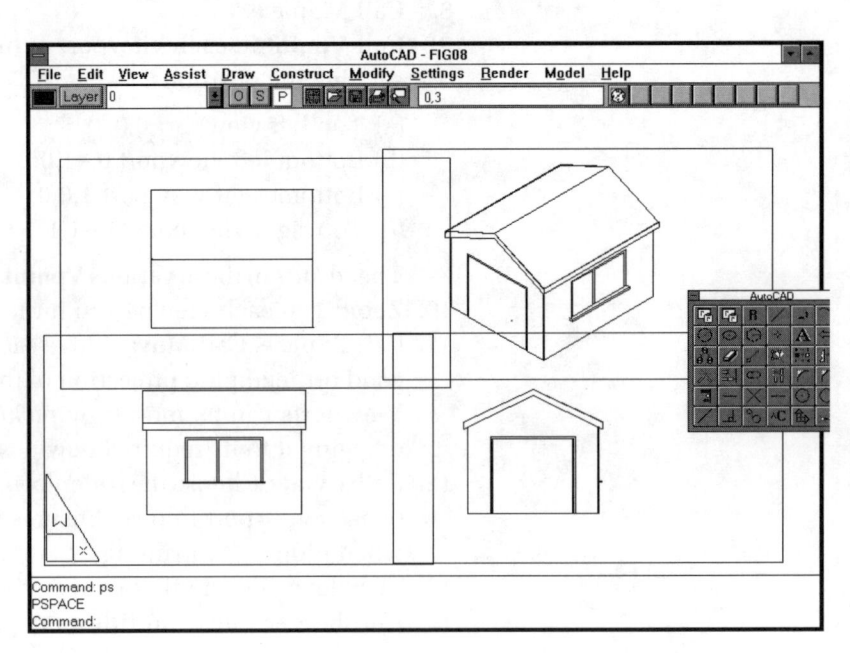

Fig. 4.14 Viewports moved to give a better layout of the views

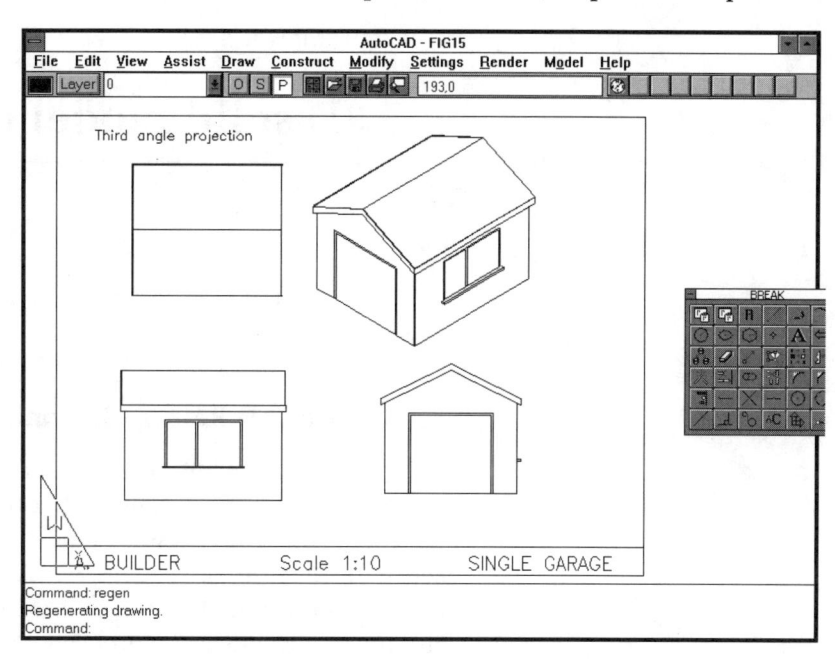

Fig. 4.15 Layer **Vport** turned off. Border and title block added

CHAPTER 5

3D solid model drawings

AutoCAD Release 12 compared with Release 13

As with AutoCAD Release 11, AutoCAD Release 12 relies upon the Advanced Modelling Extension (AME) being loaded into AutoCAD in order to construct 3D solid model drawings. The version of AME used with Release 12 is AME 2.1. AutoCAD Release 13, however, does not require the loading of AME before the construction of 3D solid model drawings can proceed, because the data controlling the use of tools concerned with 3D solids in Release 13 is part of the native AutoCAD data. When constructing 3D solids in Release 13, it will be found that work can proceed much faster than in earlier releases, because of this feature. It will also be found that the resulting solid model drawing files containing the drawing data are somewhat smaller in Release 13 than those from earlier releases. AME drawings constructed and saved in Release 12 can be loaded into Release 13, but if further work is to be carried out on the resulting loaded drawing, the drawing will need to be converted to Release 13 solid drawing data with the aid of the tool **AME Convert**. Solid models constructed in Release 12 can be saved with the tool **Save R12 DWG**, but such drawings when loaded into Release 12 are no longer solid model drawings.

Because of the differences between solid model drawing in the two releases, this chapter (Chapter 5) will be devoted to the construction of 3D solid model drawings in Release 12 and a later chapter (Chapter 7) to solid model construction in Release 13.

Loading the Advanced Modelling Extension

Before any of the tools for the construction of 3D solid models in Release 12 can commence, the AME software must first be loaded into AutoCAD. This is best carried out with a *left-click* on **Model** in the menu bar, followed by another *left-click on* **Utility** and yet another on **Load Modeler** (Fig. 5.1). The command line then shows:

3D solid model drawings 83

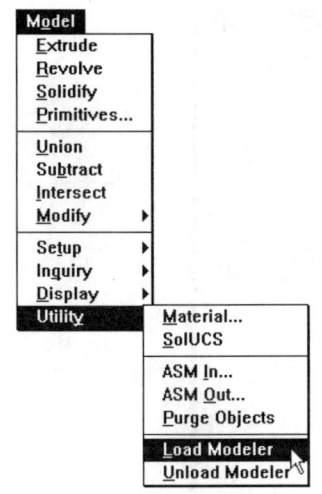

Fig. 5.1 Selecting **Load Modeler** from the **Model** pull-down menu

Command:
No modeler is loaded yet. Both AME and Region Modeler are available.
Autoload Region/<AME>: *right-click*
AME takes a few seconds to load
Command:

And solid model construction can begin. We will not be dealing with the **Region Modeler** in this book.

Another way of loading AME is to call any of the AME tools. As an example:

Command: solbox *right-click*
Initializing...
Initializing Advanced Modeling Extension.
Baseplane/Center/<Corner of box>:<0,0,0>:

And construction of a solid box can proceed.

The tools in AME

All tools from the Advanced Modelling Extension begin with **SOL** (solid). The tools can either be called by *entering* the tool name at the command line, or they can be selected from the **Draw** pull-down menu (Fig. 5.2). In this chapter all tools will be shown as called by *entering* the full tool name at the command line.

The AME primitives

There are six basic solid drawings in the AME set of Primitives. These can be called to screen either by entering the tool name preceded with **sol**, or they may be selected from the **AME Primitives** dialogue box (Fig. 5.4), which is called on screen with a *left-click* on **Primitives...** in the **Model** pull-down menu (see Fig. 5.3). The six **Primitives** are:

1. **Solbox** – for rectangular prisms or cubes.
2. **Solcone** – for either circular or elliptical cones.
3. **Solcyl** – for either circular or elliptical cylinders.
4. **Solsphere** – for spheres.
5. **Soltorus** – a closed torus can be drawn providing its tube radius is larger than the torus radius.
6. **Solwedge** – for wedge-shaped 3D solids.

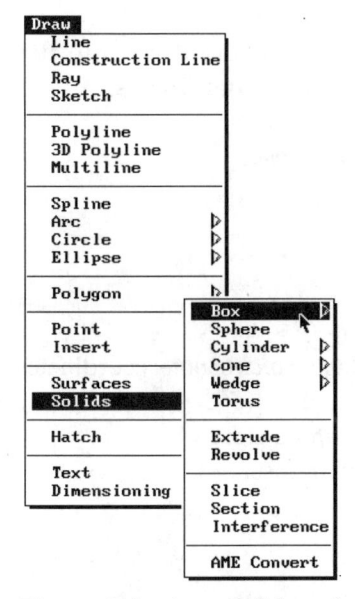

Fig. 5.2 Selecting a **Solids** tool from the **Draw** pull-down menu

84   An Introduction to 3D AutoCAD

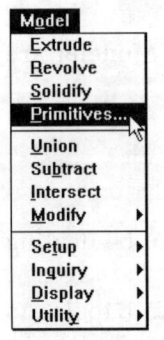

Fig. 5.3 Selecting **Primitves...** from the **Model** pull-down menu

Fig. 5.4 The **AME Primitives** dialogue box

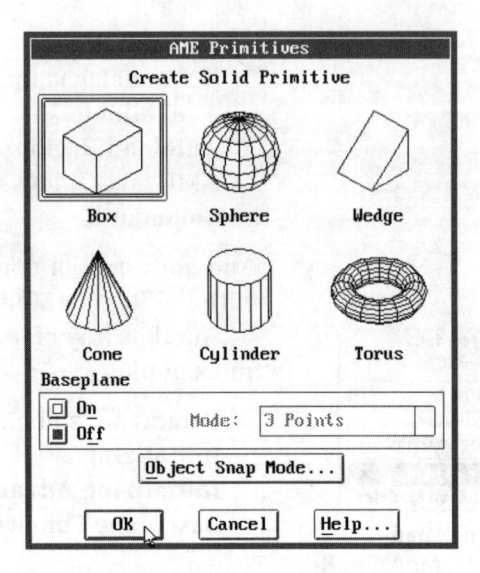

Prompts and options for the primitives

Solbox

Command: solbox *right-click*
Baseplane/Center/<Corner of box>:<0,0,0>: *pick* or *enter* coordinates
Cube/Length/<Other corner>: *pick* or *enter* coordinates
Height: *pick* two points or *enter* coordinates
    A series of statements detailing progress.
Command:

Solcone

Command: solcone *right-click*
Baseplane/Elliptical/<Center point> <0,0,0>: *pick* or *enter* coordinates
Diameter/<Radius>: *pick* or *enter* a figure
Apex/<Height>: *pick* two points or *enter* a figure
    A series of statements detailing progress.
Command:

Solcyl

Command: solcyl *right-click*
Baseplane/Elliptical/<Center point> <0,0,0>: *pick* or *enter* coordinates
Diameter/<Radius>: *pick* or *enter* a figure
Center of other end/<Height>: *pick* two points or *enter* a figure
    A series of statements detailing progress.
Command:

Solsphere

Command: solsphere *right-click*
Baseplane/<Center of sphere> <0,0,0>: *pick* or *enter* coordinates
Diameter/<Radius> of sphere: *pick* or *enter* a figure
    A series of statements detailing progress.
Command:

Soltorus

Command: soltorus *right-click*
Baseplane/<Center of torus> <0,0,0>: *pick* or *enter* coordinates
Diameter/<Radius> of torus: *pick* or *enter* a figure
Diameter/<Radius> of tube: *pick* two points or *enter* a figure
    A series of statements detailing progress.
Command:

Command:

Solwedge

Command: solwedge *right-click*
Baseplane/<Corner of wedge> <0,0,0>: *pick* or *enter* coordinates
Length <Other corner>: *pick* or *enter* a figure
Height: *pick* two points or *enter* a figure
    A series of statements detailing progress.
Command:

During the pause which occur between the stages in the construction of primitives, various statements may appear at the command line informing the operator as to what is happening while waiting for the construction to complete.

Wireframes and surface meshes

Solid models produced with the aid of AME appear on screen as wireframes, behind which lines cannot be hidden by calling the tool **Hide**. The wireframes can be changed to surface meshes by calling the tool **Solmesh** and *picking* the solid model drawing which one wishes to surface mesh. When an AME solid model drawing is acted upon by **Solmesh**, hidden lines behind faces can be hidden with **Hide**.

Command: solmesh *right-click*
Select objects: *pick*

Select objects: *right-click*
A series of statements detailing progress.
Command:

The AME variable Solwdens

The density of the mesh of those primitives which incorporate curved lines is controlled by the **Solvar** (solid variable) **Solwdens** (solid wire density). **Solwdens** can be set between 1 and 12: the higher the number, the closer the density of the mesh. Note also that each mesh of a primitive containing curves is a **Pface** with straight edges. Thus the greater the density of the mesh, the closer to accuracy will the curves of the primitive be. However, closer density means that the drawing file for an AME 3D model will become larger. To change the variable:

Command: solwdens *right-click*
Wireframe mesh density (1 to 12) <2>: *enter* the required number
Command:

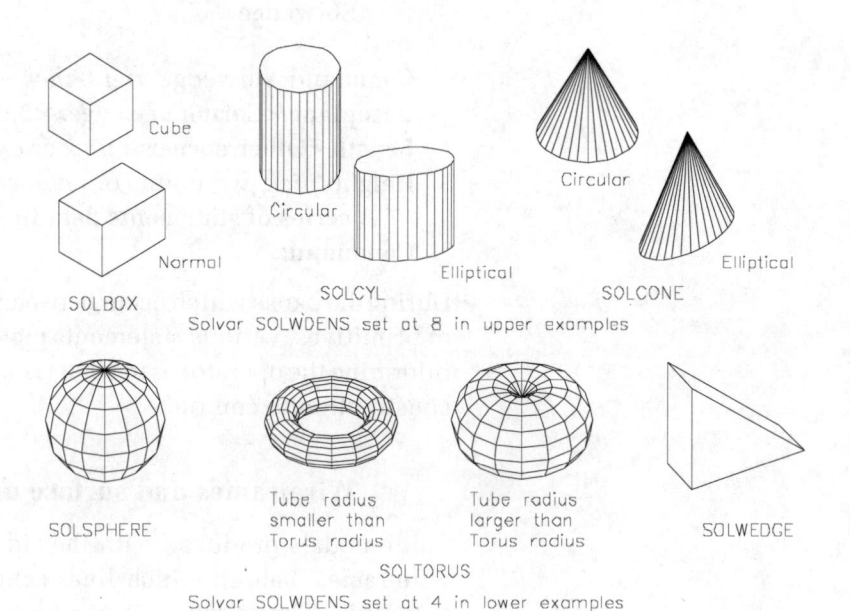

Fig. 5.5 The **Primitive** solids with **Solwdens** set to 8 or 4

The AME tool Solext

2D outlines composed of plines, circles, ellipses or polygons can be extruded with the aid of the AME tool **Solext**. Such extrusions can become surface meshed with the aid of **Solmesh**. Figure 5.6 gives

3D solid model drawings 87

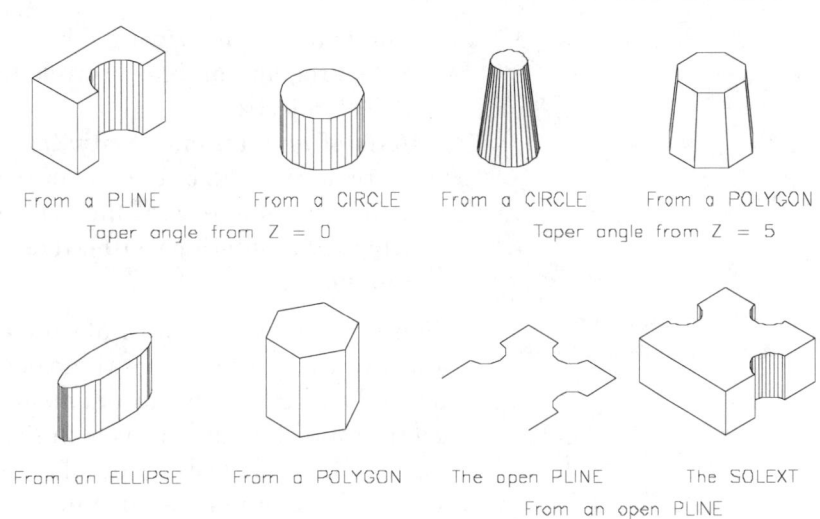

Fig. 5.6 Examples of **Solext** extrusions from pline, circle, ellipse and polygon outlines

examples of a variety of extrusions from 2D outlines. Note that if a 2D outline is open, it is automatically closed when acted upon by **Solext**.

The AME tool Solrev

Solids of revolution can be formed with the aid of the tool **Solrev**. The prompts and options are:

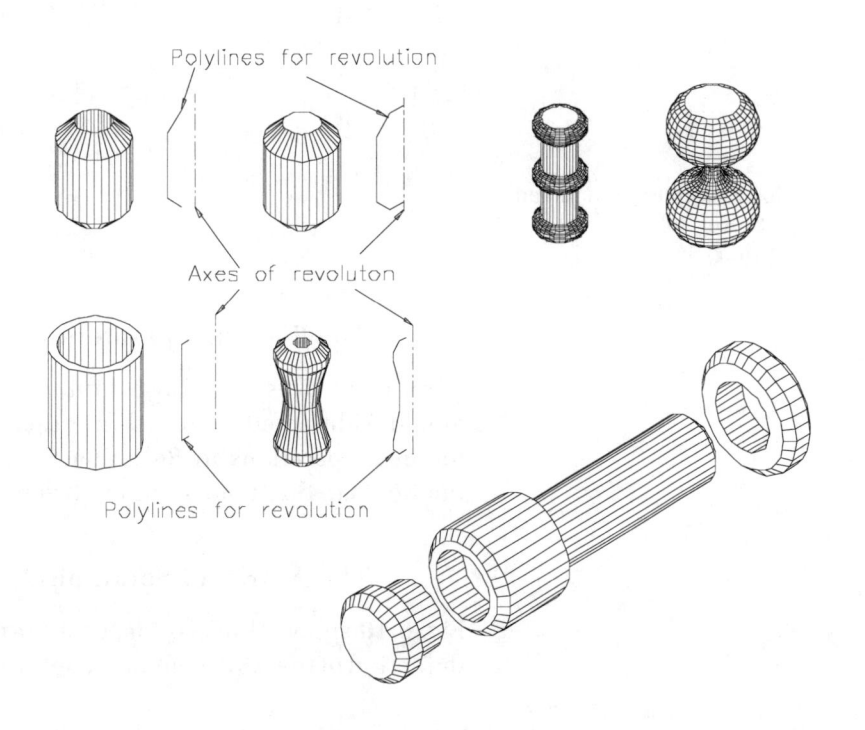

Fig. 5.7 Examples of full circle **Solrev** solids of revolution

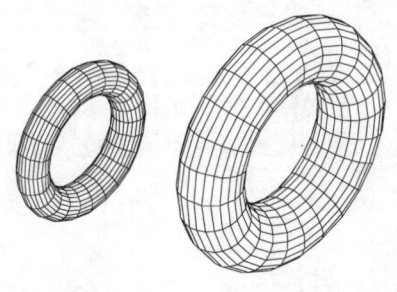

Fig. 5.8 The result of using **Solrev** on a circle is a torus

Command: solrev *right-click*
Select region polyline or circle for revolution...
Select objects:
Axis of revolution – Entity/X/Y/<Start point of axis>: *pick* the require point, or *enter* coordinates
End point of axis: *pick* the require point, or *enter* coordinates
Angle of revolution <full circle>: *right-click*
Command:

Figure 5.7 shows a number of solids of revolution formed with the aid of **Solrev**. Note that there is no need to draw an axis of revolution. It is only necessary to *pick* or *enter* the coordinates of the ends. The centre lines showing the axes in Fig. 5.7 are included to show the reader where the axes lie in relation to the plines from which the solids of revolution are generated.

Note that if a circle is selected as the basis for a solid of revolution by **Solrev**, a torus will be formed (Fig. 5.8).

Partial solids of revolution can be formed by *entering* an angle figure in response to the **Included angle <full circle>:** option (Fig. 5.9).

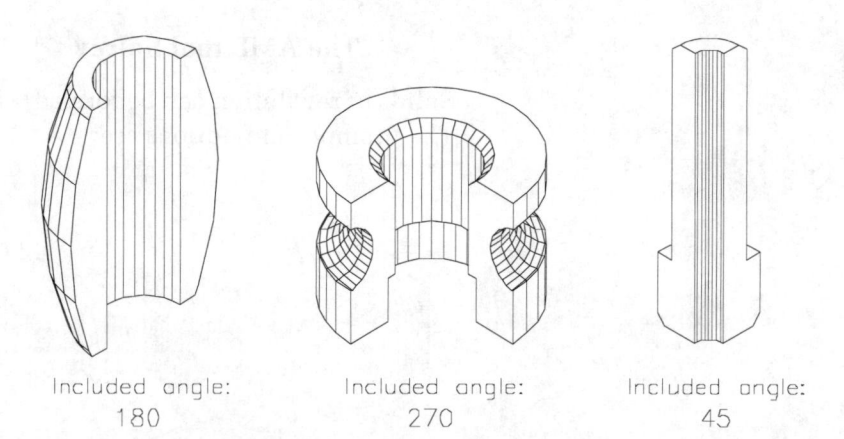

Fig. 5.9 Examples of included angle **Solrev** solid sof revolution

Included angle: 180
Included angle: 270
Included angle: 45

The Boolean operators

AME primitives and those formed by **Solext** and **Solrev** can be joined, subtracted from and intersected with each other. The tools for these operations are **Solunion**, **Solsub** and **Solint**. These produce the Boolean operations union, difference and intersection.

The AME tool Solunion

Fig. 5.10 shows three solids, each formed from two primitives, by the action of the AME command **Solunion**. When **Solunion** is called, the command line shows a series of statements as the primitives are acted upon by the tool:

Command: solunion *right-click*
Select objects: *pick* **1 found**
Select objects: *pick* **1 found**
Select objects: *right-click*
2 objects selected.
Phase 1 – Boundary evaluation begins.
3 of 20 of Phase 1 in progress.
Phase II – Tessellation computation begins.
Updating the Advanced Modeling Extension database.
Command:

The upper three drawings of Fig. 5.10 show primitives before calling **Solunion**. The lower three show the same drawings as solid model drawings after the action of **Solunion** and **Solmesh**.

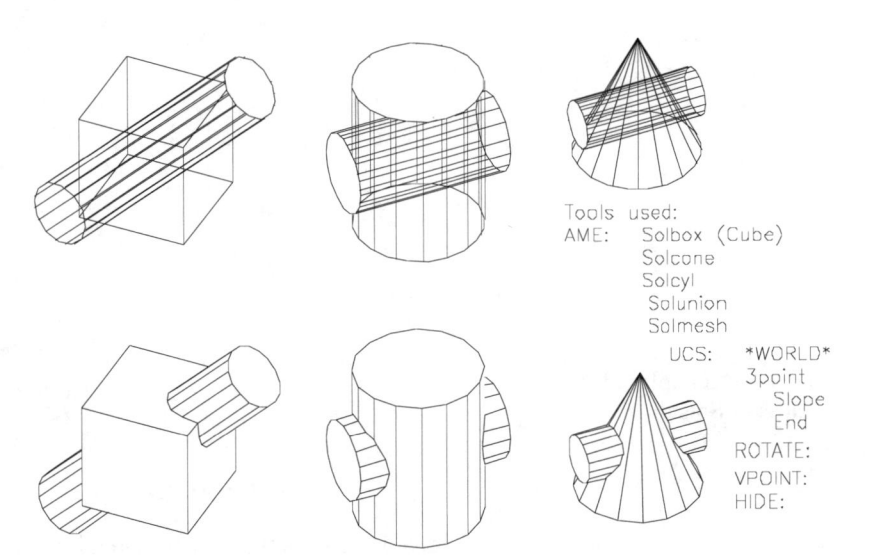

Fig. 5.10 Examples of the results of **Solunion**

The AME tool Solsub

Fig. 5.11 shows three solids each formed from two primitives by the action of the AME tool **Solsub**. When the tool is called , the command lien shows a series of statements as the primitives are subtracted one from the other.

Command: solsub *right-click*
Source objects...
Select objects: *pick* **1 found**
Objects to subtract from them...

Select objects: *pick* **1 found**
Select objects: *right-click*
Phase 1 – Boundary evaluation begins.
3 of 20 of Phase 1 in progress.
Phase II – Tessellation computation begins.
Updating the Advanced Modeling Extension database.
1 solid subtracted from 1 solid.
Command:

The upper three drawings of Fig. 5.11 show primitives before calling the tool **Solsub**. The lower three show the same drawing as solid models after the action of **Solsub** and **Solmesh**.

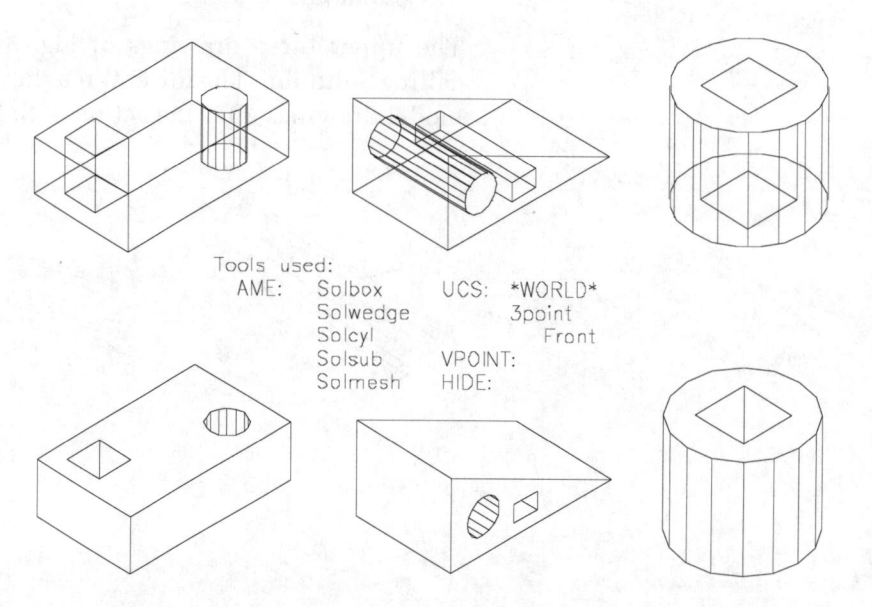

Fig. 5.11 Examples of the results of **Solsub**

The AME tool Solint

Fig. 5.12 shows three solids, each formed from two primitives by the action of the AME tool **Solint**. When the tool is called, the command line shows a series of statements as the primitives are intersected with one another.

Command: solint *right-click*
Select objects: *pick* **1 found**
Select objects: *pick* **1 found**
Select objects: *right-click*
2 solids selected.
Phase 1 – Boundary evaluation begins.
3 of 20 of Phase 1 in progress.
Phase II – Tesselation computation begins.

3D solid model drawings 91

Updating the Advanced Modeling Extension database.
2 solids intersected.
Command:

The upper three drawings of Fig. 5.12 show primitives before calling the tool **Solint**. The lower three show the same drawings as solid model drawings after the action of **Solint** and **Solmesh**.

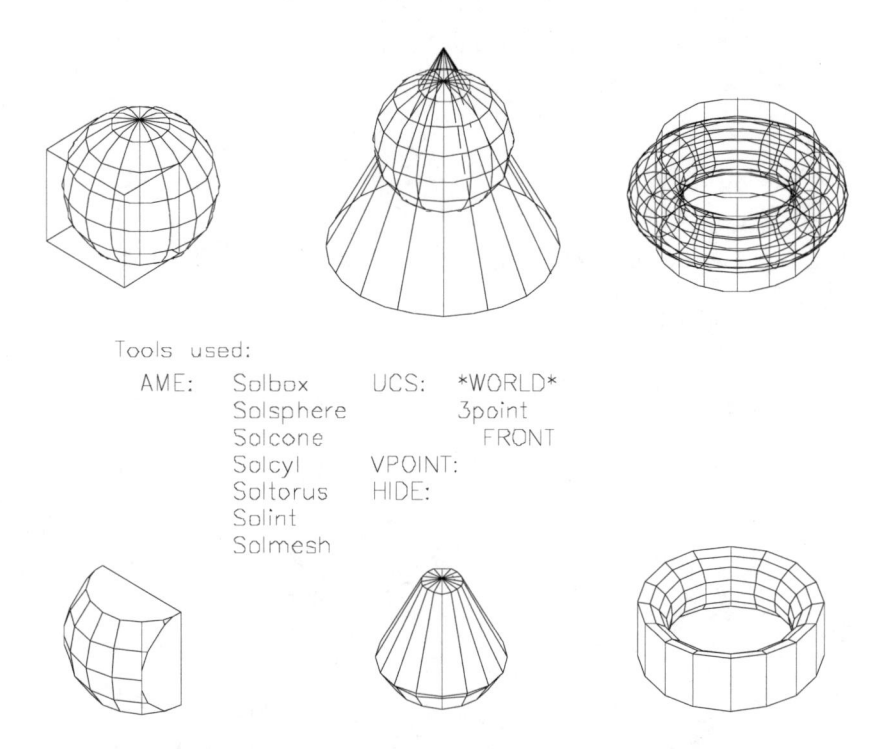

Tools used:
AME: Solbox   UCS: *WORLD*
     Solsphere   3point
     Solcone   FRONT
     Solcyl   VPOINT:
     Soltorus HIDE:
     Solint
     Solmesh

Fig. 5.12 Examples of the action of **Solint**

Figures 5.13 to 5.17 are examples of 3D solid model drawings formed from primitives, extrusions and solids of revolution with the aid of the two AME tools **Solunion** and **Solsub**. Details of the tools employed are included, together with main dimensions for the benefit of those who wish to construct these examples. Use your own judgement for those sizes which are not included.

Saving disk capacity

When AME 3D solid model drawings are saved to disk, the resulting drawing files will often be large, containing many kilobytes, depending upon their complexity. Files in excess of 0.5 megabyte (500 kilobytes) are not uncommon. If care is taken in deciding how to construct AME drawings, disk space can be saved. As examples of this, study the 3D solid model drawings in Fig. 5.18 and Fig. 5.19. It will be

92   An Introduction to 3D AutoCAD

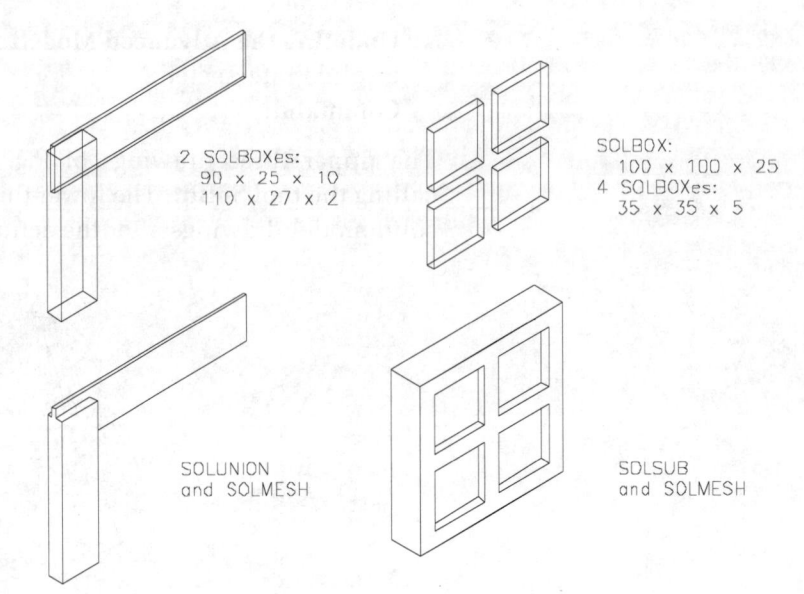

Fig. 5.13 Two examples of simple AME solids using **Solunion** and **Solsub**

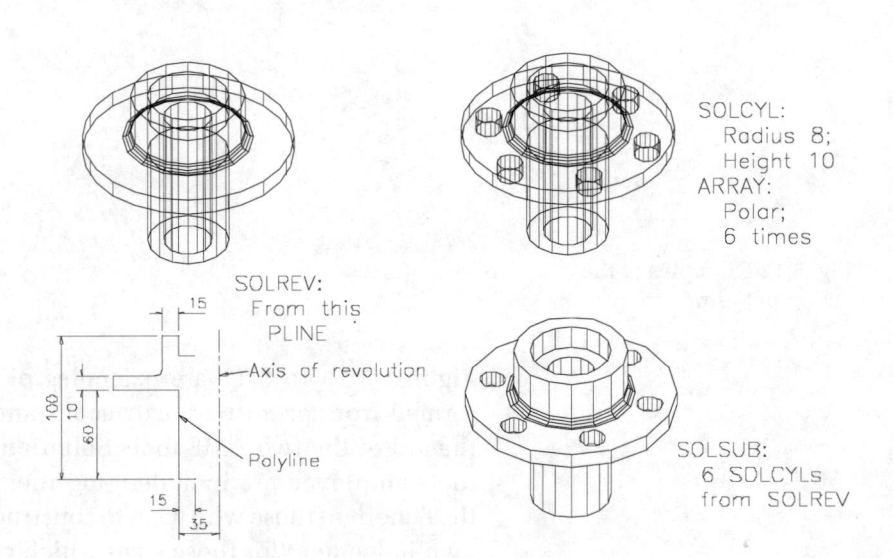

Fig. 5.14 Stage in constructing an AME solid with **Solrev**

3D solid model drawings 93

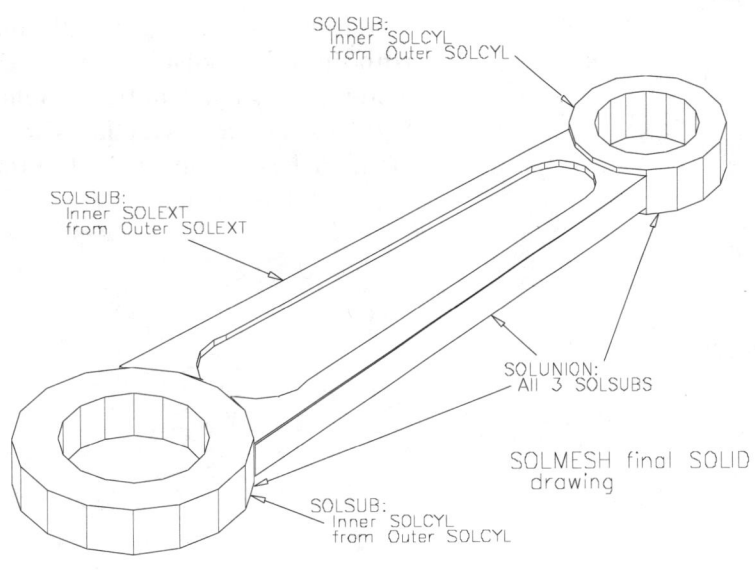

Fig. 5.15 An example of an AME solid involving several AME tools

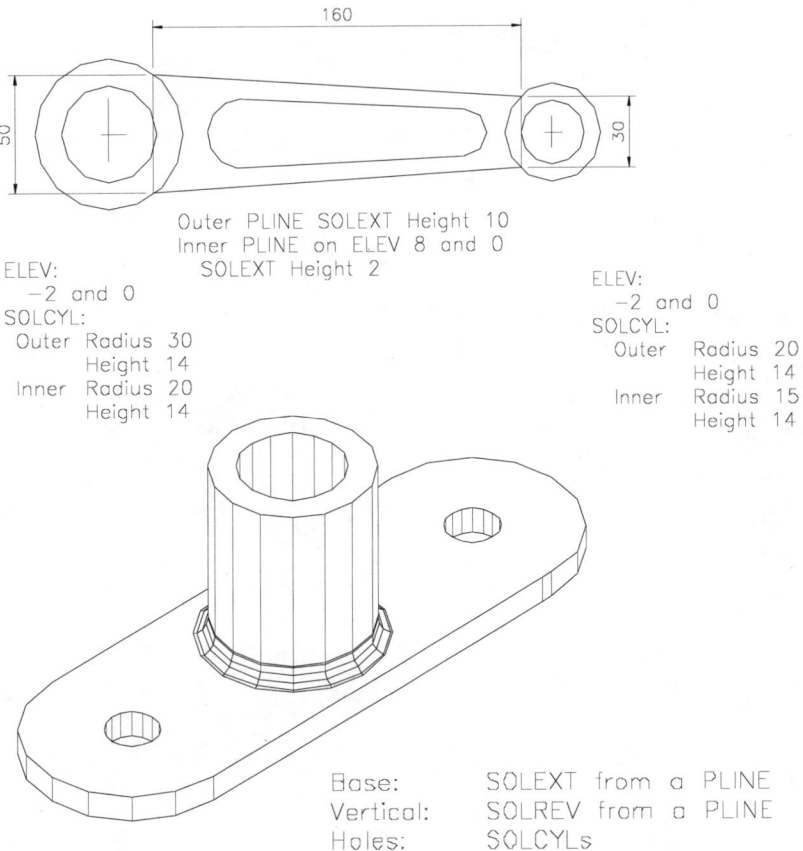

SOLSUB: Inner SOLCYL from Outer SOLCYL

SOLSUB: Inner SOLEXT from Outer SOLEXT

SOLUNION: All 3 SOLSUBS

SOLMESH final SOLID drawing

SOLSUB: Inner SOLCYL from Outer SOLCYL

Fig. 5.16 Dimensions for constructing Fig. 5.15

Outer PLINE SOLEXT Height 10
Inner PLINE on ELEV 8 and 0
SOLEXT Height 2

ELEV:
  −2 and 0
SOLCYL:
  Outer Radius 30
         Height 14
  Inner Radius 20
         Height 14

ELEV:
  −2 and 0
SOLCYL:
  Outer Radius 20
         Height 14
  Inner Radius 15
         Height 14

Fig. 5.17 An example of an AME solid involving several AME tools

Base: SOLEXT from a PLINE
Vertical: SOLREV from a PLINE
Holes: SOLCYLs
SOLSUB: Holes from base
SOLUNION: Base and vertical
SOLMESH:

seen from Fig. 5.18 that the 3D model produced from two **Solbox**es with the aid of **Solsub** requires less disk space than the similar 3D model produced from three **Solbox**es with the aid of **Solunion**. In Fig. 5.18, the various methods possible for constructing the required 3D model result in quite different file sizes as measured in the required disk capacity.

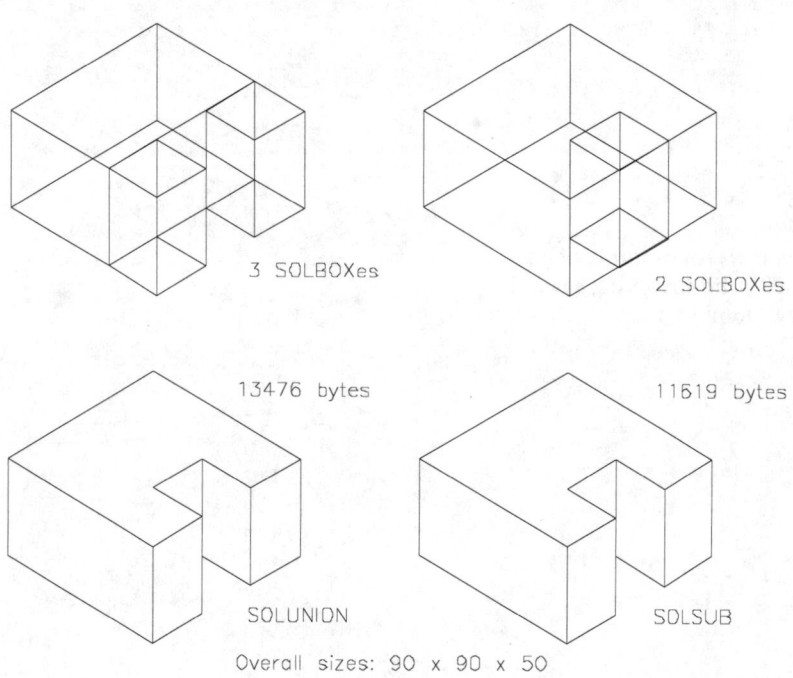

Fig. 5.18 Saving disk space

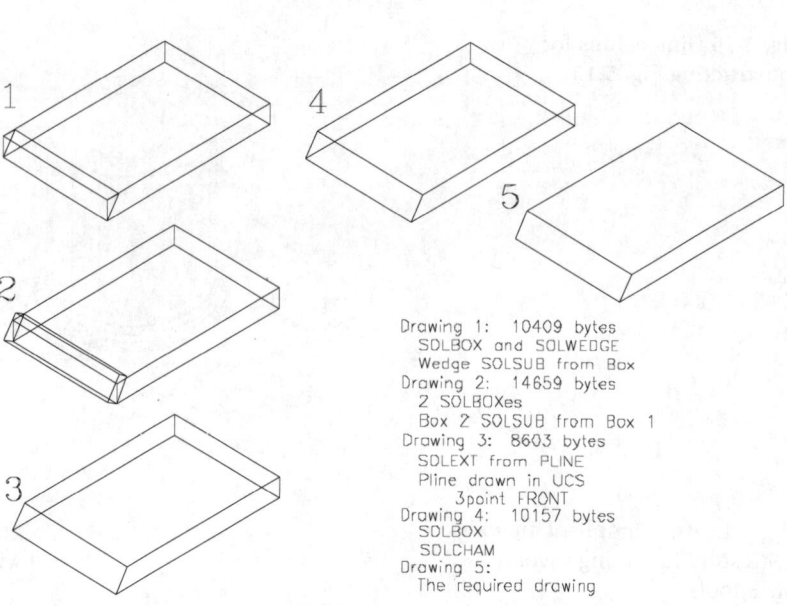

Fig. 5.19 Saving disk space

Drawing 1: 10409 bytes
  SOLBOX and SOLWEDGE
  Wedge SOLSUB from Box
Drawing 2: 14659 bytes
  2 SOLBOXes
  Box 2 SOLSUB from Box 1
Drawing 3: 8603 bytes
  SOLEXT from PLINE
  Pline drawn in UCS
  3point FRONT
Drawing 4: 10157 bytes
  SOLBOX
  SOLCHAM
Drawing 5:
  The required drawing

3D solid model drawings 95

Primitive, extrusion or revolved solid

Similar 3D model drawings can be constructed from primitives, extrusions or revolved models. An example of this is shown in Fig. 5.20.

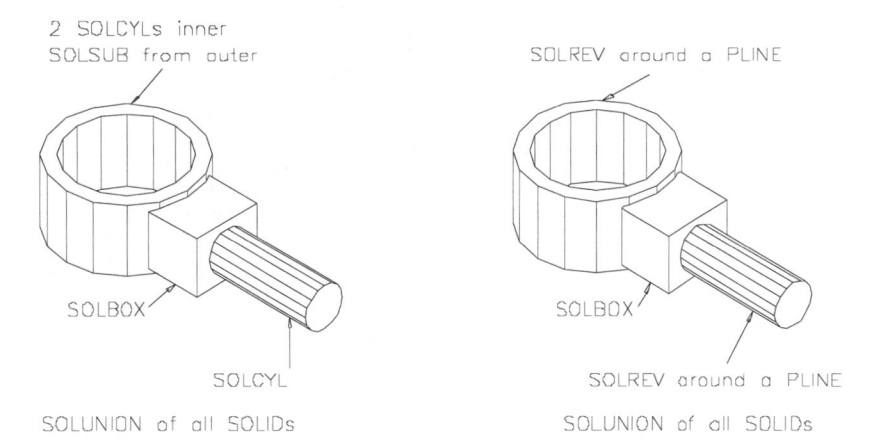

Fig. 5.20 Two methods of constructing an AME solid using different AME tools

Constructing 3D models in viewports

The method of constructing 3D model drawings, which is probably the most frequently employed, is to work in a three-viewport setup such as that shown in Fig. 5.21. The model can be constructed in the

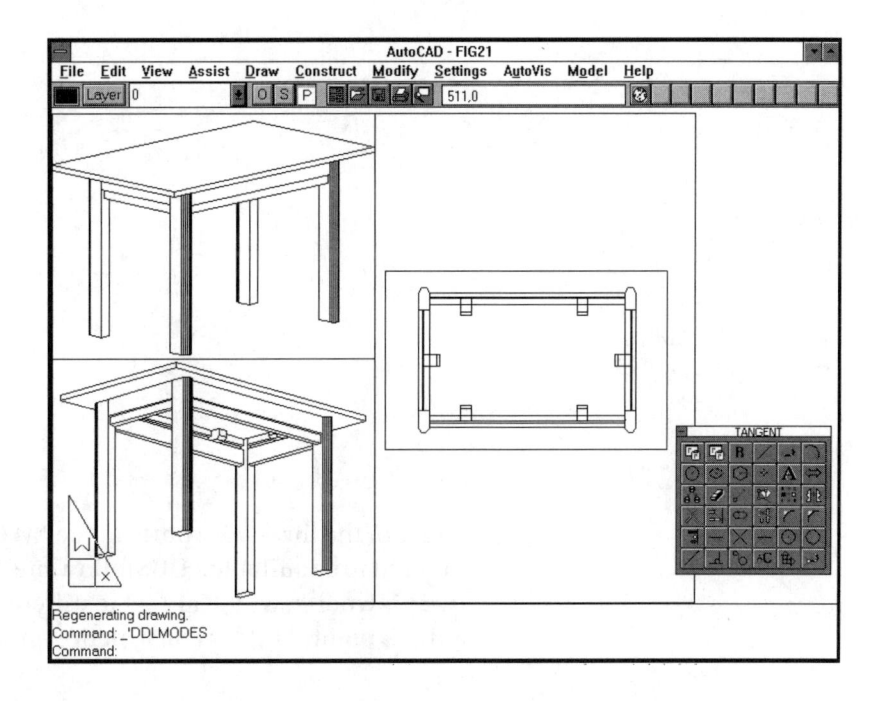

Fig. 5.21 An example of an AME 3D drawing contructed in a three-viewport setting in **MSpace** and then changed to **PSpace**

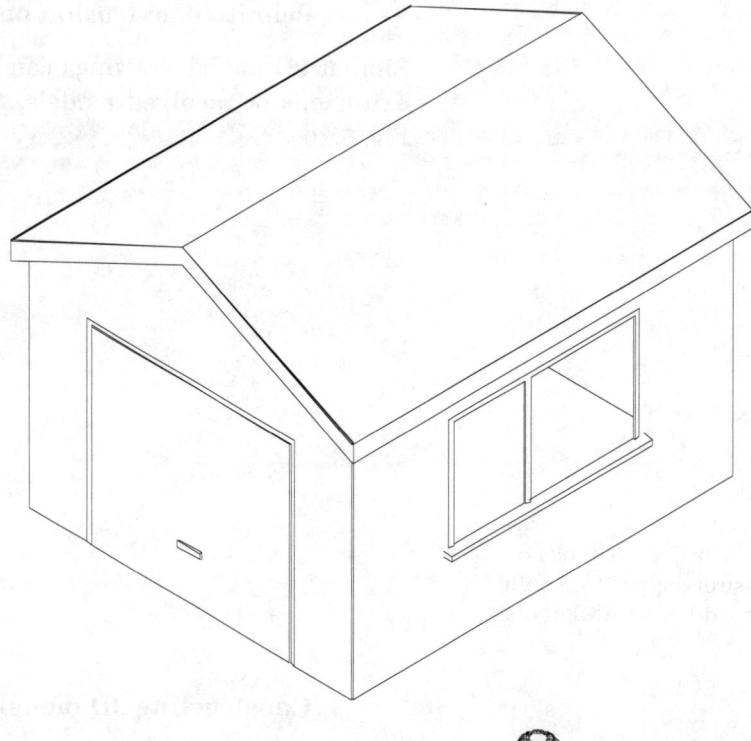

Fig. 5.22 A Vpoint view of an AME solid

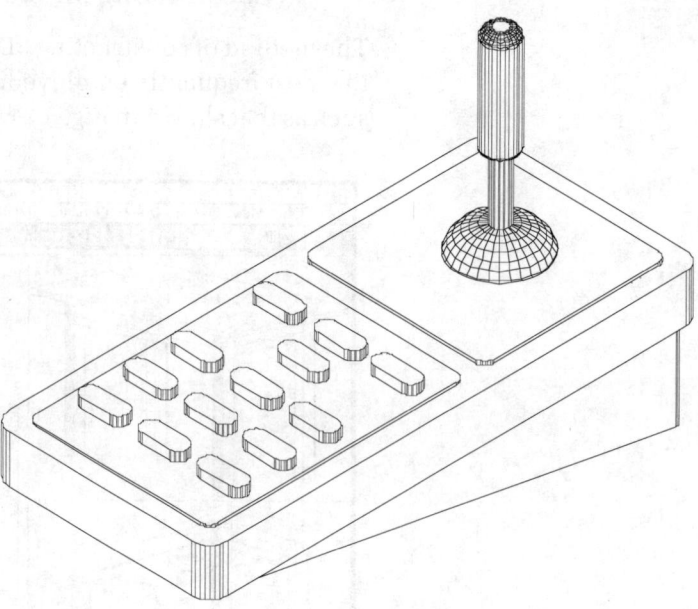

Fig. 5.23 An AME solid drawing of a joystick

larger of the three viewports in the ***WORLD** UCS (or any other UCS thought to be suitable). **UCSfollow** must be set to 0 (**OFF**) in the other two viewports, which are set to different viewing positions with the aid of **Vpoint**. Then as construction proceeds in the largest viewport, the results, in pictorial views, can be seen on the other two. Working in this manner assists in achieving accuracy.

Further examples of AME 3D model drawings

Figures 5.22 and 5.23 are two further examples of 3D solid model drawings constructed in AME.

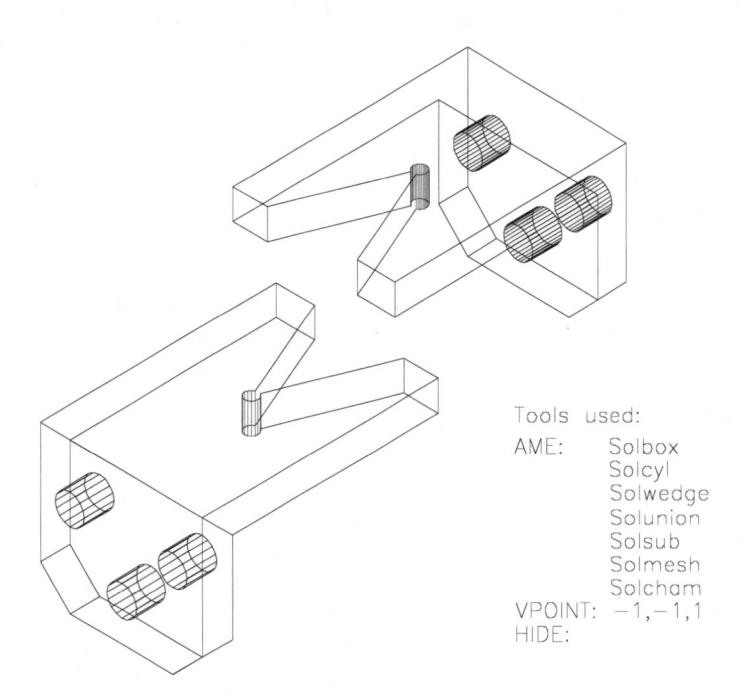

```
Tools used:
AME:   Solbox
       Solcyl
       Solwedge
       Solunion
       Solsub
       Solmesh
       Solcham
VPOINT: −1,−1,1
HIDE:
```

Fig. 5.24 Two views of an AME model drawing Exercise 1

Exercises

Five exercises are given below to allow the reader to practise constructing with the aid of the set of AME tools described in this chapter. No dimensions are included with the drawing. Work to convenient sizes.

1. Two views of a 3D solid drawing of a simple sawing board are given in Fig. 5.24. Construct the 3D drawing with the aid of the tools shown.
2. A pictorial view of a 3D drawing of a clip is given in Fig. 5.25. Working to sizes of your own choice, construct the drawing with the aid of the AME tools shown.

98 An Introduction to 3D AutoCAD

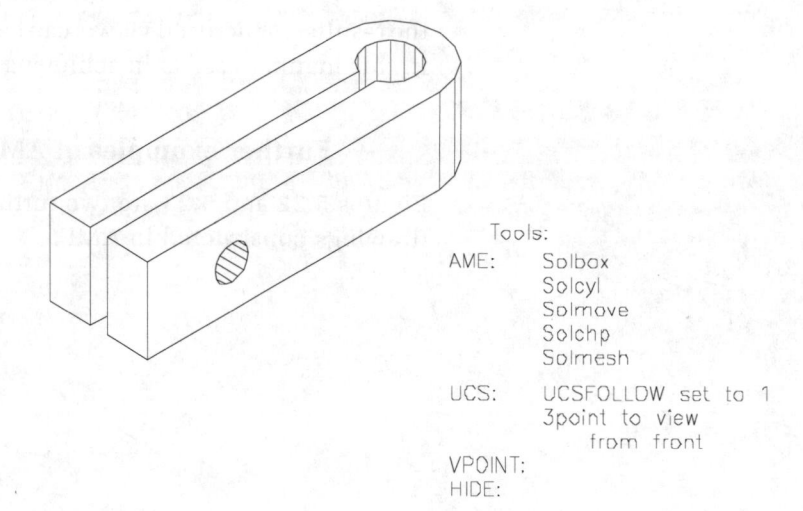

Tools:
AME: Solbox
       Solcyl
       Solmove
       Solchp
       Solmesh
UCS: UCSFOLLOW set to 1
       3point to view
              from front
VPOINT:
HIDE:

Fig. 5.25 Exercise 2

3. Figure 5.26 is a **Vpoint** view of a pipe clip drawn with the aid of AME. Construct the drawing using suitable dimensions.

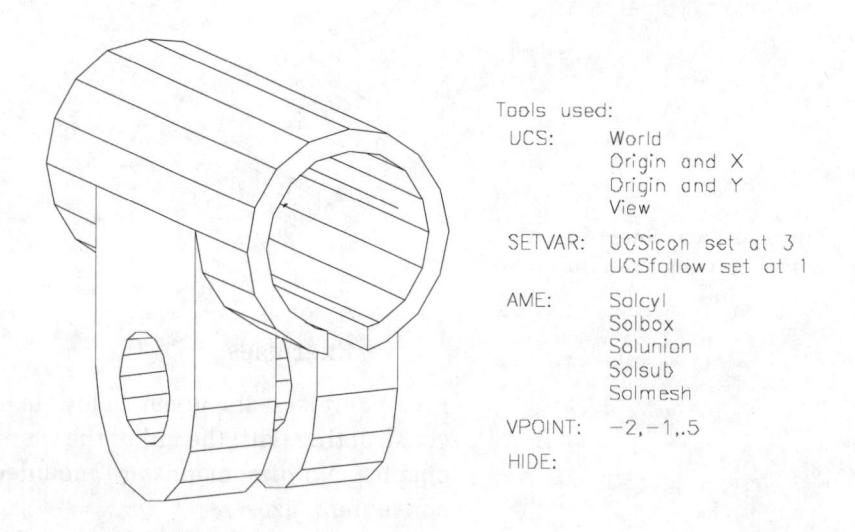

Tools used:
UCS: World
         Origin and X
         Origin and Y
         View
SETVAR: UCSicon set at 3
         UCSfollow set at 1
AME: Solcyl
         Solbox
         Solunion
         Solsub
         Solmesh
VPOINT: −2,−1,.5
HIDE:

Fig. 5.26 Exercise 3

4. Figure 5.27 is a 3D model of a clip. With the aid of the tools included with the drawing, construct the given model.

Plate I An AME solid model ready for rendering in AutoCAD Release 12 for DOS

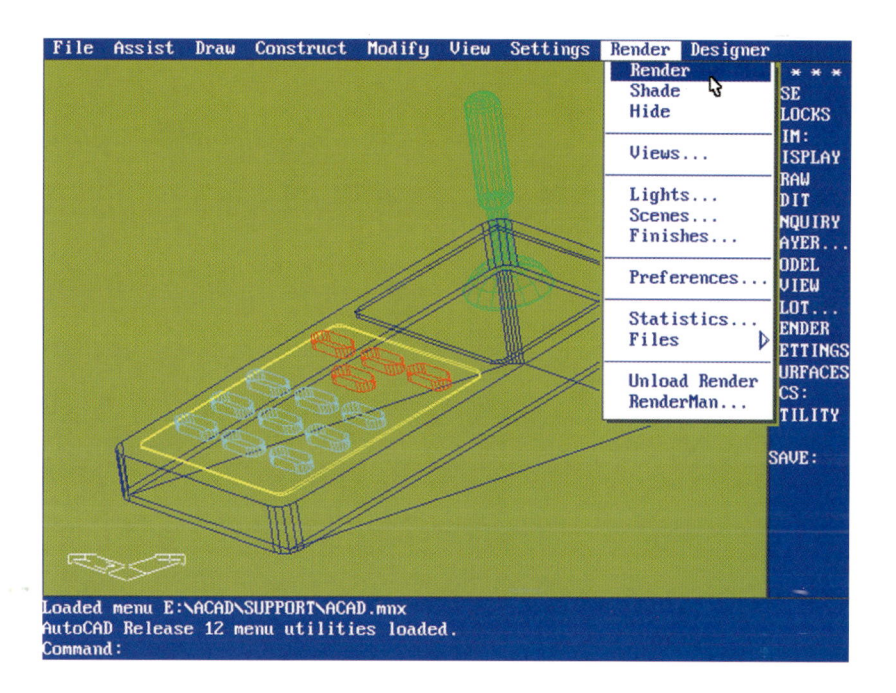

Plate II The AME model in Plate I rendered against a white background

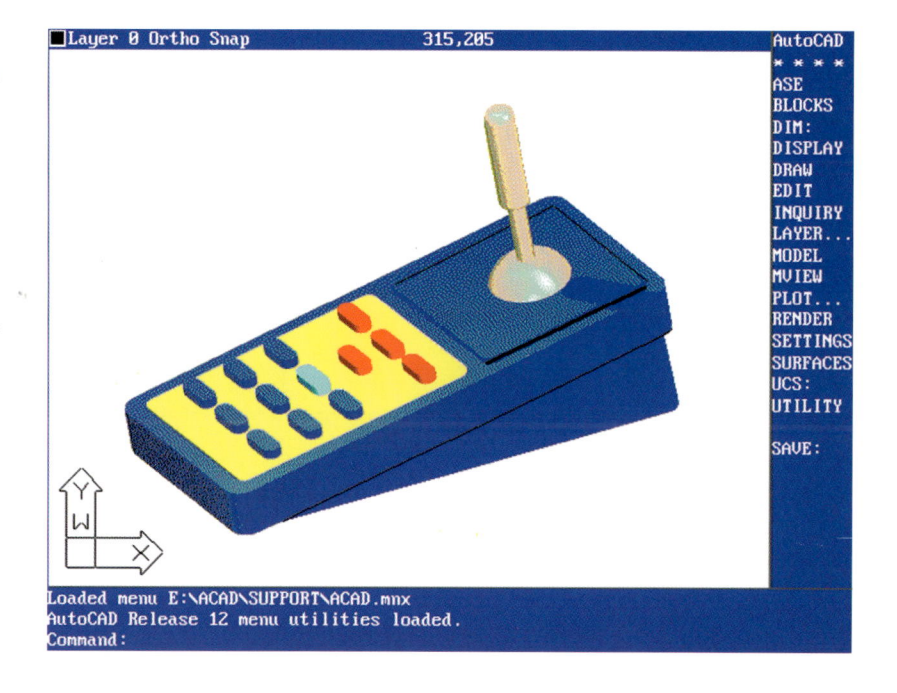

Plate III The 3D model in Plate I rendered in AutoCAD Release 13 (Windows version)

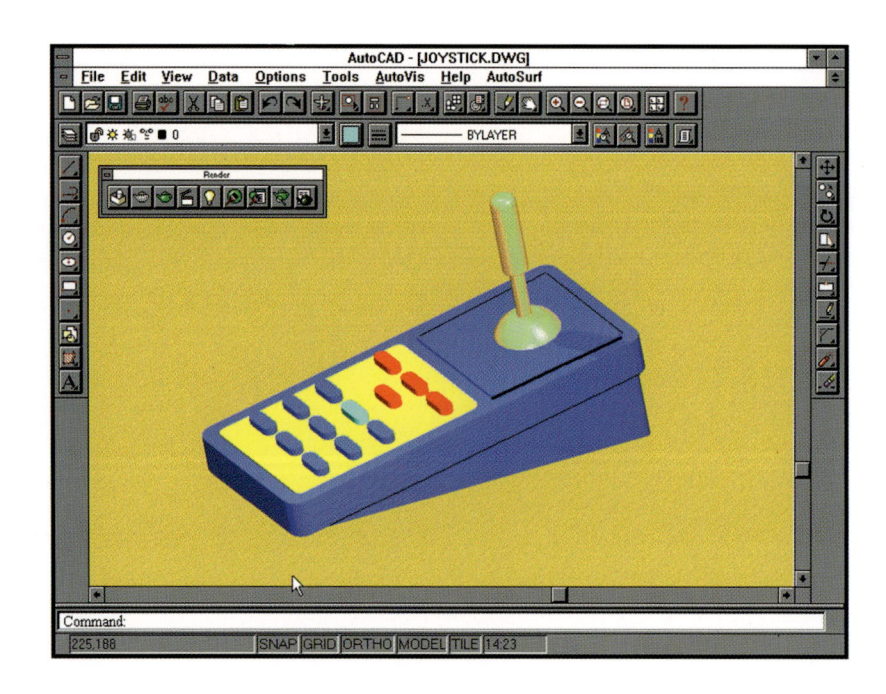

Plate IV A 3D model constructed with **Surface** commands and rendered using AutoVision within AutoCAD for Windows

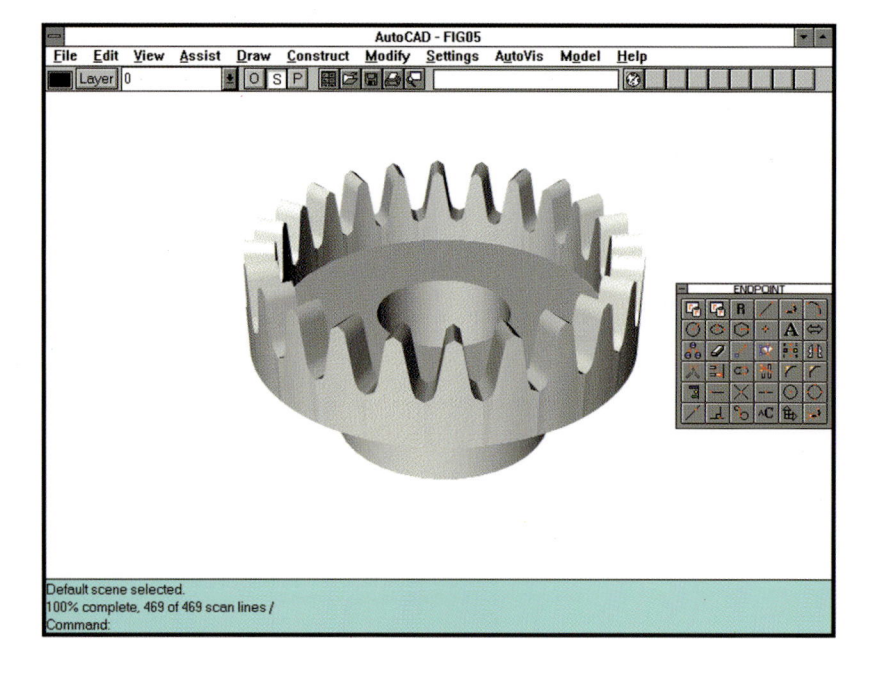

Plate V The 3D model in Plate IV rendered in copper using AutoVision Release 2 within AutoCAD Release 13 (Windows 95 version)

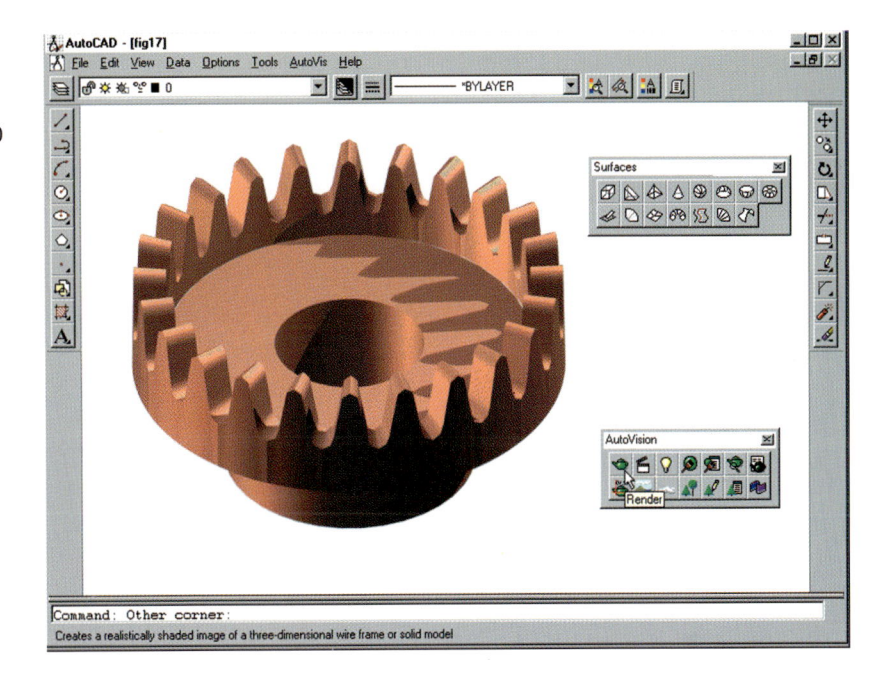

Plate VI Two poppet valves constructed with the aid of **Surfrev** and rendered in AutoCAD Release 13 (Windows 95 version)

Plate VII A perspective view of a 3D garage model ready for rendering in AutoCAD Release 13 for Windows

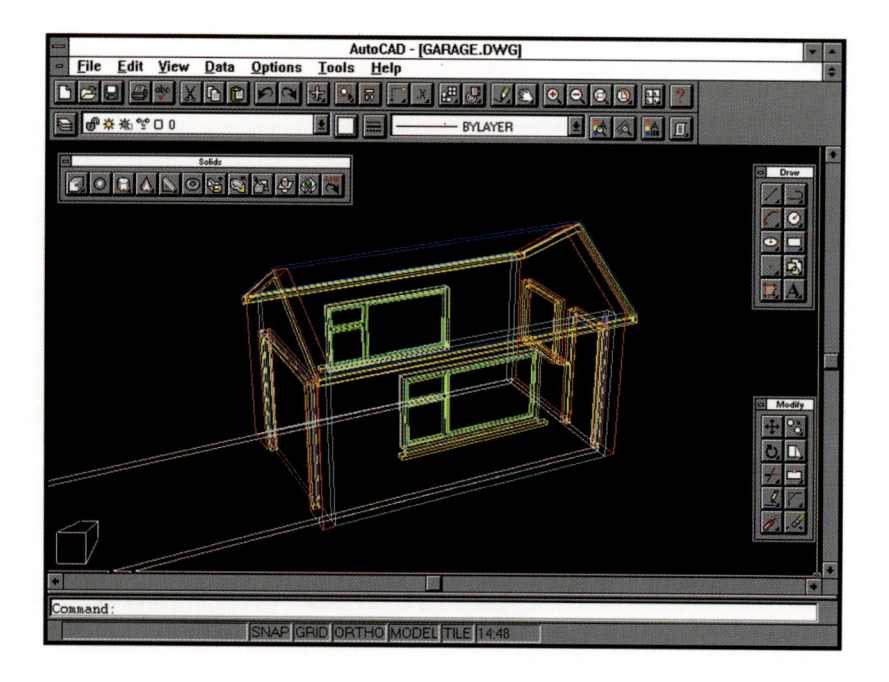

Plate VIII The result of using the **Shade** command on the garage model in Plate VII. AutoCAD has here been configured to use a background colour other than white

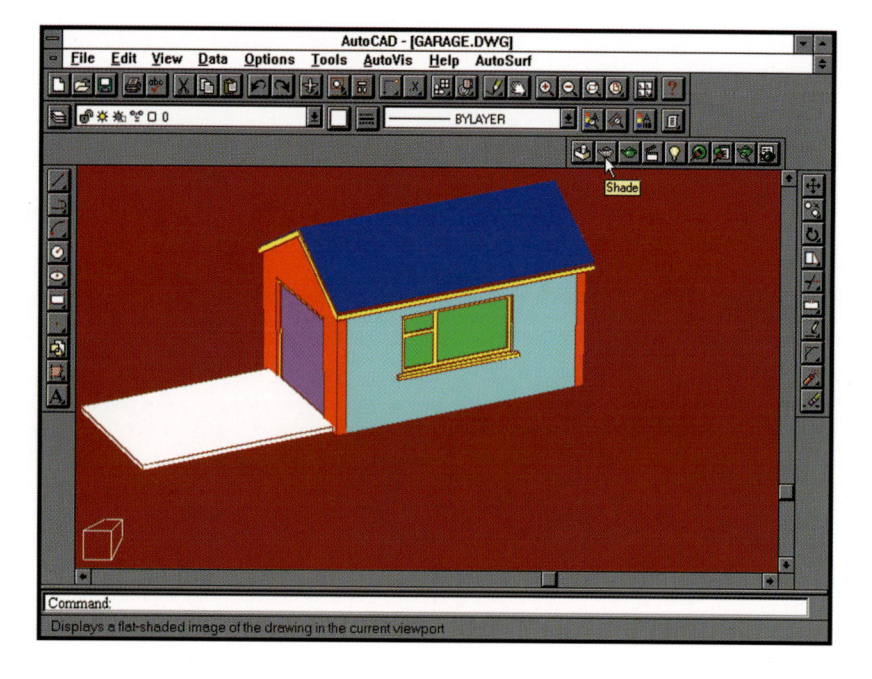

Plate IX The garage model in Plates VI and VIII rendered in the colours used when the parts were drawn

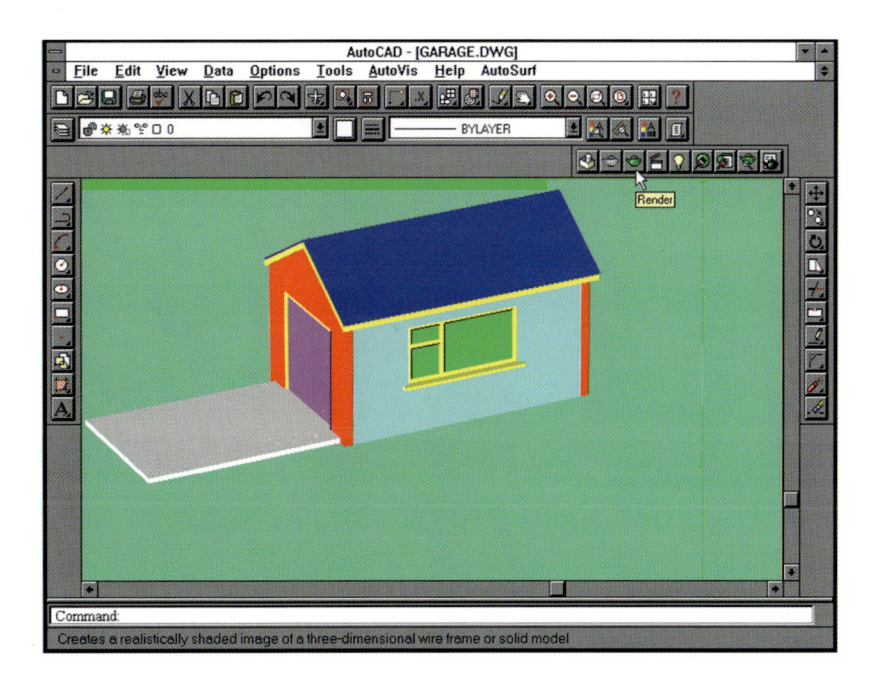

Plate X The garage model rendered using materials added in Autodesk 3D Studio

Plate XI Two solid models created in AutoCAD rendered within 3D Studio against a tiled background

Plate XII A model constructed in AutoCAD using the **Revsurf** command and rendered in 3D Studio

Plate XIII A 3D AutoCAD model rendered in 3D Studio against a brick background

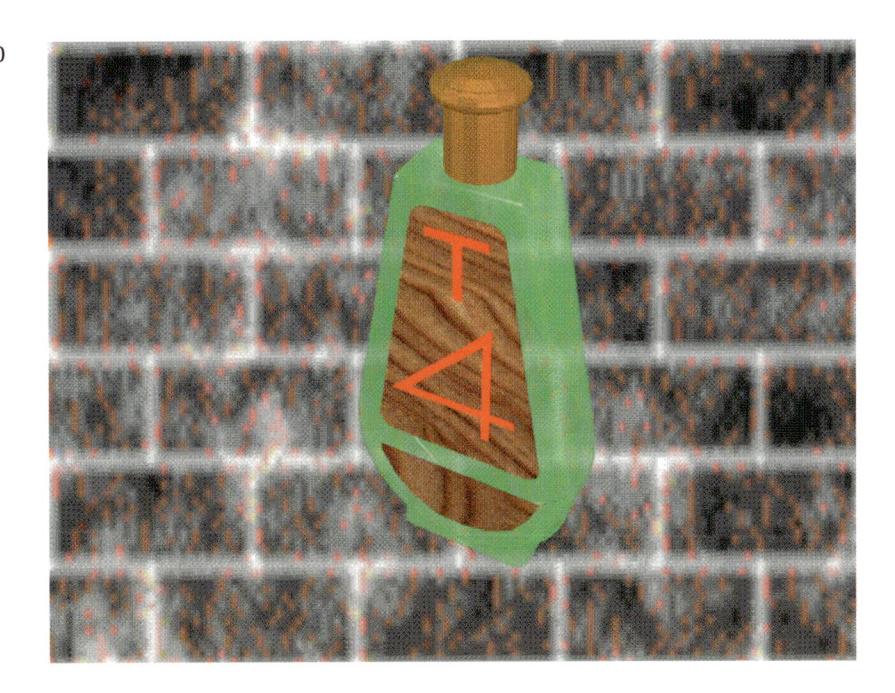

Plate XIV A model constructed and rendered in 3D Studio

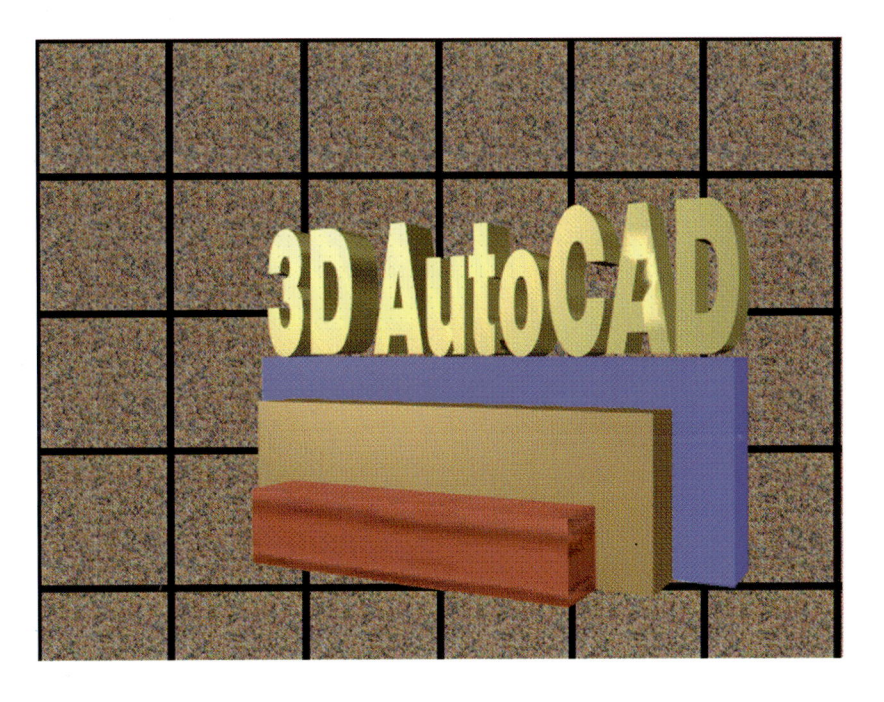

Plate XV A 3D model created in AutoCAD rendered against a background in 3D Studio

Plate XVI An AutoCAD 3D model rendered as a variety of materials within 3D Studio

3D solid model drawings 99

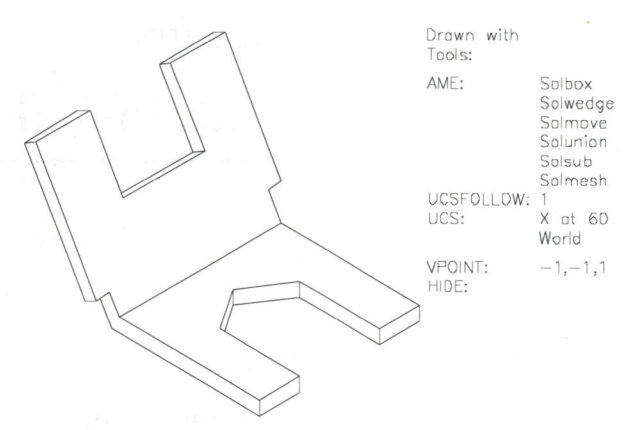

Fig. 5.27 Exercise 4

5. Figure 5.28 is a drawing of a clip drawn with the aid of the Advanced Modelling Extension. Construct the drawing with the aid of the tools shown. Note that **Solfill** is described in the next chapter.

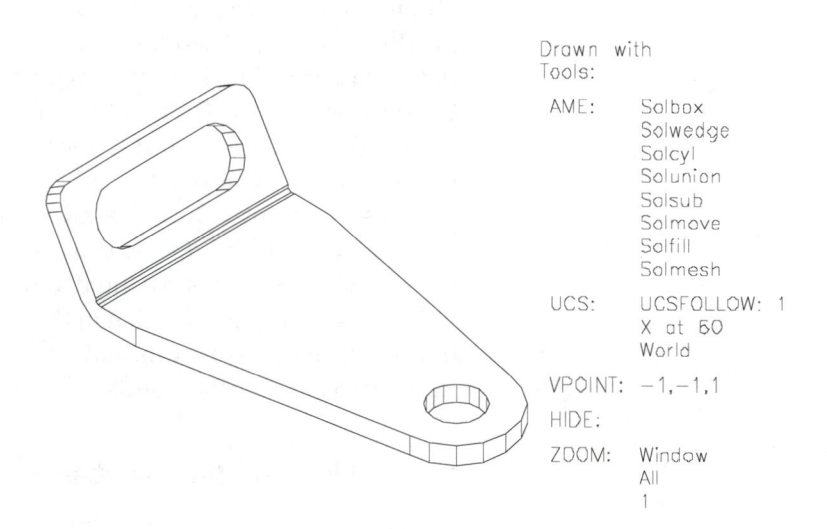

Fig. 5.28 Exercise 5

CHAPTER 6

Additional AME 3D tools

Introduction

As stated earlier 3D models are best constructed in a three-viewport AutoCAD drawing editor. As the construction proceeds in the largest viewport, details of the construction can be made to appear in pictorial views in the other two viewports from different viewing positions. This allows the operator to check whether details of the 3D model are correct while the model is being constructed. Some of the illustrations in this chapter show AME solids which were drawn in this manner. The largest viewport is in the ***WORLD*** UCS with **UCSfollow** set to 1 (**ON**). In the other two viewports, **UCSfollow** is set to 0 (**OFF**), with **Vpoint** in the upper viewport set to −1,−1,1 and in the lower viewport set to 1,-1,1.

These settings allow the UCS in the largest viewport to be changed to give the operator the opportunity to add details on a variety of UCS planes, without the UCS settings in the other two viewports changing with that in the largest. It also allows viewing of the construction as its proceeds, from two different viewing points in the two smaller viewports.

The AME tool Solcham

A chamfer is formed on an AME 3D model by *picking* an edge of a correctly chosen surface of the model. The required surface, edge and the chamfer sizes are determined by the responses to the sequence of prompts appearing when **Solcham** is called:

> **Command:** solcham *right-click*
> **Pick base surface:** *pick* an edge of the required surface
> **Next/<OK>:** *right-click* (if the selected surface is correct. If not
>   enter n (Next) *right-click*
> **Pick edge to be chamfered (Press Enter when done):** *pick right-click*
> **1 edge selected.**

Enter distance along first surface <0>: 10 *right-click*
Enter distance along second surface<10>: *right-click*
Phase 1 – Boundary evaluation begins.
3 of 15 of Phase 1 in operation.
Phase II – Tessellation computation begins.
2 of 5 of Phase II in process.
Updating the Advanced Modelling Extension database.
Command:

Examples of chamfers formed on AME models with the aid of **Solcham** are given in Fig. 6.1.

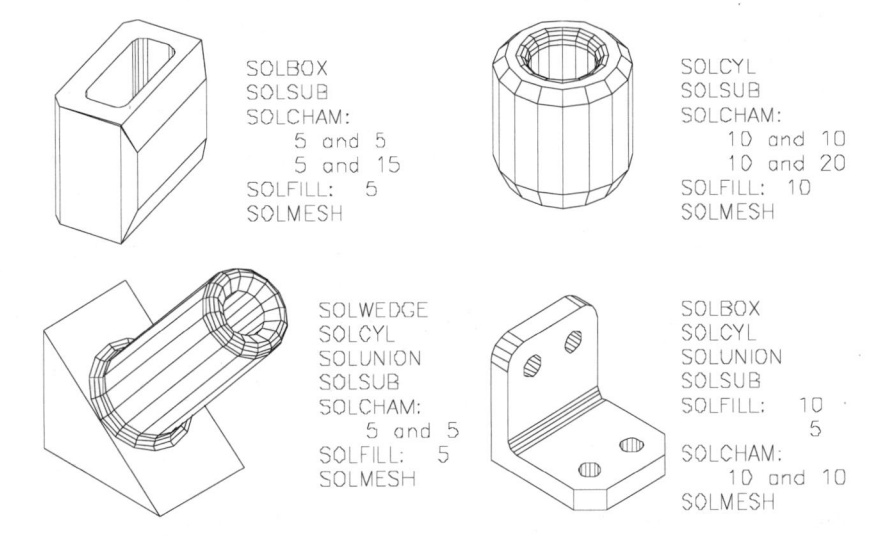

Fig. 6.1 Examples of AME solids modifed by **Solcham** and **Solfill**

The AME tool Solfill

The prompts, options and responses for **Solfill** are similar to those for **Solcham**, except that only edges need to be *picked* and only one size (radius or diameter) is required for the command to commence functioning.

Command: solfill *right-click*
Pick edges to be filleted (Press ENTER when done): *pick right-click*
1 edge selected.
Diameter/<Radius> of fillet <0>: 5 *right-click*
Phase 1 – Boundary evaluation begins.
3 of 15 of Phase 1 in operation.
Phase II – Tessellation computation begins.
2 of 5 of Phase II in process.
Updating the Advanced Modelling Extension database.
Command:

Examples of fillets formed on AME models with the aid of **Solfill** are given in Fig. 6.1.

Problems arising with Solfill and Solcham

Each AME fillet and chamfer included in 3D solid models is a separate 3D entity (a sub-model). This can give rise to undesirable results. An example of such a result arising from using **Solfill** is shown in Fig. 6.2, together with a method of overcoming the particular problem.

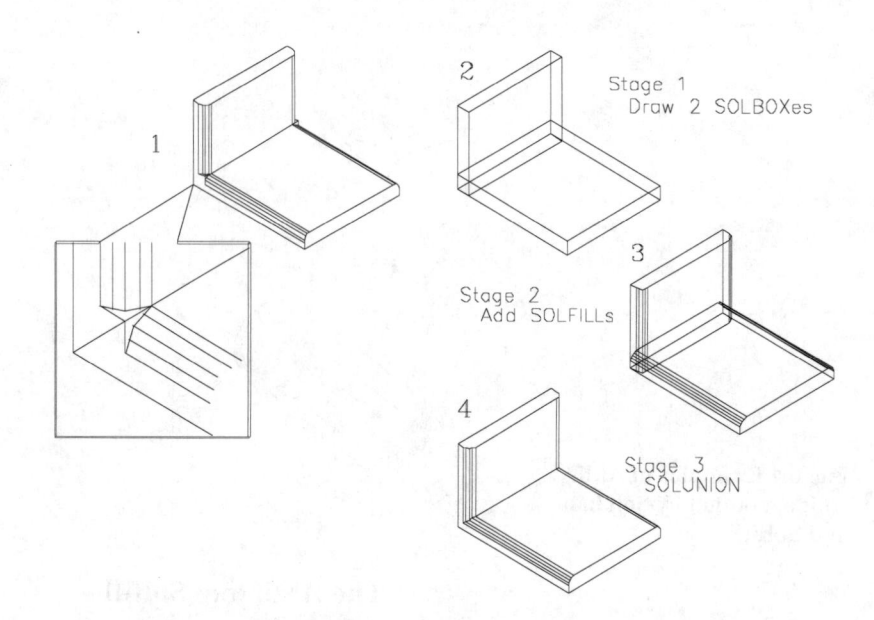

Fig. 6.2 A possible error when using **Solfill**, and its remedy

1. Drawing 1 – a solid formed from two **Solbox**es which have been acted upon by **Solunion** to form a single 3D solid model. Then fillets have been added with the aid of **Solfill**. The results are clearly undesirable.
2. Drawing 2 – the two **Solbox**es before being combined with **Solunion**.
3. Drawing 3 – fillets added with **Solfill**.
4. Drawing 4 – the two **Solbox**es are formed into a single 3D solid with **Solunion**. The results are now as desired.

An example of an undesirable result arising from the use of **Solcham** is given in Fig. 6.3, together with a method of overcoming the particular problem.

From these two examples, it can be seen that some care is required when adding fillets or chamfers to AME 3D solid models with **Solfill** or **Solcham**.

Additional AME 3D tools   103

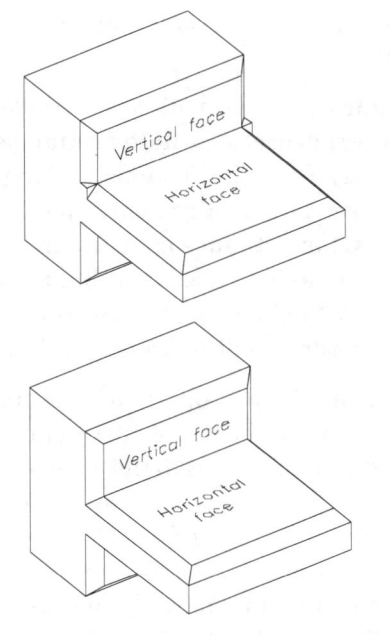

AME 3D solid model drawing formed from 2 SOLBOXes acted upon by SOLUNION

Horizontal faces chamfered with SOLCHAM before vertical faces

The same 3D solid model drawing with vertical edges chamfered with SOLCHAM before horizontal faces

Fig. 6.3 A possible error when using **Solcham** and its remedy

The AME tool Solmove

Solmove is an AME tool system which enables the user:

1. To move an AME 3D solid model in the direction of any of the three coordinate axes.
2. To rotate an AME 3D solid model around any of the three coordinate axes.
3. To align an AME 3D solid model with an edge or a face of another 3D solid model.
4. To align an AME 3D solid model with an existing UCS.
   When the tool is called the command line shows:

   Command: solmove *right-click*
   Select objects: *pick* the required AME 3D solid model
   Select objects: *right-click*
   1 solid selected.
   Redefining block SOLAXES.
   ?<Motion description>:

When the **Solaxes** are redefined, the Motion Coordinate System (MCS) icon appears at the UCS origin (0,0,0). The motion description can be defined in any of several ways as is shown when a **?** is *entered* in response to the option:

   ?<Motion description>: ? *right-click*

104   An Introduction to 3D AutoCAD

An AutoCAD text screen appears on which the following will be seen:

a(efuw) – align with selected coordinate system
r(xyz) degrees – rotate around selected axis
t(xyz) distance – translate along selected axis
e – set axis to edge coordinate system
f – set axis to face coordinate system
u – set axis to user coordinate system
w – set axis to world coordinate system
o – restore motion to original position

According to the operator's response to the motion description option, the selected AME 3D model can be manipulated as required. The **MCS** icon moves to the edge or face *picked* on the selected AME model and moves with the model as movement prompts are entered. The results of using the **r** (**R**otate) prompt and the **af** (**A**lign **F**ace) responses are shown in Figures 6.4 and 6.5. The operator will probably find that movement options most frequently required will be **t** (**T**ranslate) and **r** (**R**otate) to move or rotate an AME 3D model to new positions. Note that it is usually advisable to move (translate) or rotate a 3D model after the **Solaxes** have been transferred to an edge or to a face, although it is possible to move around the **Solaxes** situated at the UCS origin. If movement is based upon the **Solaxes** at the UCS origin, the results may not be as expected.

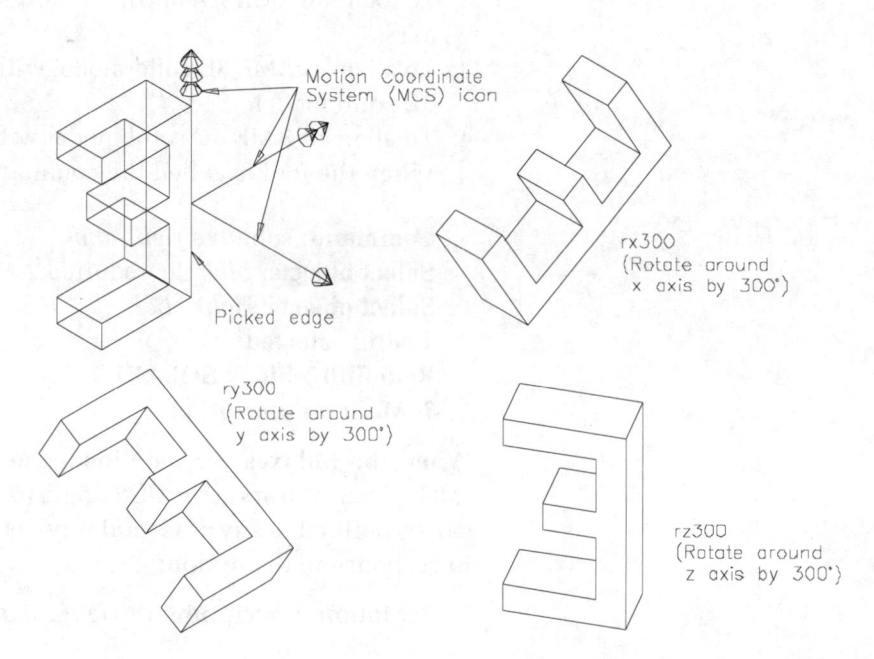

Fig. 6.4 Examples of moving an AME solid with the **Solmove** options **e** (**E**dge) and **r** (**R**otate)

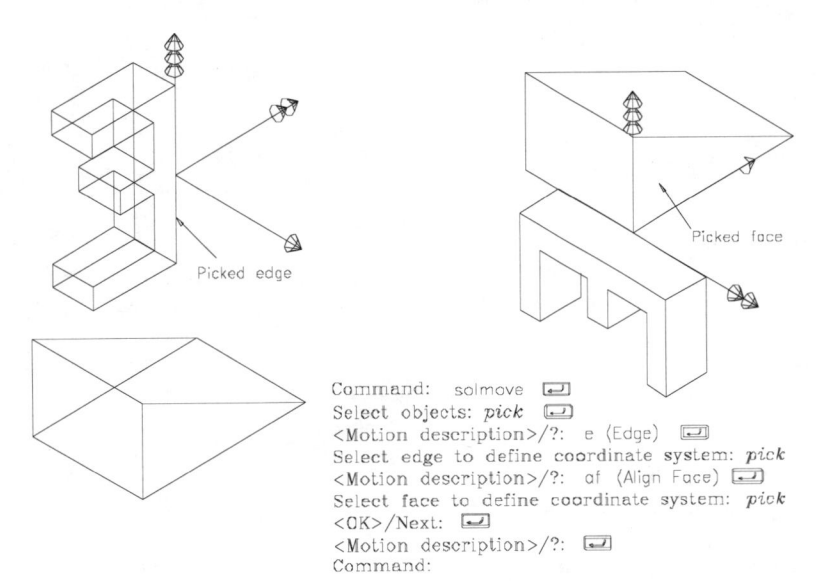

Fig. 6.5 Exaamples of moving an AME solid with the **Solmove** otpions **e (E**dge**)** and **af (A**lign Face**)**

```
Command: solmove
Select objects: pick
<Motion description>/?: e (Edge)
Select edge to define coordinate system: pick
<Motion description>/?: af (Align Face)
Select face to define coordinate system: pick
<OK>/Next:
<Motion description>/?:
Command:
```

The AME tool Solchp

This command is for changing various properties of AME primitives. When the tool is called the command line shows:

Command: solchp *right-click*
Select solid or region: *pick*
1 solid selected.
Select primitive: *pick*
Color/Delete/Evaluate/Instance/Move/Next/Pick/Replace/Size/eXit/ <N>:

From the options shown, it can be seen that with **Solchp**:

1. The colour or size of any primitive in a 3D AME solid can be changed.
2. Any primitive making up an AME 3D solid can be replaced or moved.
3. Any primitive from an AME 3D solid can be copied with the **i** (Instance) option. The copy will not be seen as it will be exactly on top of the primitive from which it was Instanced. However, the copy can be moved and then used to replace another primitive in the solid.

Examples of the **r (R**eplace**)**, **s (S**ize**)** and **m (M**ove**)** options of **Solchp** are shown in Fig. 6.6. Note that although the given 3D AME solid is composed of three primitives, the **Solunion** is retained after primitives have been amended by **Solchp**.

106 An Introduction to 3D AutoCAD

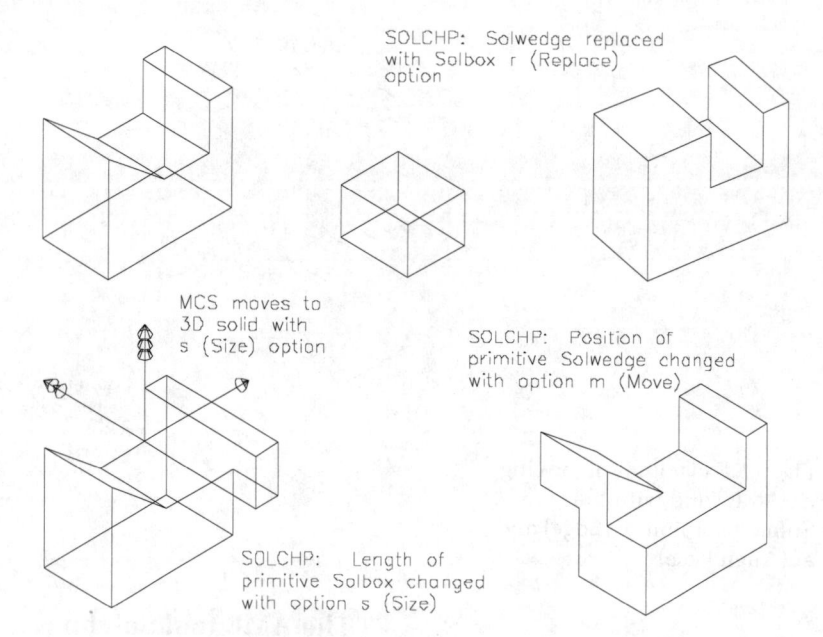

Fig. 6.6 Changing the properties of primitives with the **Solchp** options **r** (**R**eplace), **s** (**S**ize) and **m** (**M**ove)

The AME tool Solsep

Solsep reverses the action of **Solunion**. The AME solid is separated into its constituent primitives. An example is given in Fig. 6.7. This illustration also shows the effect of the AME tool **Solmesh**. **Solmesh** changes the wireframe into a series of **Pface**s, behind which hidden lines can be removed with the **Hide** tool.

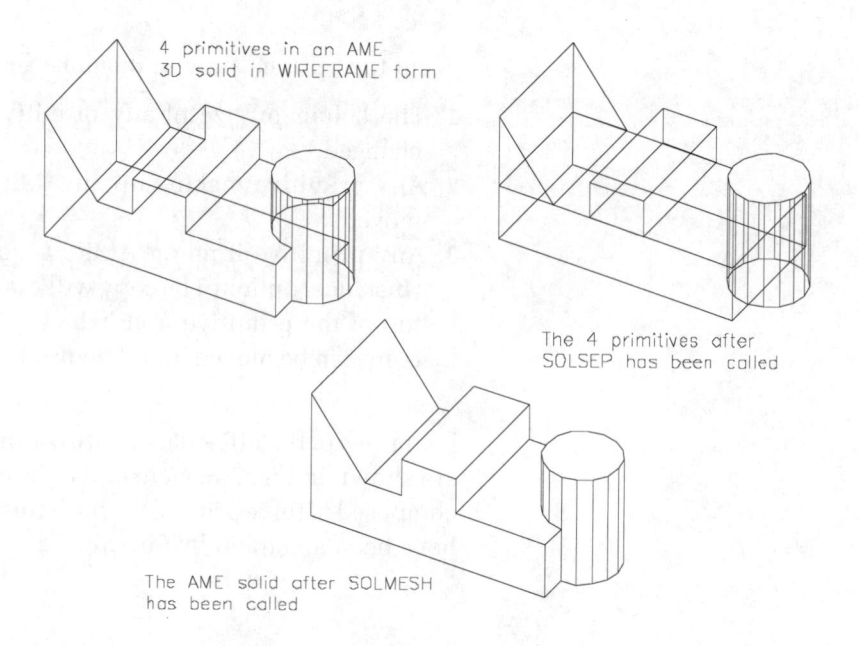

Fig. 6.7 An AME solid after the actions of **Solsep** and **Solmesh**

The AME tool Solpurge

When parts of an AME solid have been erased, it is advisable to call **Solpurge**, which can be used:

1. To clean from memory **a** (**A**ll) AME primitives or AME solids which have been erased previously.
2. To reduce the size of the drawing file by calling **m** (**M**emory), **b** (**B**file), and **p** (**P**mesh) options of **Solpurge** in turn. The size of the drawing file acted upon in this manner can be reduced by as much as 40% or more. If these options are used when the drawing is called back to the drawing editor, the solid will have to be updated by loading AME. This operation automatically occurs when an AME tool is called to work on the solid drawing. However, if the drawing is to be plotted with hidden lines removed, the file must be called back to the drawing and the required solid acted upon by **Solmesh**. Otherwise hidden lines will not be removed in the plot.

The AME tool Solucs

By calling the tool **Solucs**, a new UCS plane, on which details may be added, can be obtained very speedily. When the tool has been called, all that is required is to select either an edge or a face of the AME solid. When the selection has been made, the model automatically aligns on a new UCS on the selected edge or face. Because one

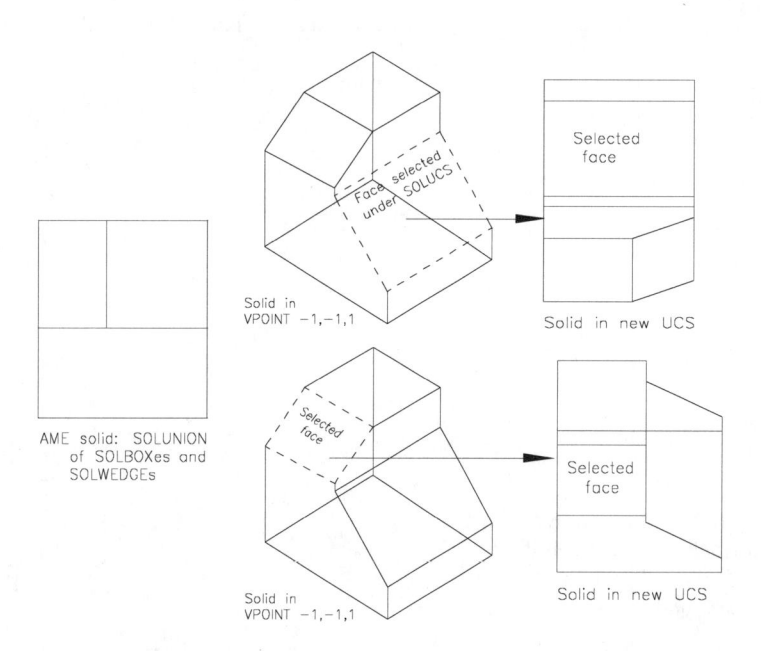

Fig. 6.8 Changing the UCS of an AME solid with **Solucs**

normally requires a face to be aligned as a new UCS, **<Face>** is the default option. It is easier to select a face when the AME model is in a pictorial view. Thus, first place the solid in a **Vpoint** viewing position, then point at the required face. That face then highlights. If the highlighted face is not that required, *enter* **N** (**N**ext) and an adjoining face is highlighted. Continue *entering* **N** for **N**ext until the required face highlights. Then a *right-click* causes the solid to assume its new UCS position based on the highlighted face. Two examples of changing the UCS plane for an AME solid with the aid of **Solucs** are given in Fig. 6.8.

> **Command:** solucs *right-click*
> **Edge/<Face>:** *right-click*
> **Select a face...**
> **Next/<OK>:** if face OK *right-click* if not *enter* n (Next) *right-click*
> **Command:**

The AME tool Solfeat

Solfeat allows edges or faces (features) to be copied from an AME solid for use in other constructions or in other parts of the current drawing. After calling the command, select the required edge or face. The selected part highlights. Next call **Move** and move the selected edge or face from the solid to wherever it is to required. Note that when an edge or face has been acted on by **Solfeat**, the solid itself has not changed. Fig. 6.9 shows all the faces from an AME solid moved away from the solid. The solid itself is unchanged.

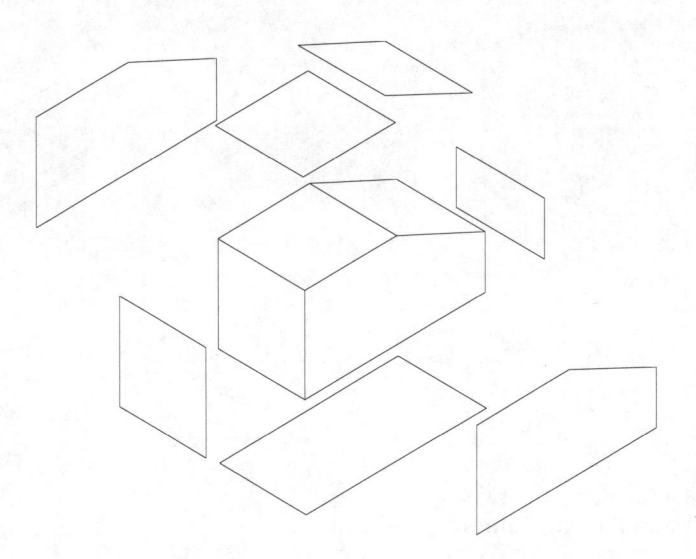

Fig. 6.9 All faces moved from an AME solid with **Solfeat**, yet the solid remains unchanged

> **Command:** solfeat *right-click*
> **Edge/<Face>:** *right-click*
> **Select a face...** *pick*
> **Next<OK>:** if face OK *right-click* if not *enter* n (Next) *right-click*
> **Command:**

The selected face highlights. If the highlighted face is not the required face, respond with **n** (**N**ext) *right-click* to the **Next/<OK>:** prompt and another face highlights. Continue with **n** *right-click* until the required face highlights then *right-click*. The selected edge or face remains highlighted. Call **Move** to move the highlighted feature away from the AME solid drawing.

The AME tool Solprof

Solprof is for removing hidden lines from AME solids, When **Solprof** is called, the command line, its prompts and possible responses show:

> **Command:** solprof *right-click*
> **Select objects:** *pick* **1 selected**
> **Select objects:** *right-click*
> **Display hidden profile lines on separate layer<Y>:** *right-click*
> **Project profile lines on to a plane <Y>:** *right-click*
> **Delete tangential edges <Y>:** *right-click*
> **1 solid selected.**
> **Profile line computation of current solid has started.**
> **Profile line computation of current solid is completed.**
> **Command:**

The hidden lines are computed on to new layers automatically formed when **Solprof** is in action. The layers are named **0-PH-2**, **0-PH-3** and so on, depending upon the number of solids which have been acted upon. The required profile lines – those which are not hidden lines are computed on to new layers named **0-PV-2**, **0-PV-3** and so on. To hide hidden lines and to show only profile lines:

1. *Left-click* on the **Layer** button (top right of the AutoCAD for Windows screen) or select **Layer Control** from the **Settings** pull-down menu.
2. Turn off hidden line layers in the **Layer Control** dialogue box which appears – those named **0-PH**.
3. Turn off Layer **0**.
4. *Left-click* on the **OK** button of the dialogue box.

Figure 6.10 shows the **Layer Control** dialogue box for the 3D model illustrated in Figs. 6.11 and 6.12.

110   An Introduction to 3D AutoCAD

Fig. 6.10 The **Layer Control** dialogue box showing the layers formed when **Solprof** is in action

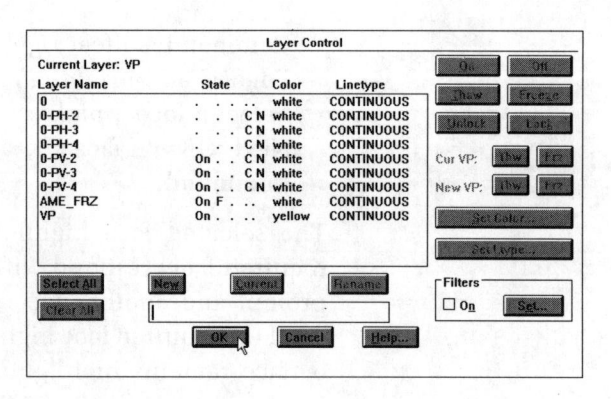

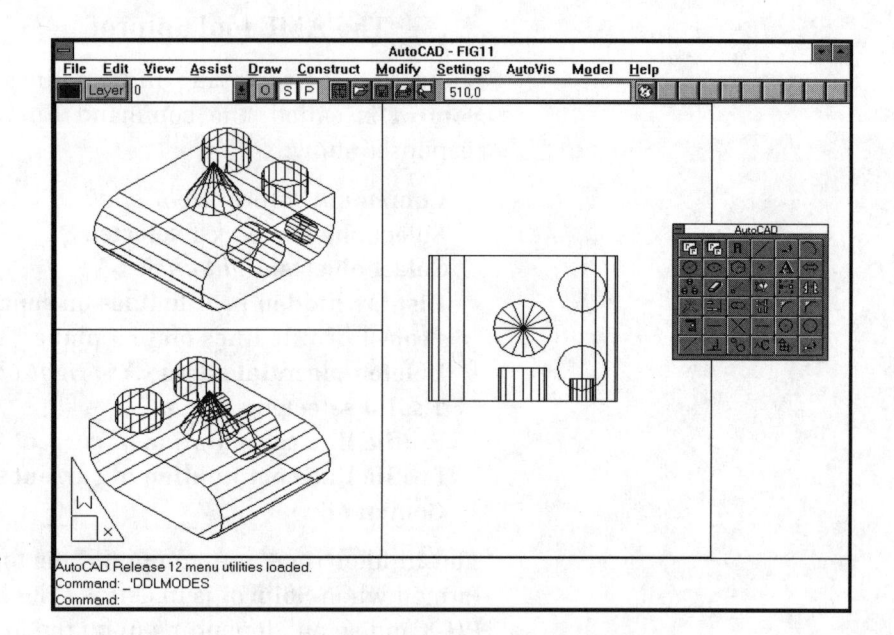

Fig. 6.11 An AME model in a three-viewport drawing editor display

Notes on the action of Solprof

1. When an AME model has been acted upon by **Solprof**, only the current view profile is correct. If the viewing position is changed, it will be seen that the profile is no longer correct,
2. The command will not function while if **PS**pace. The action of **Solprof** is only effective in **MS**pace and then only when **Tilenmode** has been turned **OFF** (set to 0) and **MS**pace called from **PS**pace.
3. When in viewports each viewport must have **Solprof** applied.
4. When plotting or printing a drawing acted upon by **Solprof** do not set the plotter/printer to remove hidden lines.

Additional AME 3D tools 111

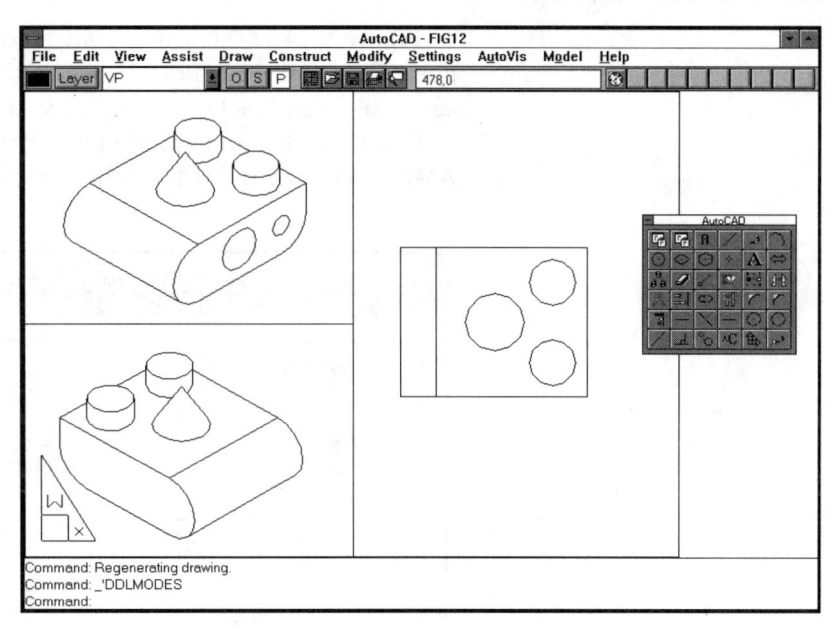

Fig. 6.12 The AME model shown in Fig. 6.11 after **Solprof**

Further examples of Solprof

Figure 6.13 is a plot of a monitor screen stand constructed from a number of AME primitives to form a single solid model. After **Solmesh** and **Hide**, the drawing was plotted with hidden lines removed.

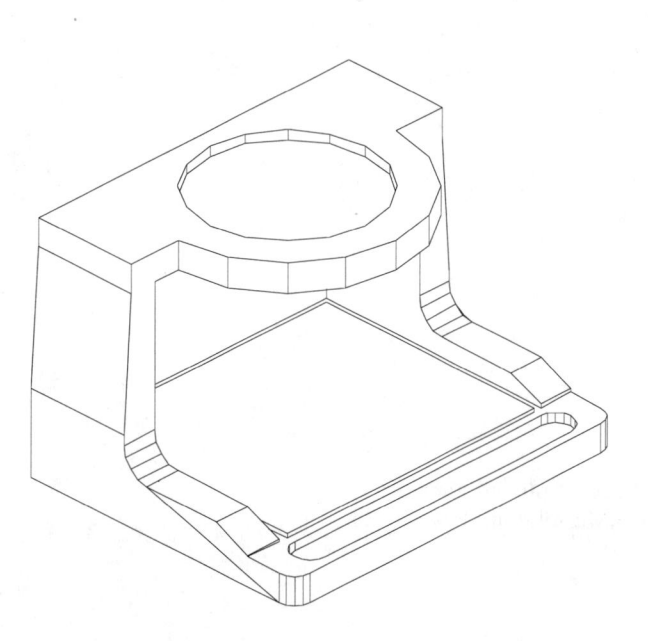

Fig. 6.13 A plot of a pictorial view of a monitor screen stand with hidden lines removed from the plot

112 An Introduction to 3D AutoCAD

Figure 6.14 is the same AME model as in Fig. 6.13. It has been placed in a four-viewport drawing editor layout and the drawing in each viewport has been profiled with the aid of **Solprof**.

Figure 6.15 is an exploded view of a bearing, each part being an AME model. Figure 6.16 is the same exploded view after **Solprof**.

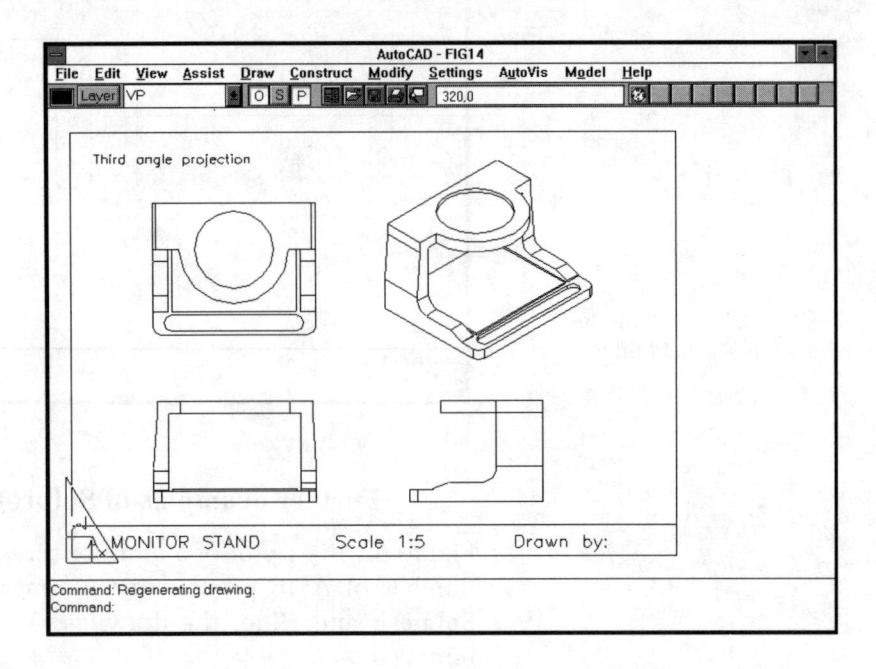

Fig. 6.14 A Third angle orthographic projection of the stand (Fig. 6.13) drawn in viewports after **Solprof**

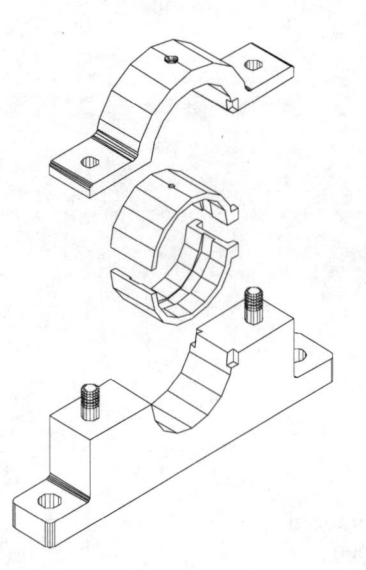

Fig. 6.15 An exploded view of a set of AME solid models

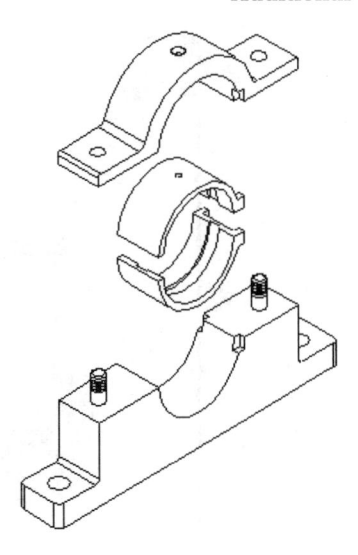

Fig. 6.16 The exploded AME model of Fig. 6.15 after **Solprof**

The AME tool Solsect

The AME command **Solsect** defines UCS planes across an AME solid. Associated with **Solsect** are the three **Solvar** variables, **Solhpat**, **Solhsize** and **Solhangle**, the settings of which determine the hatching pattern, the spacing between the hatching pattern lines and the angle at which the hatch pattern appears on the selected UCS plane in the model. This means that before **Solsect** can be used, the following settings must be made.

1. UCS – usually **3point** – to set the UCS plane on which the hatch pattern is to appear.
2. Assign a name to **Solhpat** to set the hatching pattern to be used.
3. Assign a number to **Solhsize** to set the hatching spacing.
4. Assign a number to **Solhangle** to set the angle at which the hatching will occur.

Then all that is required is to call **Solsect** and *pick* the model in the which UCS section plane has been set. An example of the use of **Solsect** is given in Fig. 6.17. A detailed description of the procedure for producing the complete drawing is given below:

The procedure for constructing Fig. 6.17

1. Load AME.
2. **UCS – 3point** 0,0,0; 1,0,0; 0,0,1.
3. **Zoom** – 1.
4. **UCS – S**ave as FRONT.
5. **Pline** – as Fig. 6.18.
6. **Solext** – extrude 60.

114   An Introduction to 3D AutoCAD

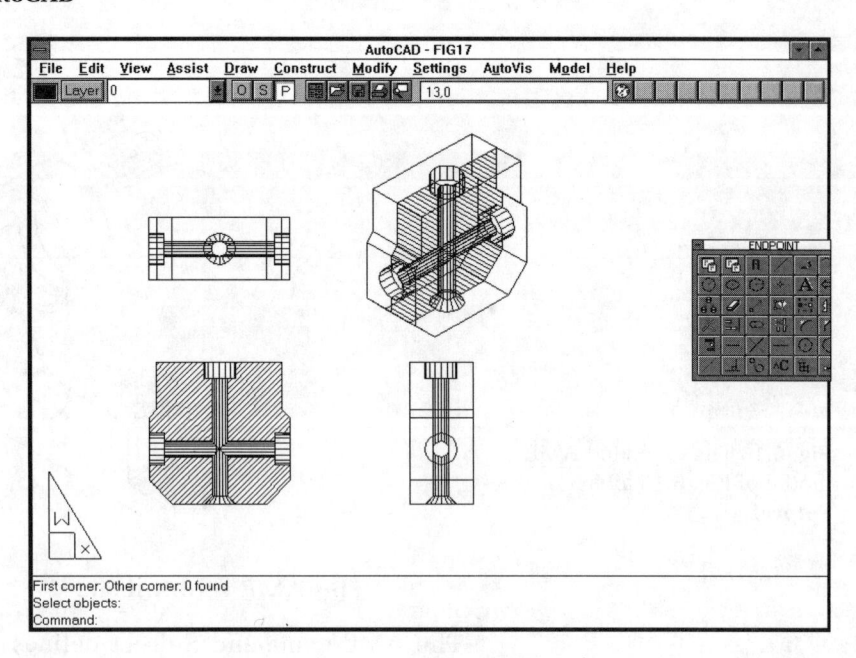

Fig. 6.17 An example of the use of **Solsect**

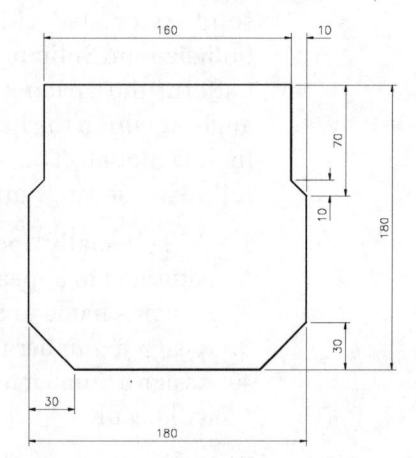

Fig. 6.18 The pline outline for the example of Fig. 6.17

7. **UCS** – w (World).
8. **Zoom** – a (All).
9. **Solmove** – place model central to screen.
10. **Solcyl** – radius 10, height 180
11. **Solcyl** – radius 20, height 20.
12. **Solcone** – radius 20, height 20.
13. **UCS** – **R**estore FRONT.
14. **Solmove** – the 20 radius **Solcyl** to top of model.
15. **UCS** – **3point** to obtain an end view.
16. **UCS** – **S**ave as ENDVIEW.
17. **Zoom** – a (All).

18. **Solcyl** – radius 10, height 180.
19. **Solcyl** – radius 20, height 20.
20. **UCS** – **R**estore FRONT.
21. **Solmove** – **Solcyls** to required position.
22. **Copy** – copy **Solcyl** of height 20 to top of model.
23. **UCS** – w (World).
24. **Zoom** – a (All).
25. **Solunion** – all **Solcyls** and the **Solcone**.
26. **Tilemode** – 0 (OFF). Model disappears. In **PS**pace
27. **Limits** – set to 420,300.
28. **Zoom** – a (All).
29. **Layer** – make a new layer **VIEWPORT**, colour 2 (Yellow).
30. **Mview** – 4 (four-viewport screen) and f (Fit).
31. **MSpace**.
32. **UCSfollow**- set to 0 in all viewports except top left.
33. **Vpoint** – top right: –1,–1,1;
    – bottom left: 0,–1,0;
    – bottom right: 1,0,0;
34. **Zoom** – each viewport to 1.
35. **UCS** – in top left viewport **3point** along vertical centre of model.
36. **Solhpat** – ansi31.
37. **Solhsize** – set to 3.
38. **Solhangle** – set to –90 (i.e. minus 90).
39. **Solsect** – in top left viewport only *pick* the model.

Another example of a model with a **Solsect** section is given in Fig. 6.19. The left-hand of the two drawings in Fig. 6.19 is before the sectioned half model was acted upon by **Solprof**. The right-hand drawing is the model after the action of **Solsect**.

Removing the section plane from a Solsect

The surface outline and hatching of a **Solsect** section consists of two blocks – the outline and the hatching. These can be moved from the model and used as two-dimensional sectional views. Some additional lines usually have to be added to complete a sectional view. **Solsect** sectional views obtained in this manner are correct, in that they have been derived from models which can be viewed from a variety of directions to check their accuracy. Figure 6.20 shows the **Solsect** plane and its hatching moved from the half-model of Fig. 6.19, together with a completed and dimensioned orthographic 2D view. Another example of an AME model acted upon by **Solsect** is shown in Fig. 6.21. This example has also been profiled with **Solprof**.

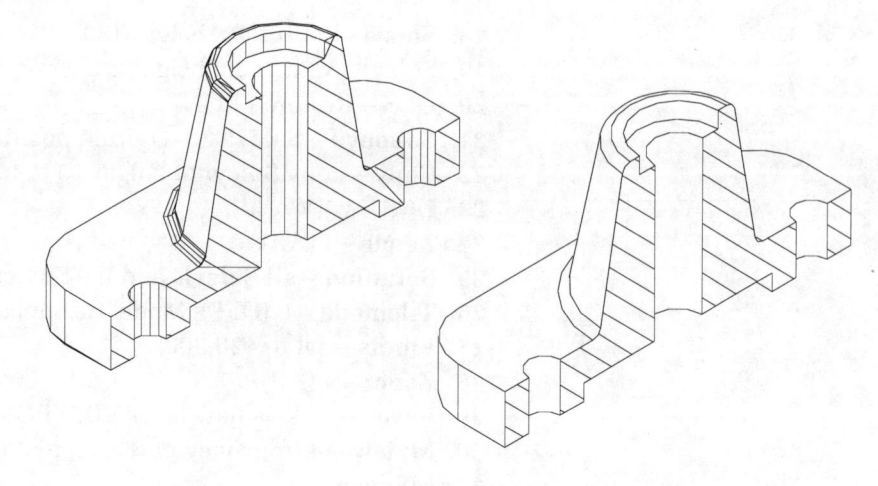

Fig. 6.19 Another 3D model showing the use of **Solsect**

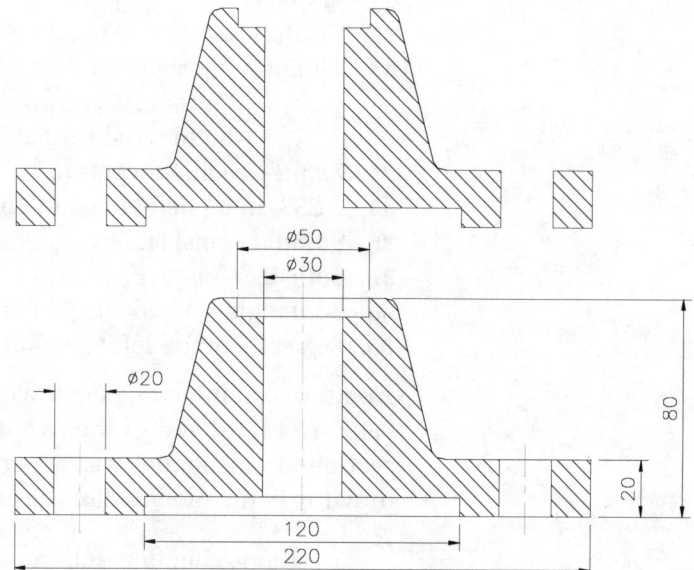

Fig. 6.20 The section plane of Fig. 6.19 used as a sectional view

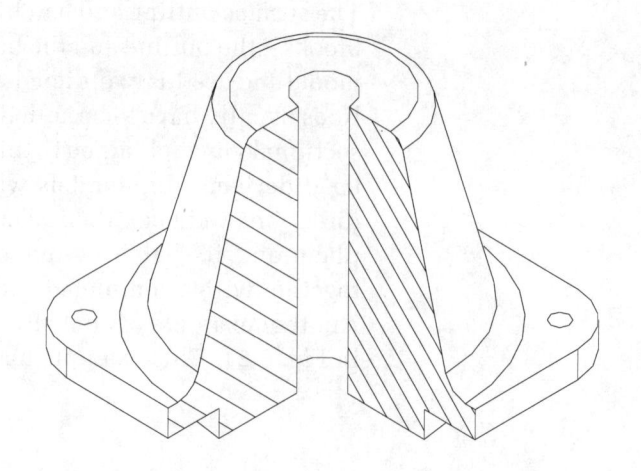

Fig. 6.21 A further example of a 3D model constructed with the aid of **Solsect** and **Solprof**

The AME Solvar variables

In the same way in which variables can be set in AutoCAD, so can variables be set in the AME extension. A list of the AME **Solvar** variables will appear on a flipped text screen if **Solvar** is called and a **?** *entered* as the response to the command line options which appear.

Exercises

The following exercises are included to allow the reader to practise the use of AME in the construction of 3D model drawings. The exercises contain elements of the tools included in the previous chapter.

1. Figure 6.22 is an AME model of an angle support. Working to suitable dimensions, construct this AME model.

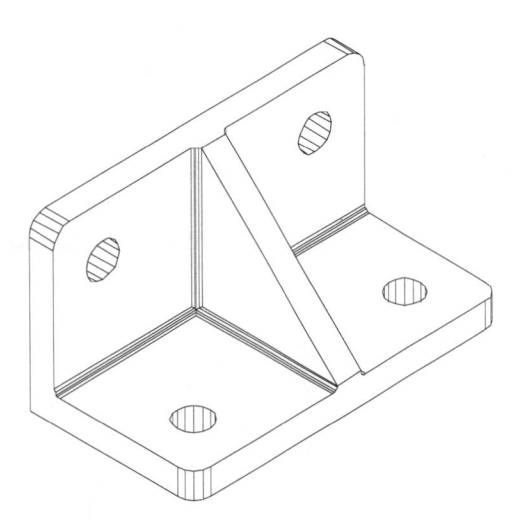

Fig. 6.22 Exercise 1

118   An Introduction to 3D AutoCAD

2. Figure 6.23 is an AME model of a supporting device. Working to suitable dimensions construct the model.

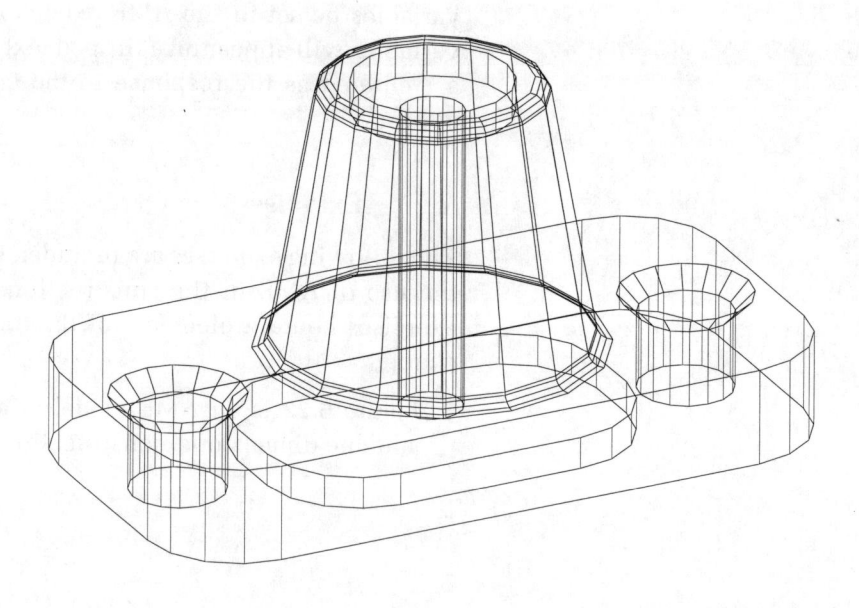

Fig. 6.23 Exercise 2

3. Figure 6.24 is a three-view orthographic projection of a simple Sellotape dispenser. Construct an AME model of the dispenser to the given dimensions.

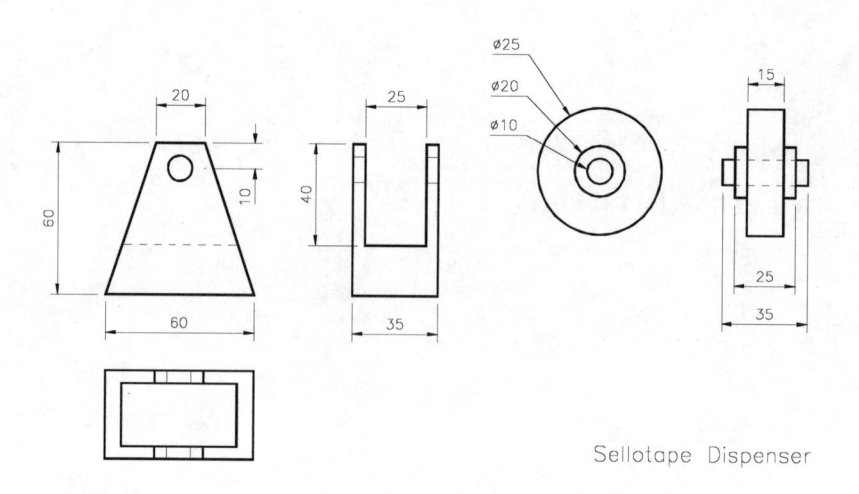

Fig. 6.24 Exercise 3

Sellotape Dispenser

4. Figure 6.25 is a three-view orthographic projection of a rotary bracket. Construct an AME solid drawing to the dimensions given.

Additional AME 3D tools 119

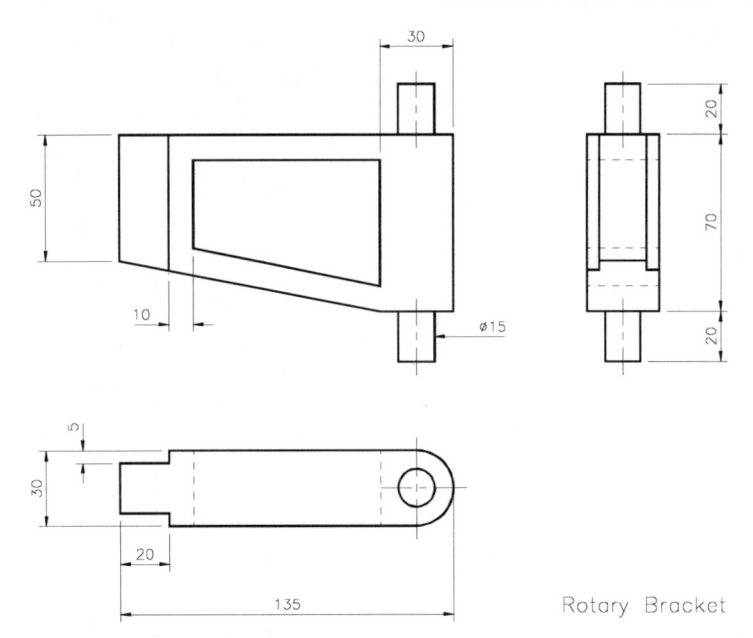

Fig. 6.25 Exercise 4

5. Figure 6.26 is a three-view orthographic projection of a support clip. Construct an AME model drawing of the clip to the given dimensions.

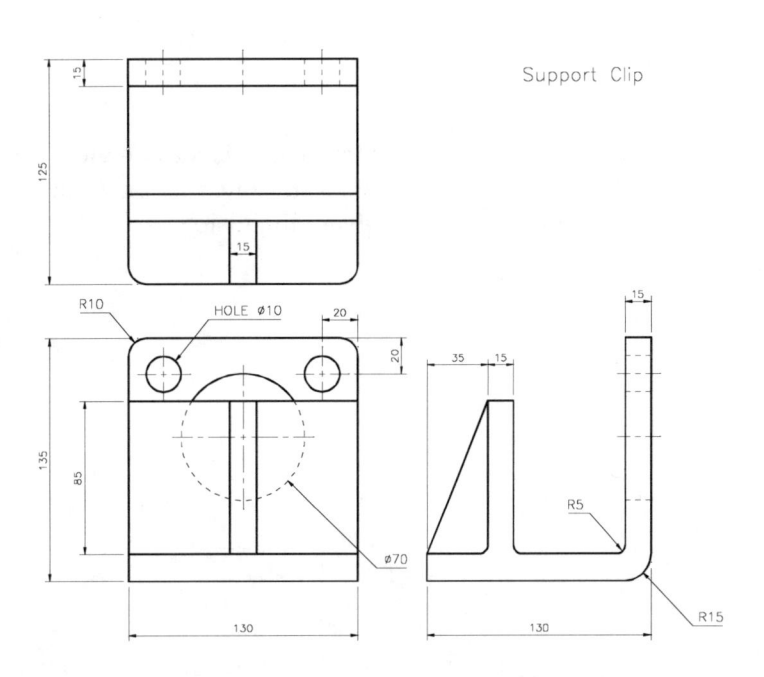

Fig. 6.26 Exercise 5

6. Figure 6.27 is a three-view orthographic projection of an electronic hand control device. Construct an AME model drawing of the device to the dimensions given.

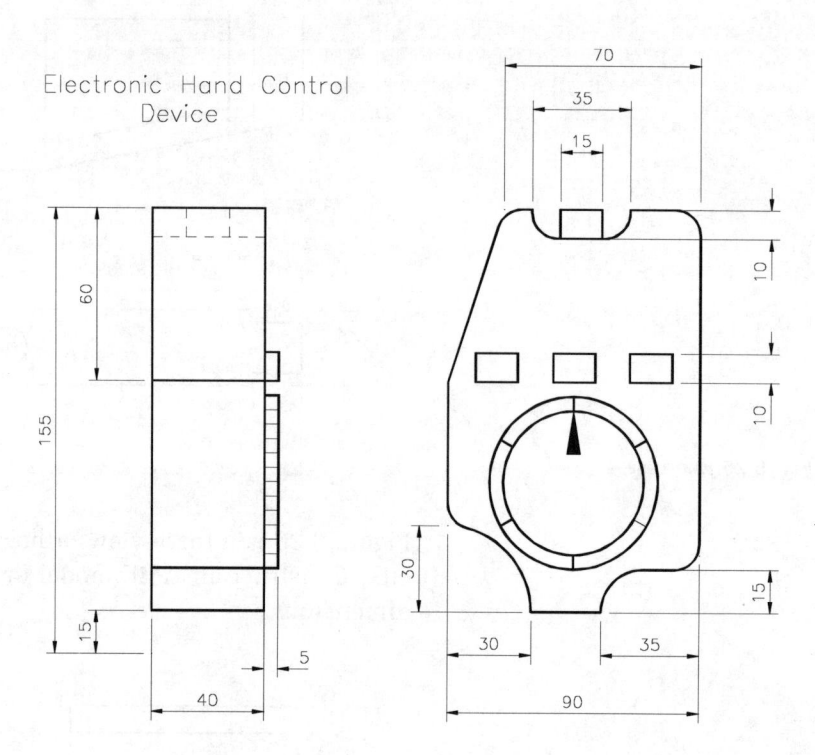

Fig. 6.27 Exercise 6

7. Figure 6.28 is a three-view orthographic projection of a hanging bracket. Construct an AME model drawing of the bracket to the given dimensions.

Additional AME 3D tools 121

Hanging Bracket

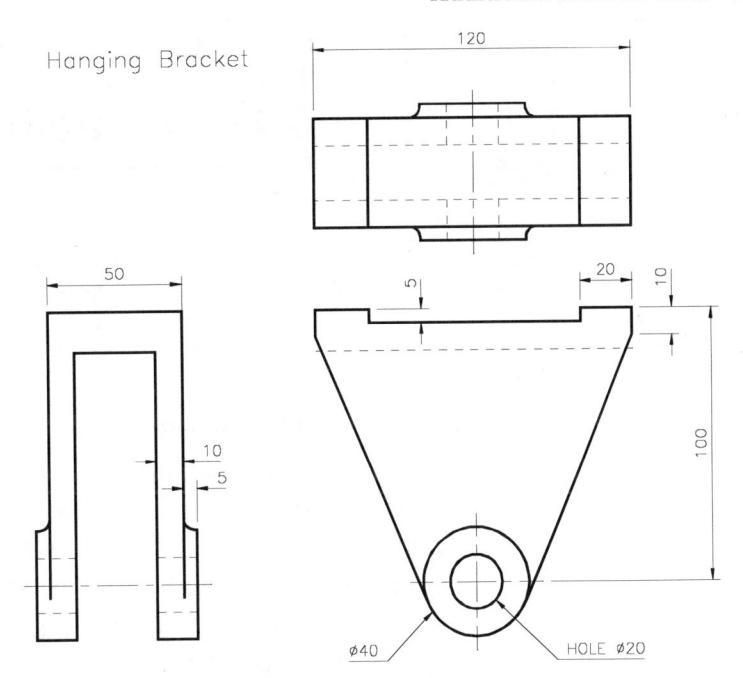

Fig. 6.28 Exercise 7

8. Figure 6.29 is a **Vpoint** view of a table constructed with the aid of AME. Using dimensions of you own choice, construct a similar model drawing.

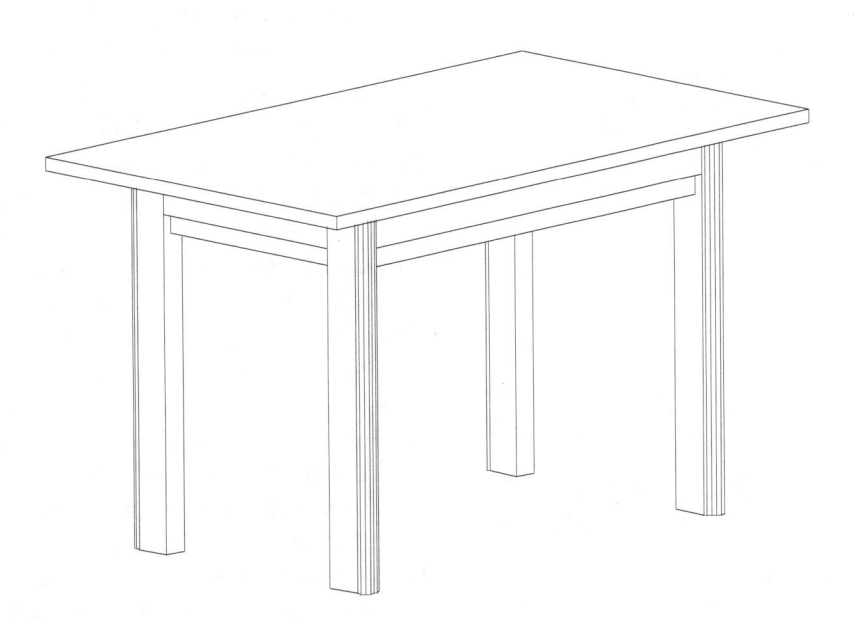

Fig. 6.29 Exercise 8

CHAPTER 7

3D solid models with Release 13

Introduction

The methods by which 3D solid model drawings are constructed in Release 13 are broadly similar to those used in Release 12. There are, however, a number of differences in the way 3D model construction operates between the two release versions:

1. The solid drawing data in Release 13 is held in native AutoCAD form. This means:
   (a) There is no need to load a modelling extension programme before being able to construct a 3D solid model drawing.
   (b) Constructing 3D models in Release 13 solid drawing tools is considerably faster than in Release 12.
   (c) The resulting drawing files are smaller in size than those for the same drawing in Release 12.
2. There is no need to *enter* **Sol** preceding the name of a **Solids** tool when calling the tool. In fact, if **Sol** is used when working in Release 13, the tool name is ignored.
3. When working in the Windows version of Release 13, all the **Solids** tools can be made to appear in the drawing editor in **icon** form, with **tool tips** in **toolbars**. Some of the icons also have **flyouts**. The operator has the choice between *entering* tool names at the command line, or selecting the tool from icons in toolbars.
4. The Boolean operators are not held on the **Solids** toolbar, but on the **Explode** flyout of the **Modify** toolbar.
5. Because some of the names of **Solids** tools are the same as those of the **3D Objects** tools, the names of the **3D Objects** tools are *entered* at the command line with **ai_** as a prefix to the tool name to avoid the **3D Objects** tools being called as **Solids** tools.
6. When primitives are called to the screen they are already surface meshed. There is therefore no **Solids** tool in Release 13 that is equivalent to the **Solmesh** tool of Release 12.

3D solid models with Release 13 123

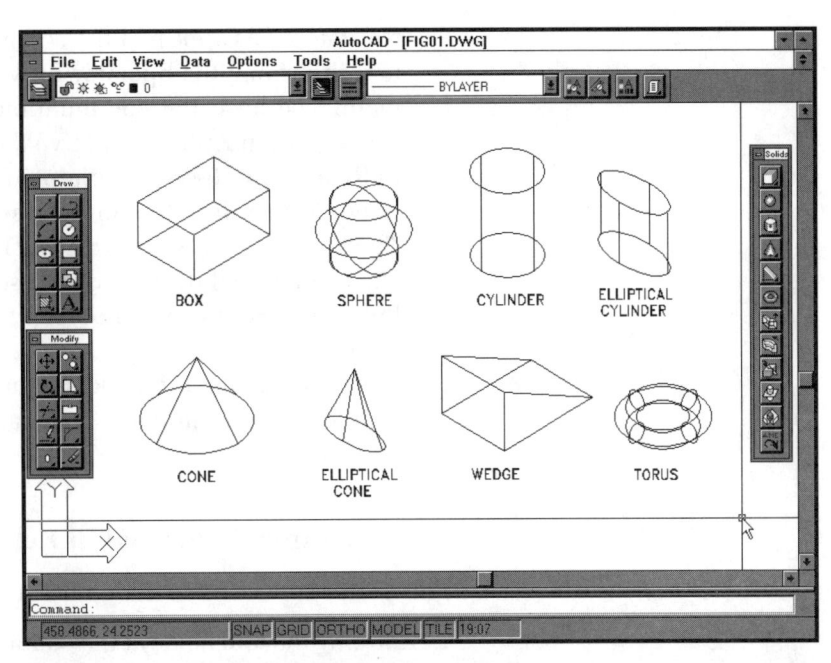

Fig. 7.1 The basic **Solids** primitives of Release 13 before **Hide**

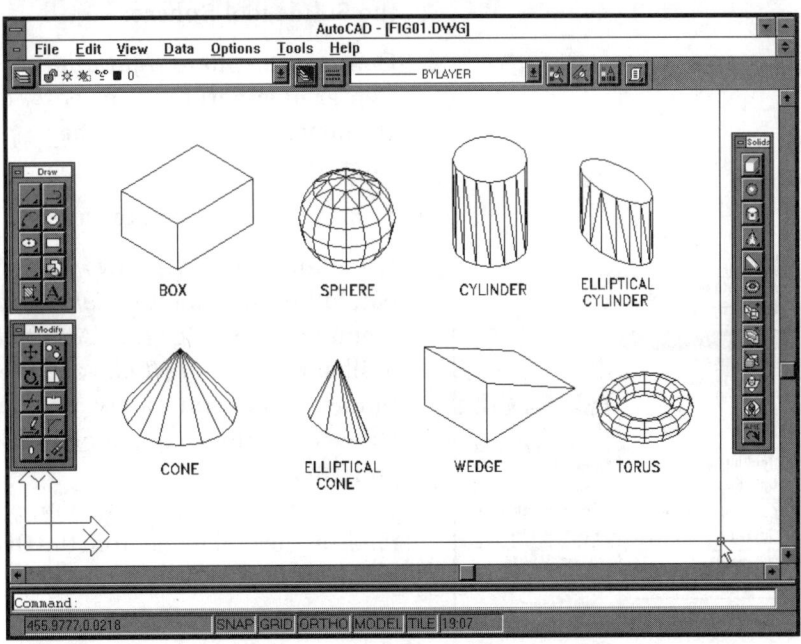

Fig. 7.2 The basic **Solids** primitives of Release 13 after **Hide**

7. There is no equivalent **Solids** tool to the Release 12 **Solwdens** variable in Release 13. When the primitives are called to the screen, they appear in a very simple outline form. When **Hide** is called to remove hidden lines the complete surface meshes are revealed. Figure 7.1 shows the basic primitives of Release 13 before **Hide** is called. Fig. 7.2 shows the same primitives after **Hide**.

8. No statements appear at the command line during the action of a tool informing the operator of what is being computed. This is mainly because the computation is much faster because it is carried out in AutoCAD native data.
9. In Release 13, there is no **Solprof** tool as in Release 12.
10. There is no **Solsep** tool in Release 13.
11. The Release 13 **Modify** tools, such as **Move**, **Copy**, **Mirror**, **Scale** etc. can be used directly on 3D solid models. Thus there are no Release 12 **Solmove** and **Solchp** tools for modifying 3D solids in Release 13.
12. The **Chamfer** and **Fillet** tools from **Modify** can be used to chamfer or fillet 3D solid models. There are thus no **Solcham** and **Solfill** tools in Release 13.

Calling Solids tool in Release 13

The **Solids** tools can be called by one of the following methods:

1. *Entering* the tool name at the command line. As an example to call the **Solids** tool **Sphere**:

   Command: sphere *right-click*
   Center of sphere: *pick* or *enter* coordinates
   Diameter/<Radius> of sphere: *pick* or *enter* a number
   Command:

   And the sphere appears on screen.

2. If working in the Windows version, *left-click* on **Tools** in the menu bar, followed by another *left-click* on **Toolbars**. The **Toolbars** sub-menu appears (Fig. 7.3). A *left-click* on **Solids** brings the **Solids** toolbar to screen. *Left-click* on the icon for the required tool in the **Solids** toolbar and follow the command line prompts. Figure 7.4 shows all the tool icons, tool tips and flyouts of the toolbars – **Solids** and **Modify**.

3. If working in the DOS version, either proceed as 1. above or *left-click* on the tool name from the **Draw** pull-down menu and its sub-menus (Fig. 7.5).

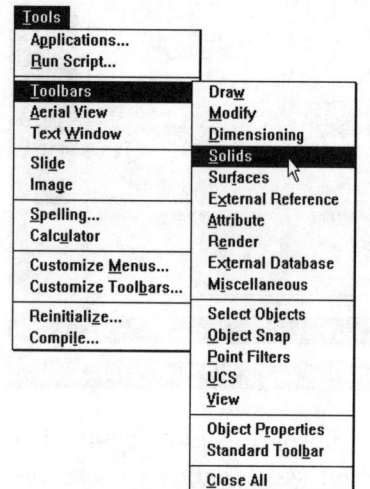

Fig. 7.3 Selecting the **Solids** toolbar from the **Tools** pull-down menu

Examples of constructing 3D models in Release 13

First example – the Union Subtract, Chamfer and Fillet tools

Fig. 7.6 shows the First example both before and after **Hide** was called. The procedure for constructing this model was as follows:

3D solid models with Release 13   125

Fig. 7.4 The **Solids** tools from the **Solids** and **Modify** toolbars

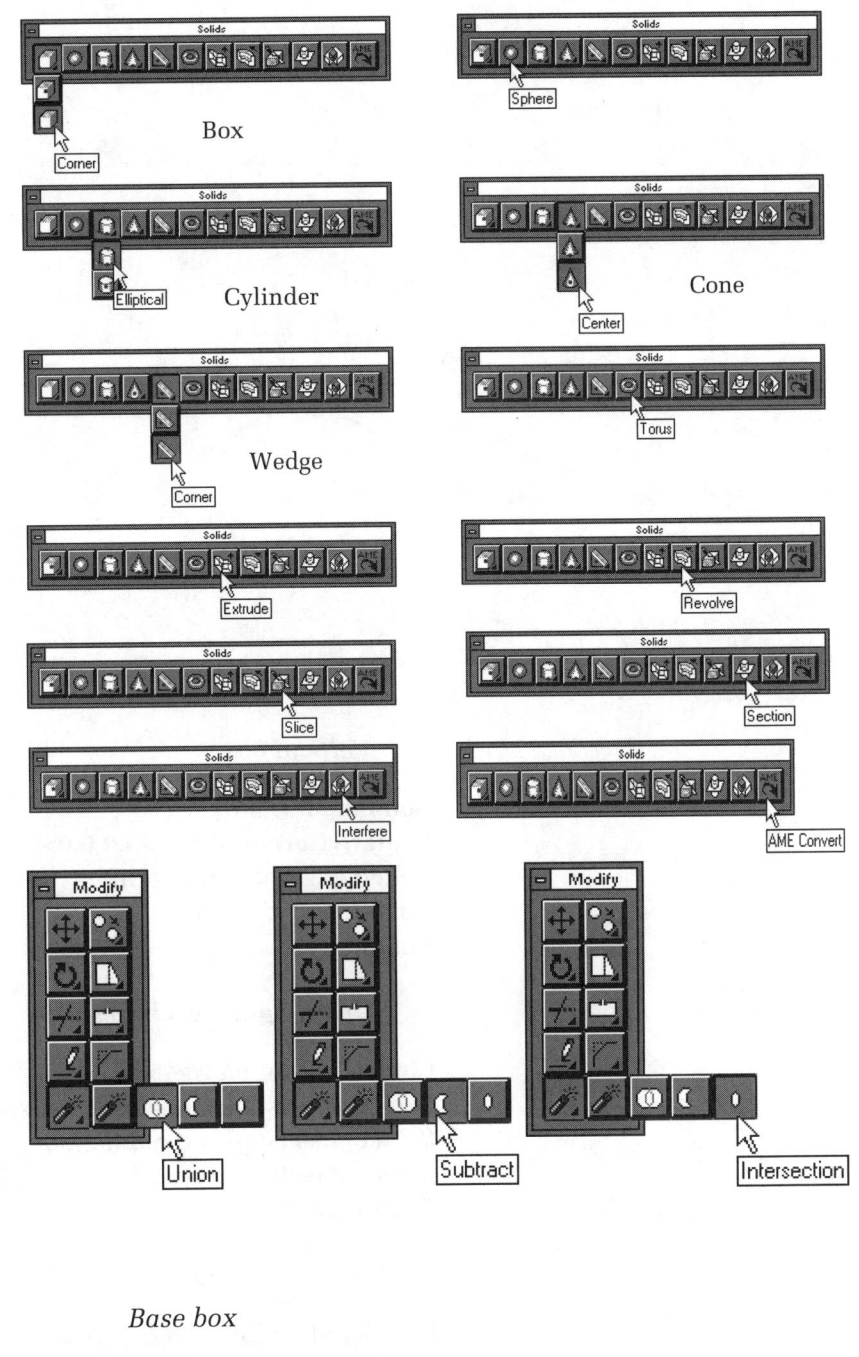

Box

Sphere

Cylinder

Cone

Wedge

Torus

Extrude

Revolve

Slice

Section

Interfere

AME Convert

Union

Subtract

Intersection

Fig. 7.5 Selecting **Solids** tools when working in the DOS version of Release 13

Base box

Command: box *right-click*
Center/<Corner of box> <0,0,0>: 100,250 *right-click*
Cube/Length/<Other corner>: 300,150 *right-click*
Height: 30 *right-click*
Command:

126   An Introduction to 3D AutoCAD

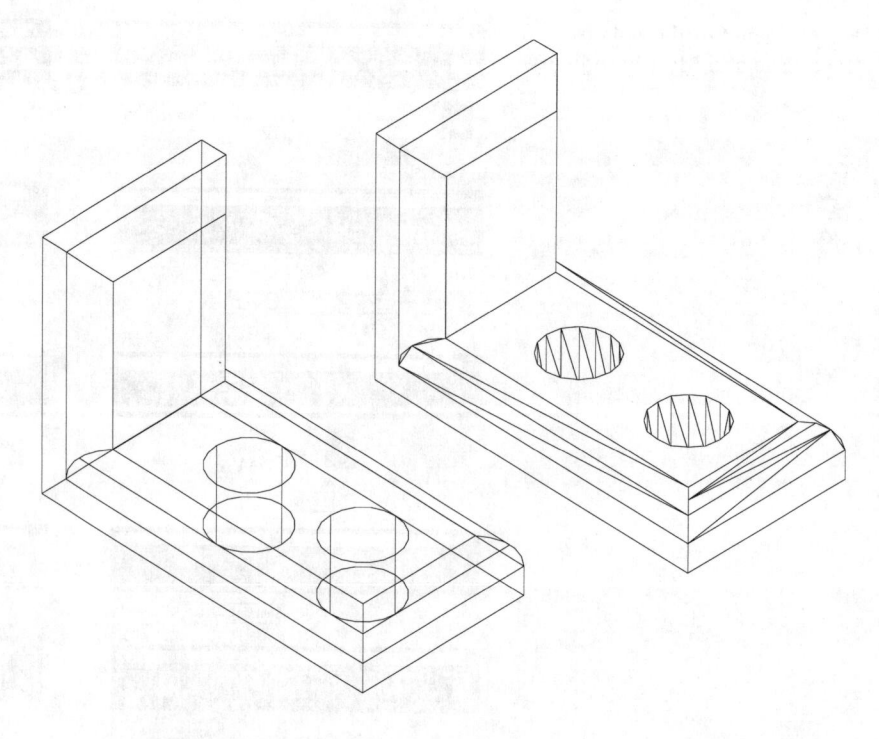

Fig. 7.6 First example

Vertical box

Command: *right-click*
Center/<Corner of box> <0,0,0>: 100,250,30 *right-click*
Cube/Length/<Other corner>: 130,150,30 *right-click*
Height: 100 *right-click*
Command:

Union of the two boxes

Command: union *right-click*
Select objects: *pick* one of the boxes
Select objects: *pick* the other box
Select objects: *right-click*
Command:

The two cylinders

Command: cylinder *right-click*
Elliptical/<Center point> <0,0,0>: 250,200 *right-click*
Diameter/<Radius>: 20 *right-click*
Center of other end/<Height>: 35 *right-click*
Command: copy *right-click*
Select objects: *pick* the cylinder

3D solid models with Release 13

Base point of displacement/<Multiple>: *pick* centre of cylinder
Second point of displacement: 180,200 *right-click*
Command:

Subtracting cylinders from the union of boxes

Command: subtract *right-click*
Select objects: *pick* the union of two boxes
Select objects: *pick* both cylinders
Command:

View point

Command: vpoint *return*
Rotate/<View point> <0,0,0>: 1,-1,1 *right-click*
Command:

The chamfers

Command: chamfer *right-click*
Polyline/Distance/Angle/Trim/Method/<Select first line>: *pick*
Next/<OK>: *right-click*
Enter base distance <10>: 15 *right-click*
Enter other surface distance <0>: 15 *right-click*
Loop/<Select edge>: *pick* three edges to be chamfered
Command:

The fillets

Command: fillet *right-click*
Polyline/Radius/Trim/<Select first object>: *pick* one edge
Enter radius: 15 *right-click*
Chain/Radius/<Select edge>: *pick* three edges to be filleted
Command:

Notes

1. The tools could have been selected from the **Solids** toolbar icons if so wished. The command line prompts and responses would have been the same except that the tool name would reappear with a dash preceding the name at the command line – e.g. **_sphere**.
2. The lack of the prefix **Sol** in front of the **Solids** tool names.
3. Differences in the prompts between Release 12 and Release 13.
4. **Copy**, **Chamfer** and **Fillet** could have been called from the **Modify** toolbar.
5. The drawing prior to **Hide** does not show all surface mesh lines.

Second example – the Revolve tool

Figure 7.7 shows the stages in the construction of a revolved solid formed with the **Revolve** tool. This example was constructed as follows:

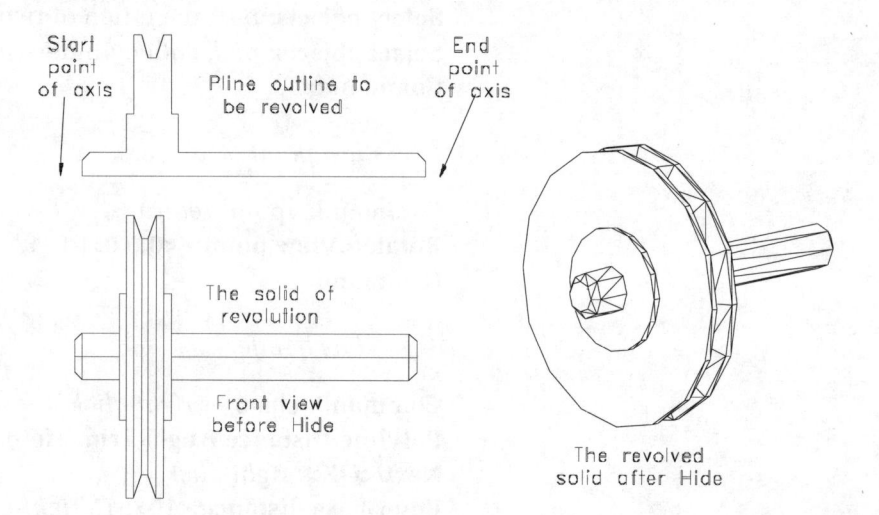

Fig. 7.7 Second example

1. Stage 1 – construct the pline outline.
2. Stage 2 – call the **Solids** tool **Revolve**:

   Command: revolve *right-click*
   Select objects: *pick the* pline outline **1 found.**
   Select objects: *right-click*
   Axis of revolution – Object/X/Y/<Start point of axis>: *pick*
   End point of axis: *pick*
   Axis of revolution <full circle>: *right-click*
   Command:

3. Stage 3 – Place solid in a new viewing position:

   Command: vpoint *return*
   Rotate/<View point> <0,0,0>: 1,-1,1 *right-click*
   Command:

4. Stage 4 – call the **Hide** tool

   Command: hide *right-click*
   Command:

Third example – the Extrude tool

Figure 7.8 shows a 3D solid drawing of a short length of aluminium extrusion, constructed from two pline outlines. The two outlines were drawn, then the **Solids** tool **Extrude** was called. When the extrusions had been constructed, the inner one was subtracted from the outer.:

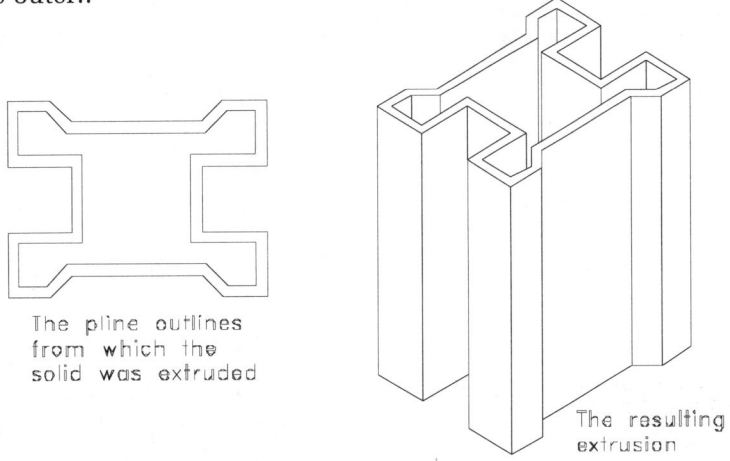

Fig. 7.8 Third example

The extrusion

Command: extrude *right-click*
Select objects: *pick* one pline
Select objects: *pick* the other pline
Select objects: *right-click*
Path/<Height of extrusion>: 150 *right-click*
Extrusion taper angle <0>: *right-click*
Command:

Subtracting inner from outer extrusion

Command: subtract *right-click*
Select objects: *pick* the outer extrusion
Select objects: *pick* the inner extrusion
Command:

Fourth example – The Section tool

This example shows the use of the **Solids** tool **Section**. The stages in constructing the section were:

1. Stage 1 – Fig 7.9.

    (a) Three **Box**es acted upon with **Union**.

130   An Introduction to 3D AutoCAD

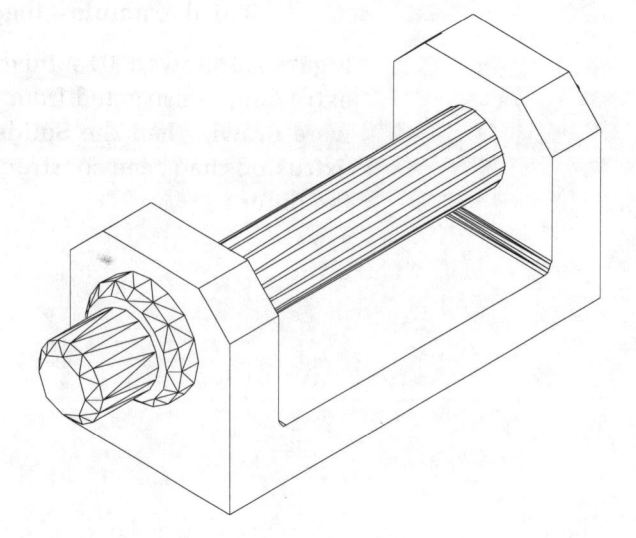

Fig. 7.9 Fourth example – Stage 1

    (b) Two **Cylinder**s added with **Union**.
    (c) **Chamfer**s and **Fillet**s.
    (d) **Pline** acted upon by **Revolve**.
    (e) **Hide**.

2. Stage 2 – Fig. 7.10.
   Call **Section**:

   Command: section *right-click*
   Select objects: *pick* the union of three boxes **1 found**.
   Select objects: *right-click*
   Section plane by Object/Zaxis/XY/YZ/ZX/<3points>: 3 *right-click*
   1st point on plane: *pick*
   2nd point on plane: *pick*
   3rd point on plane: .xy *right-click*
   of *pick* 1st point again
   (need Z): 1 *right-click*
   Command:

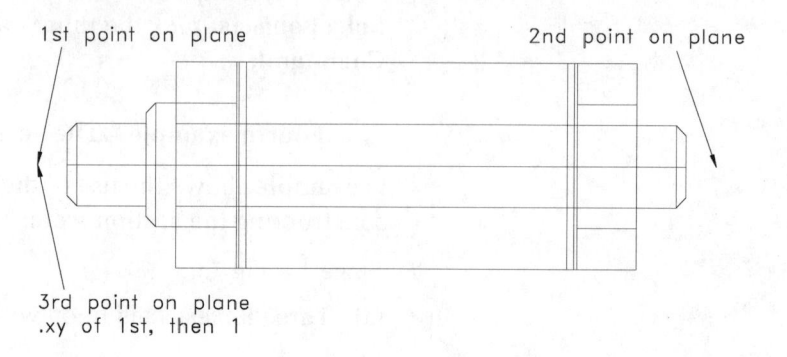

Fig. 7.10 Fourth example – Stage 2

3D solid models with Release 13   131

3. Stage 3 – Fig. 7.12

   (a) Set the **UCS** to a **3points** setting using the same three points as in Stage 2 for setting the **Section** plane:

   Command: ucs *right-click*
   Origin/ZAxis/3point/OBject/X/Y/Z/Prev/Restore/Save/Del/ ?<World>: 3 *right-click*
   Origin point <0,0,0>: *pick* 1st point again as in Fig. 7.10
   Point on positive portion of the X-axis: *pick* the 2nd point (Fig. 7.10)
   Point on positive – Y portion of the UCS XY plane: .xy *right-click*
   of *pick* the 1st point (Fig. 7.10)
   (need Z) 1 *right-click*
   Command:

   (b) Call the **Boundary Hatch** dialogue box – Fig. 7.11. Set the hatching parameters as shown in the dialogue box (Fig. 7.11). *Pick* inside the hatch boundary area of the section outline set by the **Section** tool.

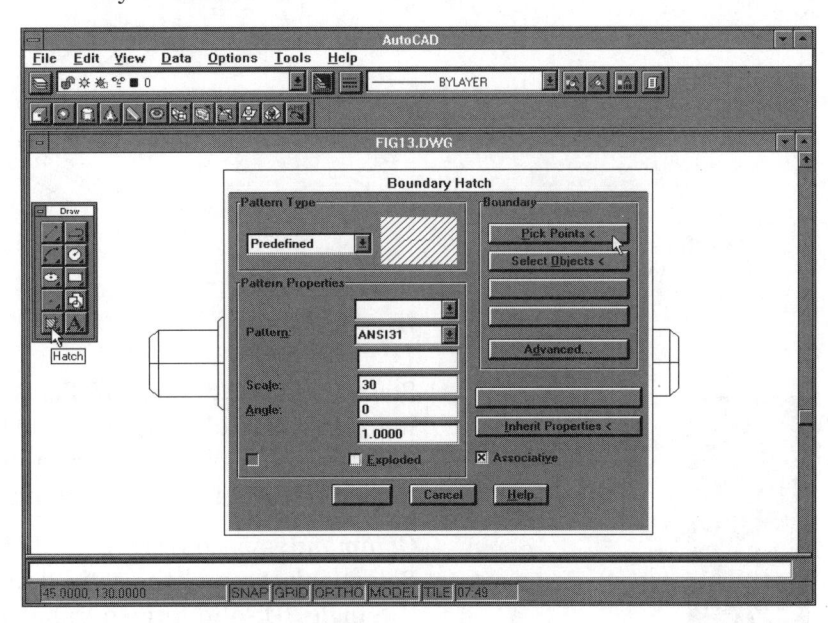

Fig. 7.11 Calling the **Boundary Hatch** dialogue box

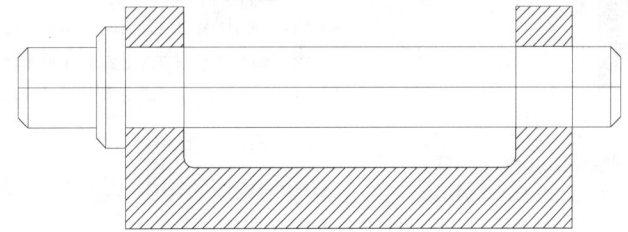

Fig. 7.12 Stage 3 – The resulting sectional view within the 3D solid model

132 An Introduction to 3D AutoCAD

(c) Check that the hatching is satisfactory (Fig. 7.12) and **Apply** the hatching from the **Boundary Hatch** dialogue box, if it is OK.

Notes

1. When hatching the section, the plane of the section outline must be in the *x,y* plane of the current UCS – hence the **3 point** ucs setting.
2. Hatch patterns are placed within the section outline with the aid of the **Hatch** tool from the **Draw** toolbar. This calls the **Boundary Hatch** dialogue box, which can also be called by:

Command: bhatch *right-click*

Fifth example – the AME Convert tool

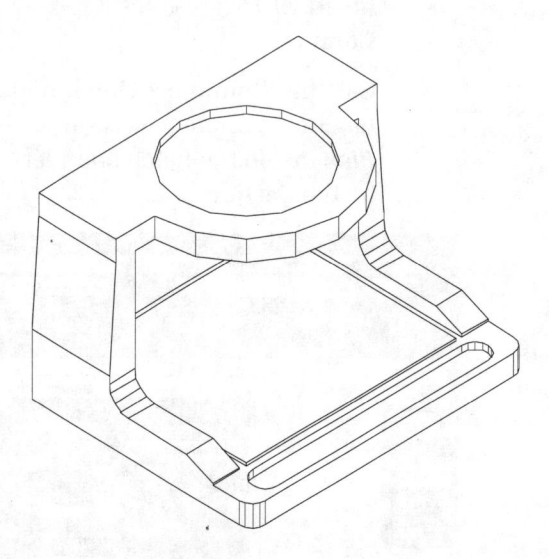

Fig. 7.13 Fifth example – Stage 1 – the AME solid from Release 13

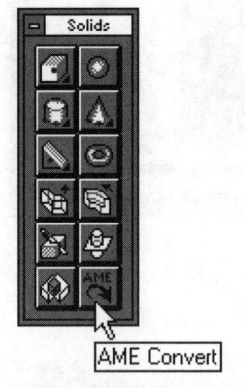

Fig. 7.14 Selecting the **AME Convert** tool from the **Solids** toolbar

1. Stage 1 – load the AutoCAD Release 12 drawing from Chapter 6 – Fig. 6.13. Call **Hide**. This results in the drawing shown in Fig. 7.13.
2. Stage 2 – Either *left-click* on the **Ame Convert** tool icon in the **Solids** toolbar (Fig. 7.14), or at the command line:

Command: ameconvert *right-click*
Select objects: *pick* the solid drawing on screen. It is, in fact, a single 3D solid formed from a number of primitives
Processing 1 of 22 Boolean operations.
Processing 2 of 22 Boolean operations.
Processing 3 of 22 Boolean operations.

And so on until all Boolean operations have been processed.

Command: hide *right-click*
Command:

3D solid models with Release 13   133

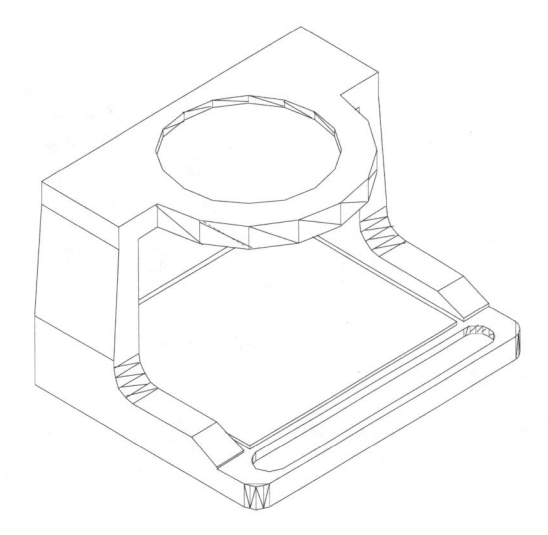

Fig. 7.15 Fifth example – Stage 2 – changing the AME solid to a Release 13 solid

The result of the converting the solid drawing from Release 12 AME solid drawing methods to Release 13 solid drawing methods is shown in Fig. 7.15.

Sixth example – the Slice tool

This example is included here to show the action of the **Slice** tool from the **Solids** toolbar. The action is similar to that of the **Section** tool, except that part of a 3D model can be sliced from the model.

1. Stage 1

    (a) Construct the 3D model – the base is a **Box**, the stand is a **Revolve**d pline, as is the dish at the top of the model. All three parts have been joined with the aid of the **Union** tool.

    (b) Call the **Slice** tool – either *left-click* on its icon in the **Solids** toolbar (Fig. 7.16) or at the command line:

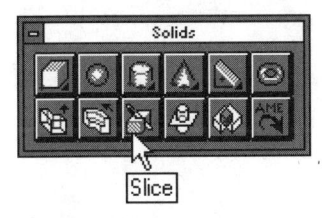

Fig. 7.16 Selecting the **Slice** tool from the **Solids** toolbar

Command: slice *right-click*
Select objects: *pick* the model
Select objects: *right-click*
Slicing plane by Object/Zaxis/View/XY/YZ/ZX/<3points>: *right-click*
1st point on plane: *pick* (Fig. 7.17)
2nd point on plane: *pick* (Fig. 7.17)
3rd point on plane: .xy *right-click*
of *pick* 1st point again
(need Z): 1 *right-click*
Both sides/<Point in desired side of the plane>: *pick* (Fig. 7.16)
Command:

134 An Introduction to 3D AutoCAD

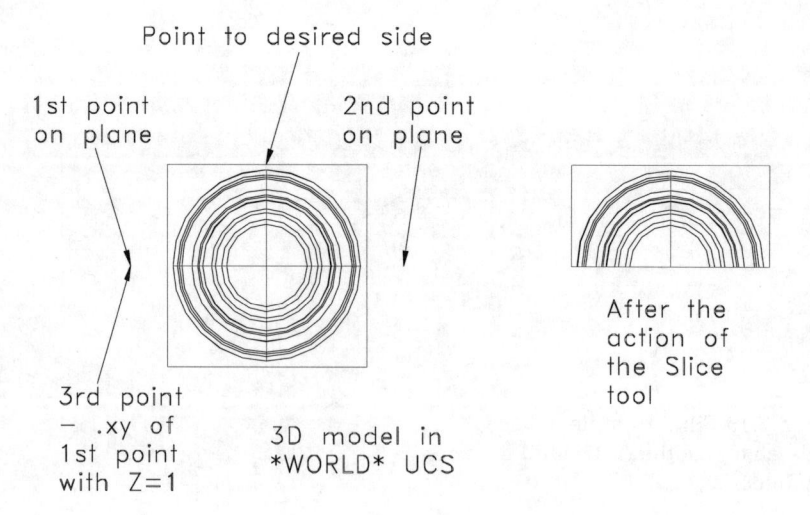

Fig. 7.17 Sixth example – The 3D model in the UCS *WORLD*

2. Stage 2
   (a) Place the sliced model in a new viewing position with the aid of **Vpoint** (Fig. 7.18).
   (b) Call the **Hide** tool.

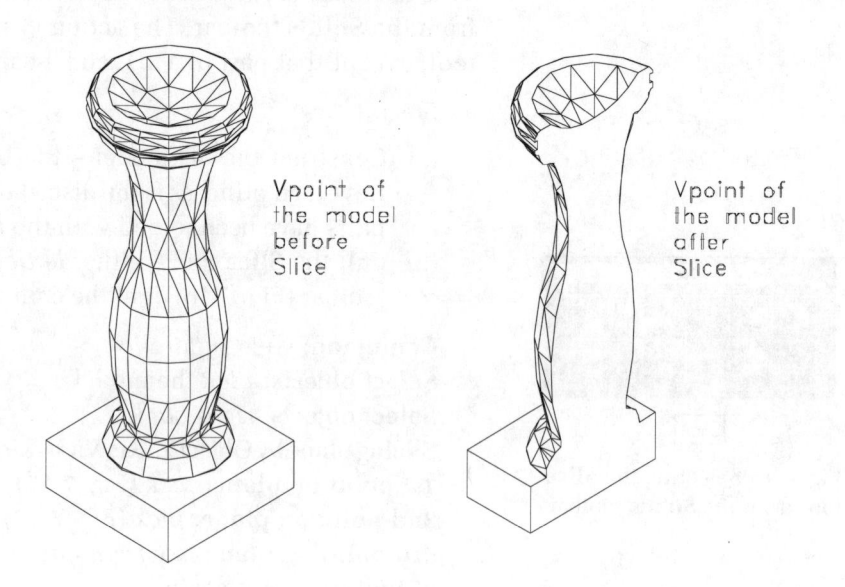

Fig. 7.18 Vpoint views of the model before and after **Slice**

Exercises

The reader is advised to attempt constructing exercises from previous chapters in AutoCAD Release 13.

CHAPTER 8

The command DVIEW

Introduction

The command **Dview** (dynamic view) allows the dynamic movement of 3D drawings on screen to produce pictorial views, including perspective views, of the model being drawn. The manipulation of the drawing can be controlled, either by movement of the pointing device or by entering values at the keyboard in response to the **Dview** prompts appearing at the command line. A ghosted copy of the 3D model drawing is dragged in response to movements of the pointing device or to the values entered, allowing the operator to see and so choose that view which shows the drawing to best advantage.

No matter whether one is working in the MS_DOS version of R12, in AutoCAD for Windows or in R13, **Dview** can be called either from the **View** pull-down menu or by *entering* dview at the command line. Figures 8.1 to 8.3 show the various versions of the **View** pull-down menu, each with **Dview** being selected.

When working with a complicated 3D drawing, either only a part of the drawing, or the Dviewblock (Fig. 8.4) can be called to screen to replace the 3D drawing. The positions of the 3D model are mimicked by those of the Dviewblock or by the part drawing. When the required positioning of the Dviewblock has been selected,

Fig. 8.1 The R13 **View** pull-down menu with **Dview** selected

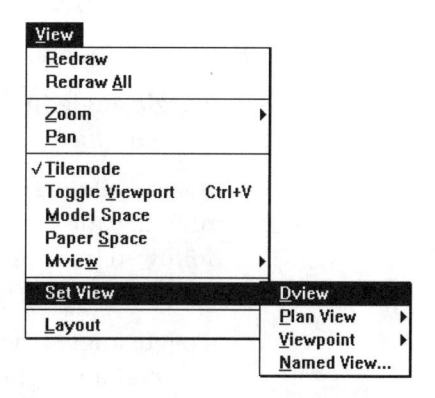

Fig. 8.2 The R12 (DOS) **View** pull-down menu with **Dview** selected

136 An Introduction to 3D AutoCAD

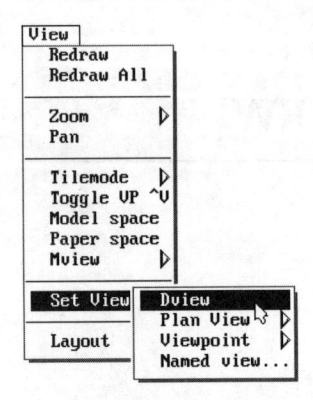

Fig. 8.3 The AutoCAD for Windows **View** pull-down menu with **Dview** selected

pressing *Return* (or *entering* X for eXit) regenerates the original 3D drawing in the position chosen with the aid of the Dviewblock. The value of using the Dviewblock is that, being a 3D line drawing, it will regenerate much more quickly as it is moved to new positions, than would a complicated 3D model.

The Dviewblock (Fig. 8.4) can be made to appear on screen with a *right-click* in response to the **Select objects:** prompt of the **Dview** command or by pressing the *Return* key.

When **Dview** is called – by *entering* **dv** (**dv**iew) or by selection from the **View** pull-down menu, the following prompts appear at the command line:

Command: dv *right-click*
Select objects: usually in a window *right-click*
**CAmera/TArget/Distance/POints/PAn/Zoom/TWist/CLip/Hide/Off/
    Undo/<eXit>:**

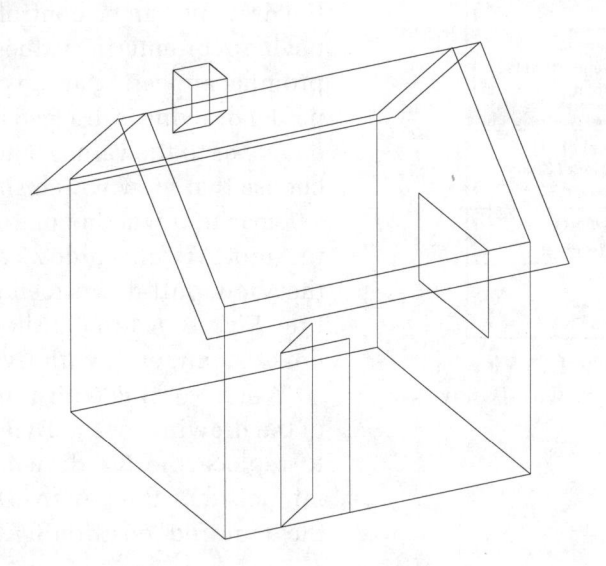

Fig. 8.4 The **Dviewblock**

The CAmera option

Enter ca (**CA**mera) and the prompt changes to:

Toggle angle in/Enter angle from XY plane<35>: *enter* an angle *right-click*

1. Instead of *entering* an angle, move the pointing device until the 3D drawing (or Dviewblock) is in a suitable position for viewing, followed by a *right-click*.
2. The 3D drawing (or Dviewblock) regenerates in a ghosted form.

Toggle angle from/Enter angle in XY plane from X-axis<-135>:
    enter an angle *right-click*

The command DVIEW   137

3. Or move the pointing device to position the drawing (or Dviewblock) as required, followed by a *right-click*.

   CAmera/TArget/Distance/POints/PAn/Zoom/TWist/CLip/Hide/ Off/Undo/<eXit>:

4. *Right-click* and the drawing regenerates in its original form in the required camera viewing position.

Figure 8.5 shows a **CAmera** viewing position among viewing positions resulting from responding to other prompts.

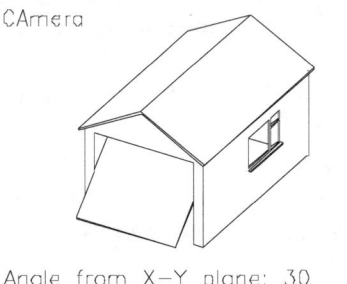

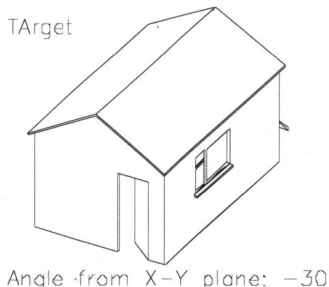

Fig. 8.5 Drawings resulting from four of the **Dview** options

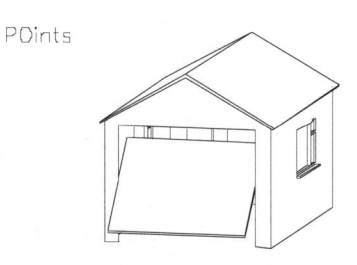

CAmera
Angle from X–Y plane: 30
Angle in X–Y plane: 30

TArget
Angle from X–Y plane: –30
Angle in X–Y plane: 30

POints
Target point: 280,150,20
Camera point: 400,180,40

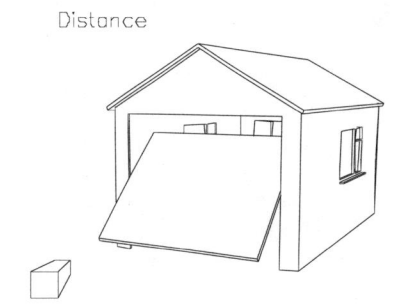

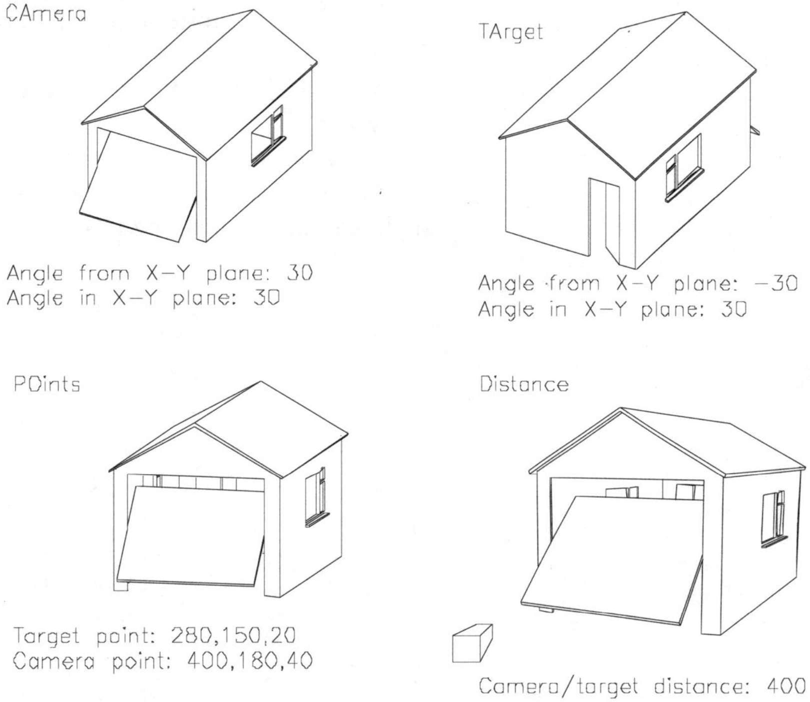

Distance
Camera/target distance: 400

The figures in brackets (< >) after each prompt are the default angles from and in the *x-y* plane of the last position relative to the **WCS**.

The TArget option

Enter ta (**TA**rget) and the prompt changes to:

Toggle angle in/Enter angle from XY plane<–40>: *enter* an angle

1. Instead of *entering* an angle, move the pointing device until the 3D drawing (or Dviewblock) is in a suitable position for viewing,

followed by a *right-click*. The 3D drawing regenerates in its original form in the selected target position.
2. If an angle is *entered* to the first prompt, a second prompt appears – the same prompt as when **CA**mera is the chosen option.

Toggle angle from/Enter angle in XY plane from X-axis<–135>:
enter an angle *right-click*

When the **TA**rget option is chosen, if you wish to choose a view from above the model, the angle **from** the *x-y* plane must be negative. The angle **in** *x-y* plane from the *x*-axis can, however, be positive. To view from above, the camera must be above the model, hence the target (the point on the model at which the camera is aimed) must be below the camera.

An example of a view produced with the **TA**rget option is given in Fig. 8.5.

Figure 8.6 shows imaginary camera and target positions in plan, rear, side and front views. Note the **angle in the x-y plane** and the **angle from the x-y plane** positions.

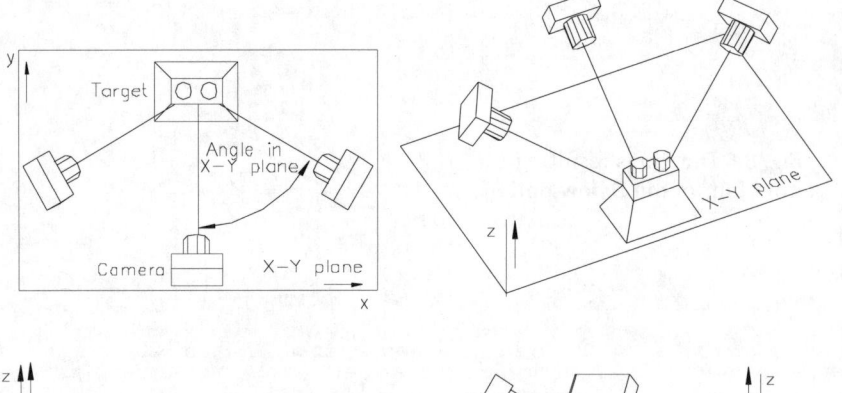

Fig. 8.6 Plan, view from rear, side view and pictorial view of imaginary camera and target positions

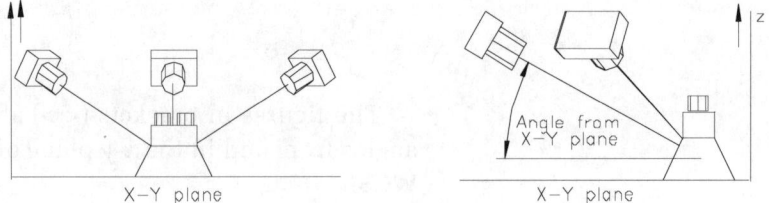

The POints option

Enter po (**PO**ints) and the prompt changes to:

Enter target point<300,40,65>:

Either select an *x,y,z* coordinate point by pointing with the aid of the .xy filter or *enter* an *x,y,z* coordinate from the keyboard. When the

The command DVIEW 139

target point has been selected, the prompt changes to:

Enter camera point<300,40,65>:

Again, either select and *x,y,z* coordinate point by pointing with the aid of the .xy filter or *enter* an *x,y,z* coordinate from the keyboard. The ghosted drawing on screen regenerates in its selected viewing position. An example is given in Fig. 8.5.

The Zoom option

Enter **z** (**Z**oom) and the prompt changes to:

Adjust zoom scale factor<1>:

And a slider bar appears at the top of the screen. Either move the pointer in the slider bar with the aid of the pointing device, watching the ghosted drawing changing size as the movement takes place, or *enter* a figure at the keyboard (see Figs. 8.7 to 8.9, in which the slider bar is shown in three versions of AutoCAD).

Note when using **Z**oom in **Dview** that the pictorial representation of the model is in parallel projection and not in perspective projection. Perspective views can only be obtained when using the **D**istance option of the command (see below). But when in a **D**istance screen and the **Z**oom option is used the perspective viewing remains. If in parallel projection when working in R12 with

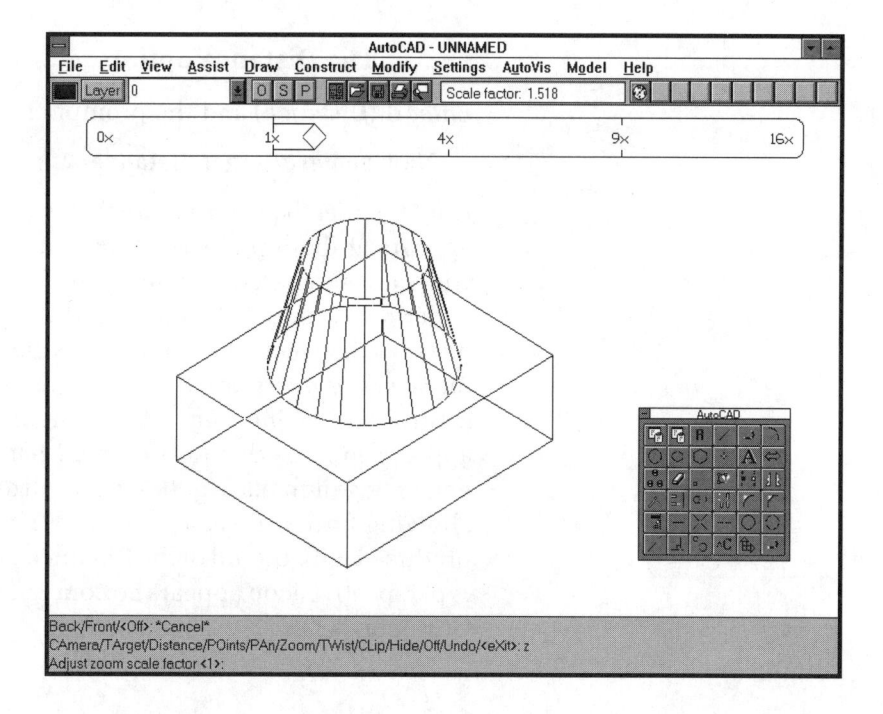

Fig. 8.7 The Zoom option of **Dview** when working in AutoCAD for Windows

Dview, when **Z**oom is called the zoom scale factor shows in the status bar (Windows), or in the menu bar (DOS). When in R13 the Scale Factor statement appears in the Coords display window at the bottom left of the screen (Fig. 8.8). When in **Dview** in R13, x,y,z coordinates do not show in the Coords window.

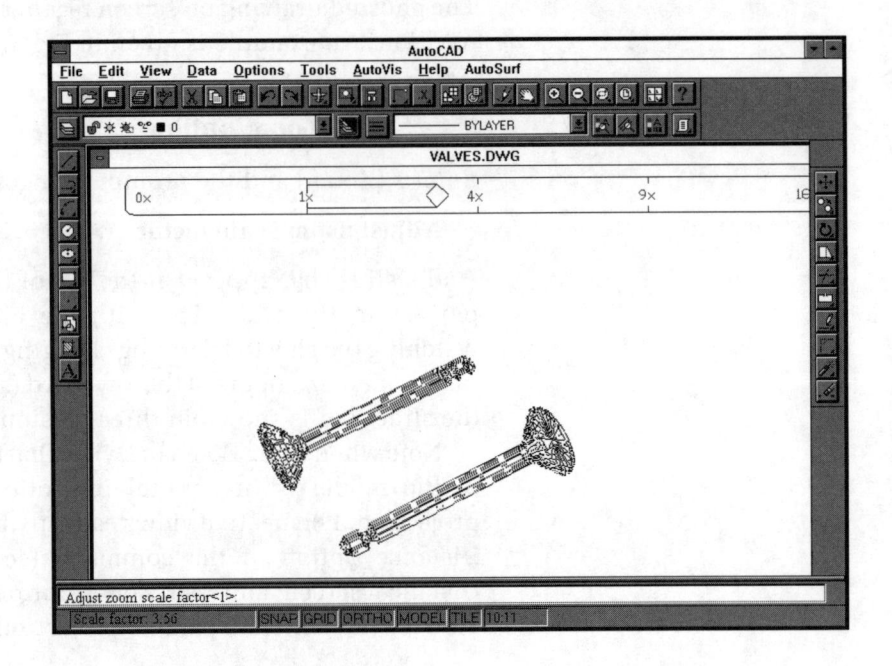

Fig. 8.8 The Zoom option of **Dview** when working in R13

The Distance option

Enter **d** (**D**istance) and the prompt changes to:

New camera/target distance<2>:

And a slider bar similar to that showing when **Z**oom is called, appears at the top of the graphic area of the screen. Points on the slider are numbered from 0x to 16x (0 times to 16 times). Moving the slider arrow under the control of the pointing device changes the distance between the target drawing and the camera and either increases or decreases the size of the drawing. Its size can also be controlled by *entering* a figure at the keyboard. If the drawing appears so large that only a small part of it is showing on screen, *enter* a large number, e.g. 400. This will decrease the size considerably, allowing further distance changes to be made. Note that drawings produced with the aid of the **Distance** prompt are perspective views. A perspective icon appears bottom left of the screen – but only if the UCS icon is **ON**.

The command DVIEW 141

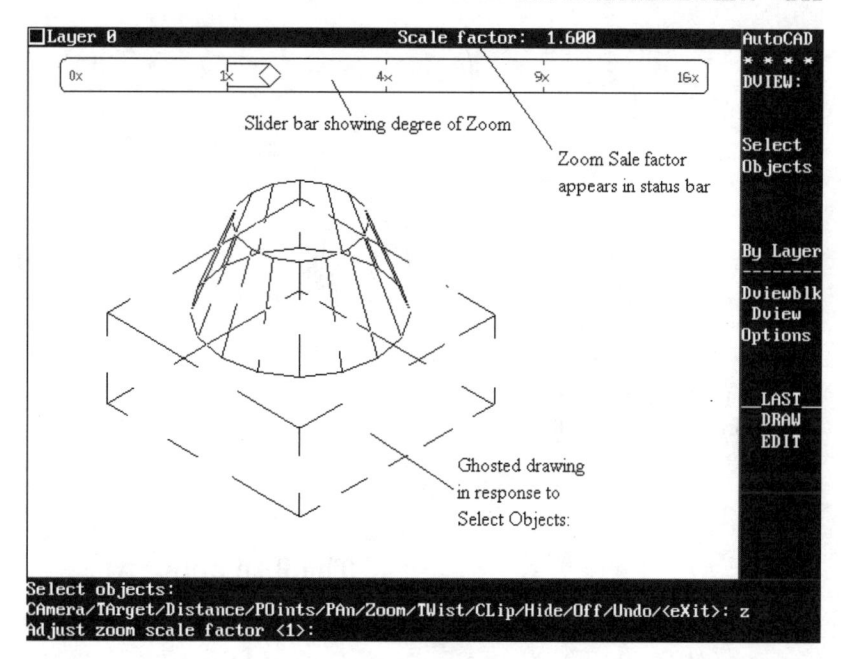

Fig. 8.9 The Zoom option of **Dview** when working in R12 (DOS version)

An example of a perspective drawing is included in Fig. 8.10. A second example of a more complicated 3D model is given in Fig. 8.11.

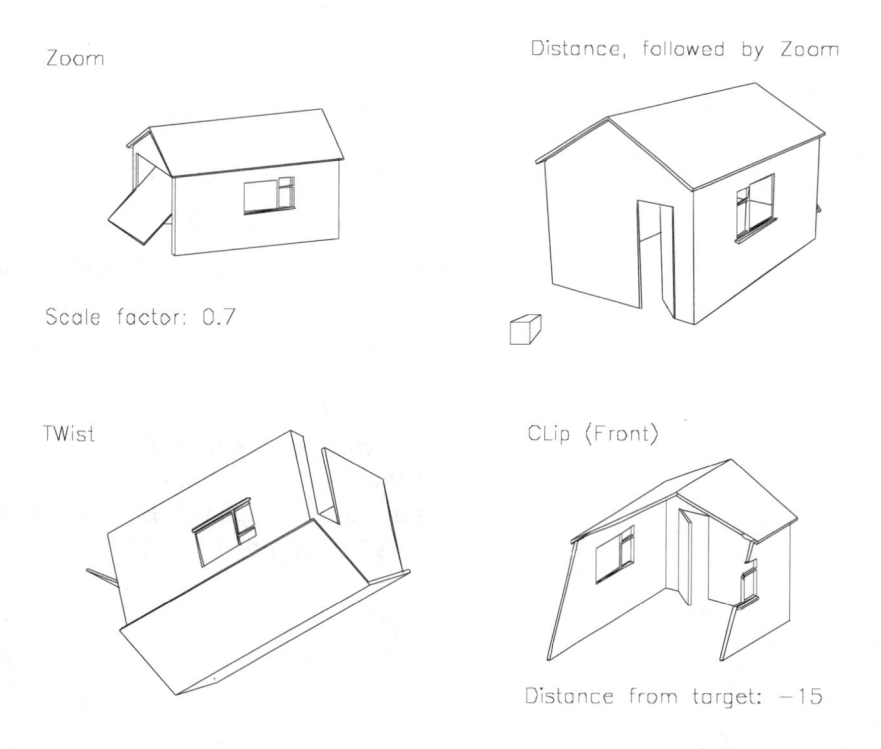

Fig. 8.10 Drawings resulting from four further **Dview** option

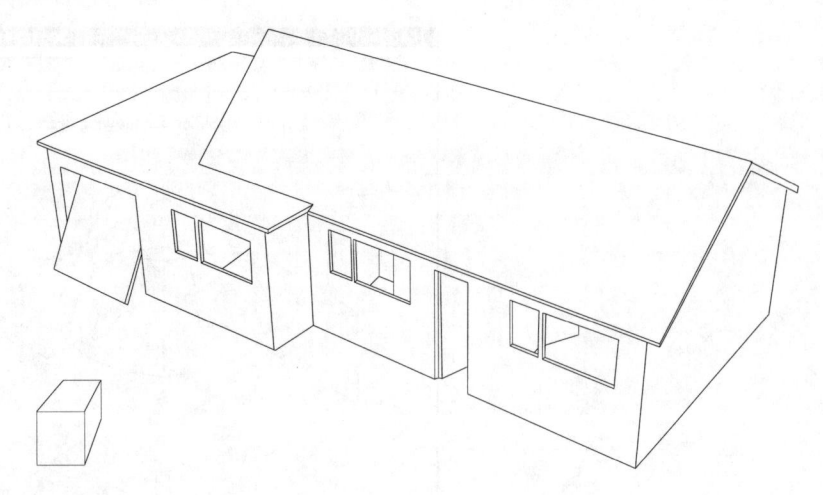

Fig. 8.11 A perspective view of a more complicated 3D drawing model

The PAn option

Enter **pa** (**PA**n) and the prompts change to:

Displacement base point: *pick* a suitable point
Second point: *pick* another point

And the drawing pans between the two picked points. The drawing can either be dragged between the two points, or two coordinate points can be entered from the keyboard. A *right-click* regenerates the drawing at the required panned position.

The TWist option

Enter **tw** (**TW**ist) and the prompts change to:

New view twist<2.00>:

And a rubber band line appears attached between the 3D drawing (or Dviewblock) and the cross-cursor hairs. Moving the cursor cross-hairs under pointing device control rotates (twists) the ghosted model to new positions in a rotary manner. When satisfied with a position, a *right-click* regenerates the drawing in its new position.

Entering figures from the keyboard rotates the drawing to new positions at angles to the original position – e.g. *enter* 90 and the twist occurs through 90°. *Enter* 180 and the drawing rotates through 180°. An example of using **TW**ist is given in Fig. 8.9.

The CLip option

Enter **cl** (**CL**ip) and the prompts change to:

Back/Front/<Off>:

Either the back or the front of the drawing can be clipped, by keying a **b** or an **f**. Figure 7.10 shows a 3D drawing which has been clipped at a distance of −15 from the camera.

If a front clip is required *enter* **f** and the prompt changes to:

Eye/ON/OFF/<Distance from target><430>:

And a slider appears at the top of the drawing area. If the slider is operated under the control of the selection device, the clipping can be seen on the ghosted drawing (or Dviewblock) on screen. The slider moves in sympathy with the movement of the selection device. The **Distance** number appears at the menu bar, status bar or Coords window depending upon which release of AutoCAD is in use. The drawing regenerates as clipped with a *right-click*.

Entering **e** (**E**ye), when in perspective view places the clipping plane at the camera. Any objects behind the camera do not appear on screen. Eye also causes a previously placed front clipping plane to revert to camera position.

The Hide option

Enter **h** (**H**ide) and the prompts change to:

Hiding lines 40% done.

And hidden lines are automatically removed.

This has the same effect in **Dview** as when Dview is not in operation.

The Off option

Entering **o** (**O**ff) turns perspective views off thus into parallel views. When Distance is invoked, perspective views are turned on again.

The Undo option

Entering **u** (Undo) reverses (undoes) the last **Dview** operation without coming out of the **Dview** options sequences.

The eXit option

Enter **x** (e**X**it) and the **Dview** command is cancelled, leaving the drawing on screen as amended in **Dview**. A *right-click* or pressing the *Return* key has the same result.

General notes about the Dview command

1. Any details entered while in **Dview** – e.g. points – are relative to the World Coordinate System (WCS) and not to the current UCS (unless it is the UCS World).
2. If a filter (e.g. *.xy*) is required, *enter* **.xy**, followed by a *right-click*. *Pick* a point on screen for the *x,y* coordinates. The command line then shows **(need Z)**. Now *enter* the *z* coordinate figure.
3. If working in AutoCAD R13, another method of using a filter is to press the **Shift** key of the keyboard and *right-click*. An Object Snaps and Filters menu appears at the cursor point (Fig. 8.12). The required filter (usually .xy) can be *picked* from the menu.
4. After each prompt option is completed, the command line reverts to:

CAmera/TArget/Distance/POints/PAn/Zoom/TWist/CLip/Hide/ Off/Undo/<eXit>:

ready for the next option. To get out of the **Dview** command sequences, *right-click*, press *Return* or *enter* **x** (e**X**it).

5. When a drawing has been placed in perspective view, the **Draw** commands, such as **Pline**, **Circle** etc. cannot be used to add to the drawing by *picking* points with the aid of the selection device. They can, however, be used by *entering* coordinate points at the command line.

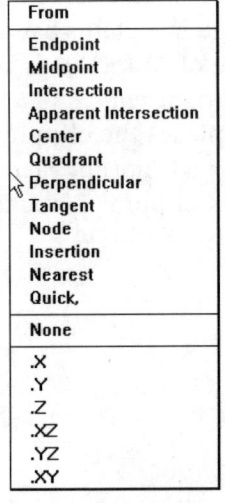

Fig. 8.12 The Object Snaps and Filters menu of AutoCAD R13

CHAPTER 9

AutoVision

Introduction

AutoVision is an Autodesk software package that works inside AutoCAD. There are two releases of the software to date – AutoVision Release 1, which works in AutoCAD Release 12 and AutoVision Release 2 which works in AutoCAD Release 13. The software is designed for the rendering of 3D models constructed in AutoCAD. Operating the software for either of the two releases is practically identical, so in this chapter the use of AutoVision in AutoCAD R13 will be described. Before attempting to work in AutoVision, try the AutoCAD tool **SHADE**.

The tool Shade

Examples of the results of using the command are given in Figs. 9.1 and 9.2. A further example is given in Plate VIII. All that is required is to call the command and the model is shaded according to the colours in which each part is constructed. The type of shading resulting from using the command is controlled by the settings of the variable **Shadedge**:

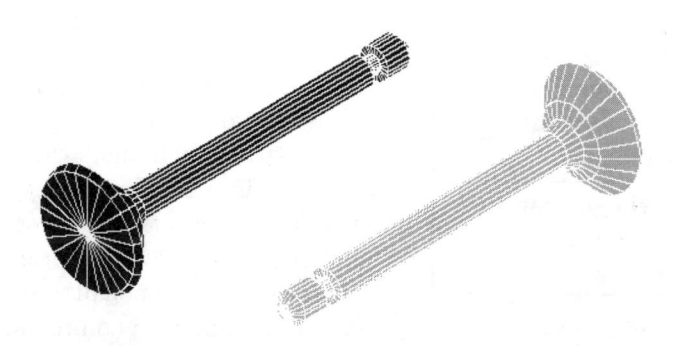

Fig. 9.1 A 3D model drawing acted upon by **SHADE** with **Shadedge** set to 3

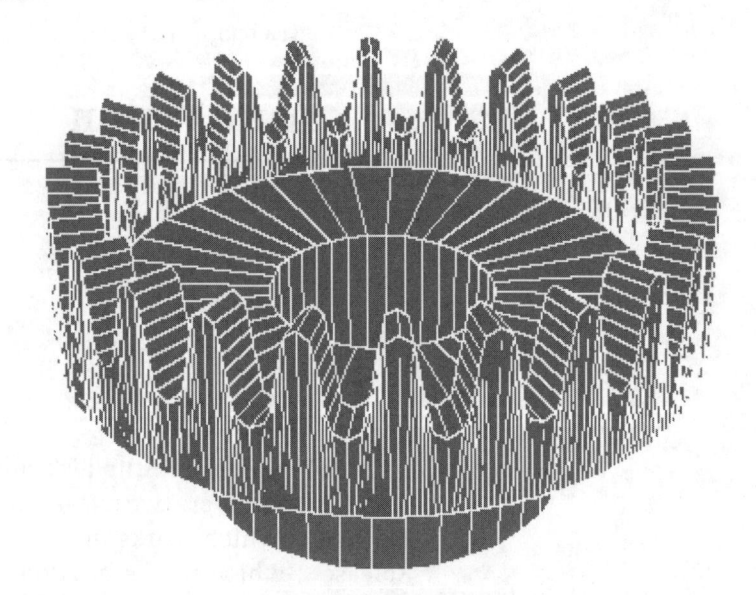

Fig. 9.1 A 3D model drawing acted upon by **Shade** with **Shadedge** set to 3

Shadedge set at 0: Faces are shaded, but edges not highlighted – but only with a 256 colour display.
Shadedge set at 1: Faces are shaded, but edges not highlighted in background colour – but only with a 256 colour display.
Shadedge set at 2: Faces are shaded in the colour in which the faces were drawn. Faces are black. Hidden edges are hidden.
Shadedge set at 3: Faces are shaded in the colour in which they were drawn.

AutoVision

Renderings in AutoVision are dependent upon the positioning of lights, shadows cast by the lights and the materials attached to parts of the 3D model being rendered. Backgrounds for AutoVision renderings can be added if desired. For good quality renderings at least a Super Video Graphic Array (SVGA) colour screen with a minimum of 256 colours is advisable.

All settings for lights, shadows, materials, colours and backgrounds are made in a number of dialogue boxes called from the **AutoVis** pull-down menu (Fig. 9.3) or, if it is on screen, from the **AutoVis** toolbar (R13). It will be seen from Fig. 9.3 that there are three fullstops (...) after each of the command names in the **AutoVis** menu, indicating that each command is related to a pull-down menu.

To fully describe the use of AutoVision would require a book in its own right. Because of this, in this chapter we will only be

Fig. 9.3 Selecting **Lights...** from the **AutoVis** pull-down menu concerned with settings for lights and materials. Also with most of the settings the default values will be accepted. However, the reader is advised to experiment with the possibilities of settings for fog, landscapes and animations as well as attempting changing default settings.

AutoVision lighting

Four types of lights are available from AutoVision – **Ambient**, **Point**, **Direct** and **Spot**:

> **Ambient Light** – general all round lighting, which does not lessen with distance.
> **Point Light** – sheds light in all directions.
> **Direct Light** – sheds light in the direction in which is pointing.
> **Spot Light** – sheds light in a cone onto the object being lit.

With the three types **Point**, **Direct** and **Spot**, the further the object being lit is from the light source, the less will be the amount of light falling on the object. The **Intensity** of these lights can be changed in the appropriate dialogue boxes.

As the settings for lights are made for any particular scene, so icons representing the forms of light appear in the scene. There is no icon for **Ambient Light**. The icons representing the other three types are shown in Fig. 9.4.

Setting Lights for a scene – First example

The **Vpoint** view of a 3D model drawing of two poppet valves given in Fig. 9.5 is taken as a first example for the production of a rendering. The stages in producing a rendering of the model follow a sequence such as:

1. Place the model in the **WCS** (World Coordinate System) and if necessary, **Zoom** to a lower scale and **Pan** to place the plan view into a suitable position for setting lighting.

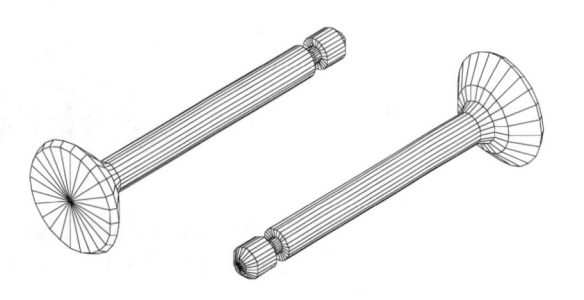

Fig. 9.4 The icons representing **Point**, **Distant** and **Spot** lights

Fig. 9.5 The model for the first example

148   An Introduction to 3D AutoCAD

2. From the **AutoVis** menu select **Lights....** The **Lights** dialogue box appears (Fig. 9.6). Note that the **Intensity** slider bar for the **Ambient Light** is set so that the reading is at **0.3**. This is the default (30%) lighting for ambient light. Note also that the type of light showing in the list box is **Point Light**. *Left-click* on the **New...** button.

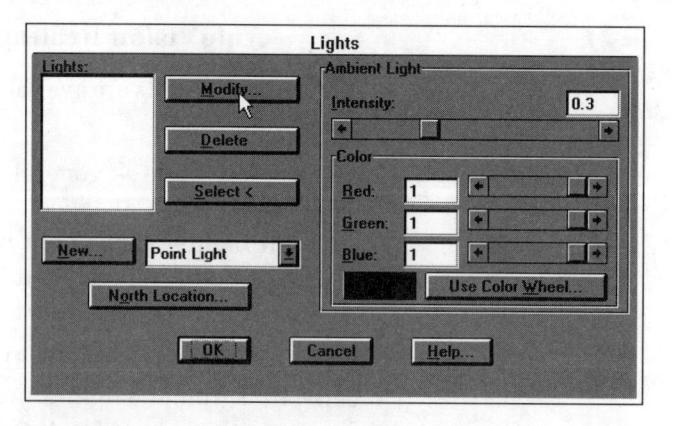

Fig. 9.6 The **Lights** dialogue box

3. The **New Point Light** dialogue box appears (Fig. 9.7). *Enter* the name **LIGHT01** in the **Light Name:** box. Adjust the **Intensity** slider as thought fit. In the example given, the intensity has been set to **180.60**. Check that **Shadow On** is off (check box with no diagonals). If diagonals are in the check box, *left-click* in the box to remove them. *Left-click* on the **Modify** button.

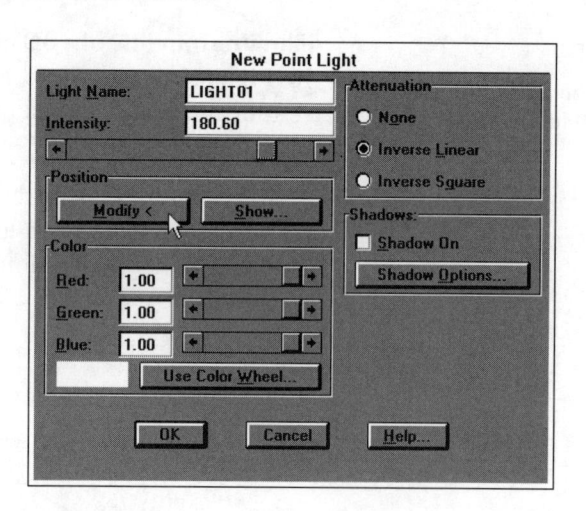

Fig. 9.7 The **New Point Light** dialogue box

4. The **Modify Point Light** dialogue box appears (Fig. 9.8). *Left-click* on the **Modify** button and, at the command line:

AutoVision 149

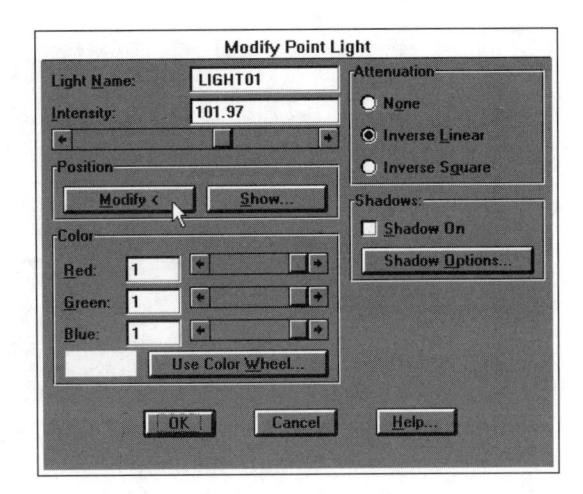

Fig. 9.8 The **Modify Point Light** dialogue box

Enter light location<current>: *enter* 320,230,300 *right-click*

or:

Enter light location<current>: *enter* .xy *right-click*
of. *pick* the point 320,230
(need Z) *enter* 300

The icon for the light appears at the selected spot (Fig. 9.9).

LIGHT04 at 90,290,100

LIGHT01 at 320,230,300

LIGHT02 at 125,40,70

LIGHT03 at 390,30,150

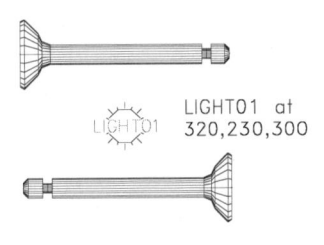

Fig. 9.9 The lighting icons showing for the first example

5. The **Lights** dialogue box reappears with the name of the **LIGHT01** showing in the **Lights** list box (Fig. 9.10). *Left-click* on **Point Light**

150   An Introduction to 3D AutoCAD

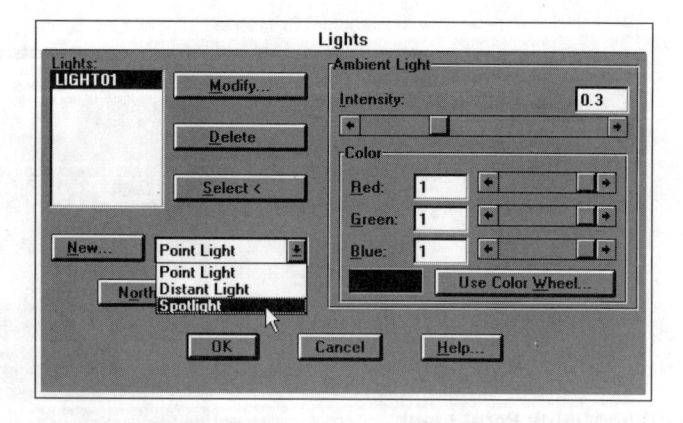

Fig. 9.10 Beginning to set up the light **LIGHT03**

and the **Lights** list box pops up. Select **Spotlight** and go through a similar routine to set **LIGHT03** and **LIGHT04** (Fig. 9.9). In a similar fashion set **LIGHT02** which is a **Distant Light**.

6. *Left-click* on **Materials...** in the **AutoVis** pull-down menu (Fig. 9.3). In the **Materials Library** dialogue box which appears (Fig. 9.11) *left-click* on the **Materials Library...** button. The library names appear in the **Library List:** list box. Select any name, followed by a *left-click* on the **Preview** button. The material is previewed in the **Preview** box. Select the two materials **BRASS GIFMAP** and **COPPER** and *left-click* on the **Import** button. The names appear in the **Materials List** box. *Left-click* on the **OK** button of the dialogue box.

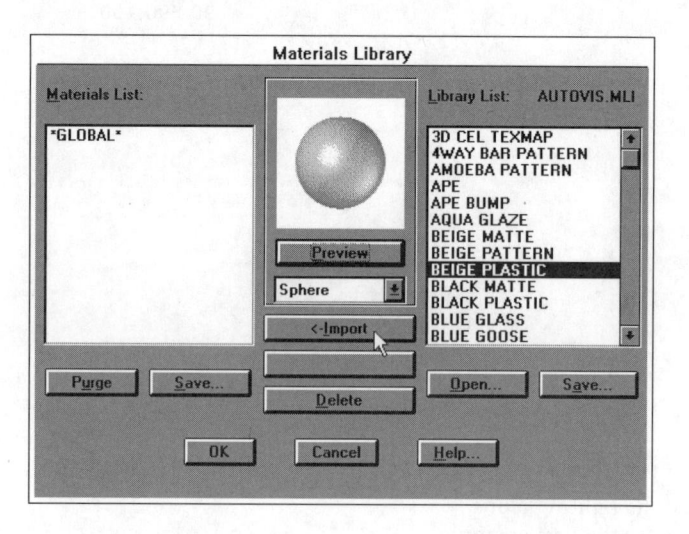

Fig. 9.11 The **Materials Library** dialogue box

7. The **Materials** dialogue box (Fig. 9.12) appears. *Left-click* on **COPPER** in the **Materials** box. *Left-click* on the **Attach** button. Then *left-click* on the nearest of the two poppet valves in the model

AutoVision 151

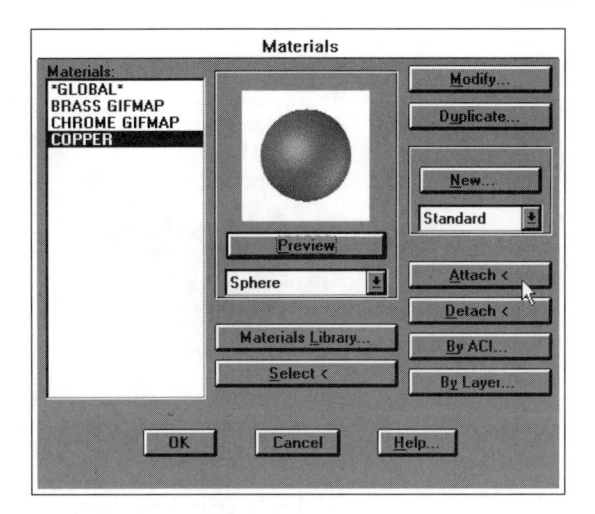

Fig. 9.12 The **Materials** dialogue box

drawing. In a similar fashion, attach the material **BRASS GIFMAP** to the furthest of the two poppet valves. *Left-click* on the **OK** button of the dialogue box.

8. Place the drawing in a **vpoint** view and if necessary, **Zoom** window to obtain a reasonably good size drawing to render. *Left-click* on **Render...** in the **AutoVis** pull-down menu. The **Render** dialogue box appears (Fig. 9.13). Check that the **Shadows** check box is **OFF**. Accept the **current view** and *left-click* on the **OK** button of the dialogue box. After some time (depending upon the speed of the computer in use) the model becomes rendered. Fig. 9.14 shows the results of the rendering of the poppet valves drawing. A coloured rendering of the poppet valves drawing is given in Plate VI.

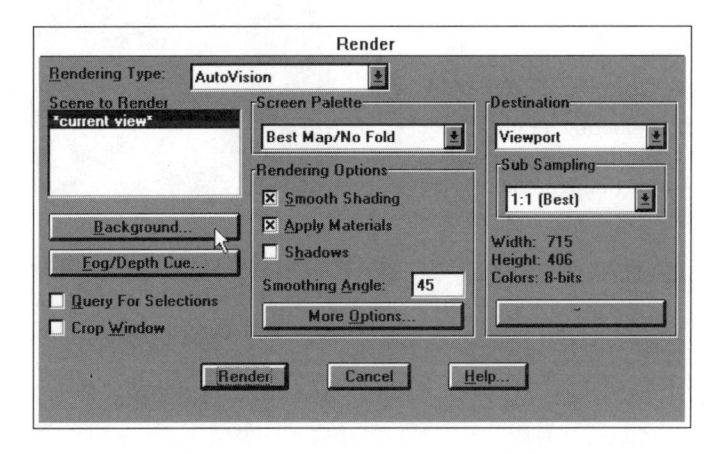

Fig. 9.13 The **Render** dialogue box

152 An Introduction to 3D AutoCAD

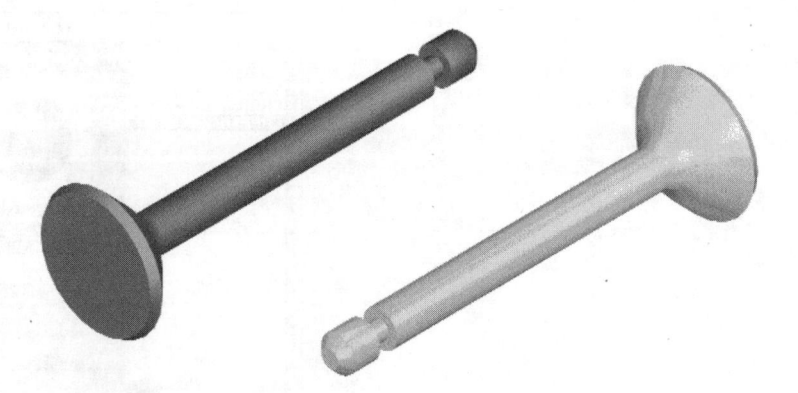

Fig. 9.14 The rendering of the first example

Notes

1. Lights can be coloured. In the **Lights** dialogue box a light colour can be set by adjusting the red, green and blue sliders in the **Color** area of the dialogue box. Alternatively *left-click* on the **Use Color Wheel** button and the **Color** dialogue box appears (Fig. 9.15). In the dialogue box *left-click* on the **Select from ACI...** button and then select a colour in the colour wheel which appears.

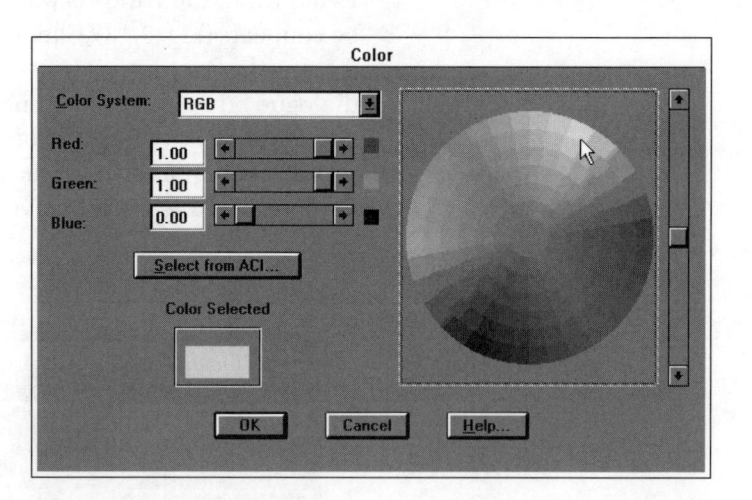

Fig. 9.15 Selecting a light colour from the colour wheel in the **Color** dialogue box

2. A *left-click* on the **Background** button in the **Render** dialogue box brings the **Background** dialogue box on screen (Fig. 9.16). If the **AutoCAD Background** check box is **OFF** a colour can be settled from the colour wheel by a *left-click* on the **Use Color Wheel** button, followed by selecting a colour from the wheel.

AutoVision 153

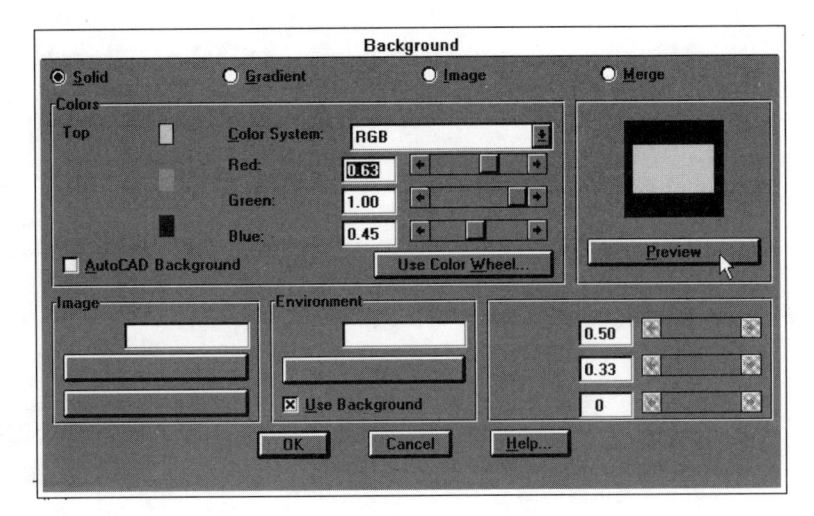

Fig. 9.16 The **Background** dialogue box

Setting Lights for a scene – Second example

A second example is given in Fig. 9.17. The rendering for this example is given in Fig. 9.18. The material **BRASS GIFMAP** was attached to the 3D drawing before rendering started. The rendering was of a perspective view produced by using the **D**istance option of the **DVIEW** command system. Figure 9.19 shows such a perspective view of the 3D model drawing. It is included here to show that rendering of perspective views is possible with **AutoVision**.

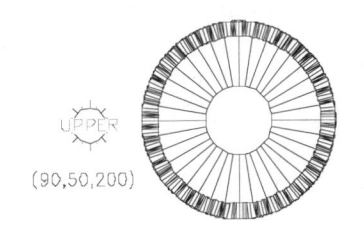

Fig. 9.17 Second example

154   An Introduction to 3D AutoCAD

Fig. 9.18 A rendering of the second example

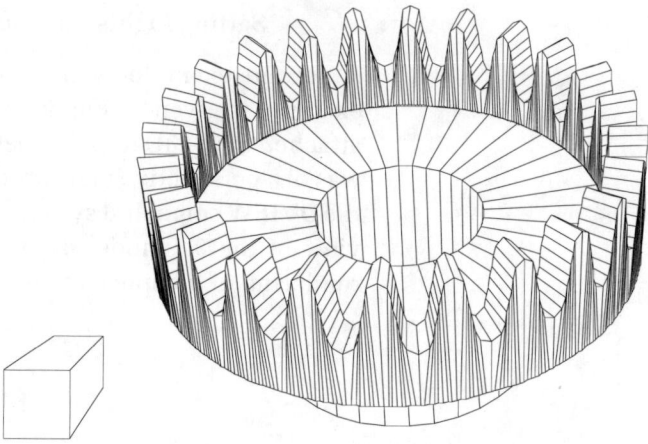

Fig. 9.19 A perspective view of the model for the second exmaple

Setting Lights for a scene – Third example

A third example (a garage scene) is shown in the three illustrations Figures 9.20 to 9.22. Figure 9.20 shows the three-viewport layout in which the 3D model drawing was constructed. Figure 9.21 shows the lighting for the model and Fig. 9.21 a **Dview** perspective view of the model. Several of the plates in the colour section involve this 3D model. In the colour plates of the garage scene a path has been added to the views. Plate VIII is a **Shade** view of the garage scene. Plate IX is an AutoVision rendering of the garage scene in the colours in which the drawing was constructed. Plate X is a rendering of the garage scene in Autodesk 3D Studio. Plate X includes a variety of materials from the 3D Studio materials libraries.

AutoVision 155

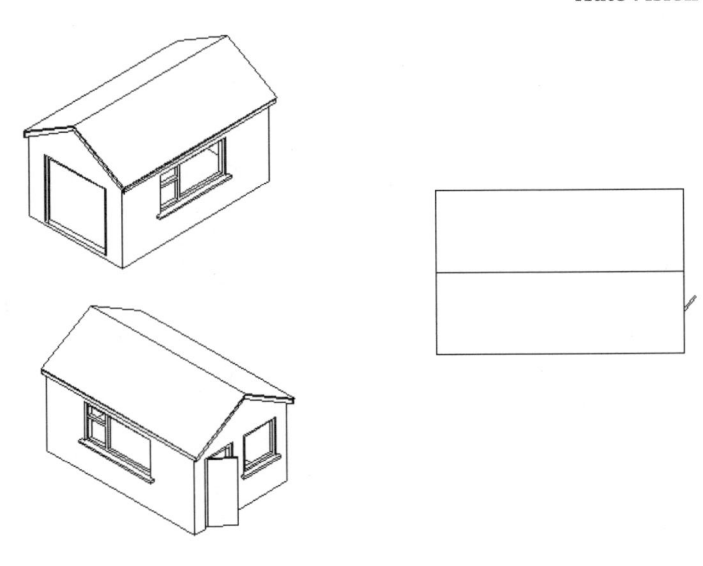

Fig. 9.20 The three-viewport layout in which the thrid example was constructed

```
LIGHT1  (P):   300,240,200
LIGHT2  (D):   420,50,100
LIGHT3  (D):   50,300,150
LIGHT4  (D):   80,40,120
```

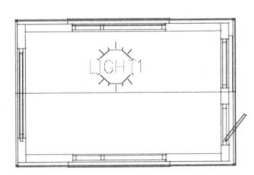

Fig. 9.21 The AutoVision lighting for the third example

Setting Lights for a scene – Fourth example

This example describes the sequence for the construction of an AME (Advanced Modelling Extension) 3D model of a dressing table bottle in AutoCAD R12 before adding lights and then rendering in **AutoVision**. The model could just have well been constructed in R13 using the native **Solid** tools of R13. A 3D Studio rendering of the model is shown in Plate XIII. See Chapter 10 for details about 3D Studio.

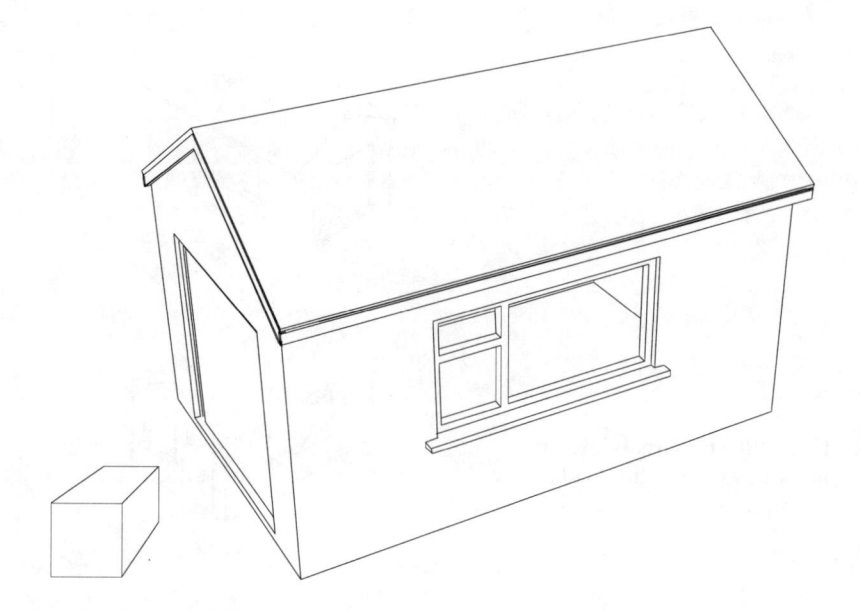

Fig. 9.22 A **Dview** perspective of the third example

The procedures for constructing the model were:

1. **UCSfollow:** set to 1.
2. Call **UCS FRONT** from the UCS Orientation dialogue box.
3. **Zoom** 1.
4. With **Pline,** draw the outline on **UCS FRONT** as shown in Fig. 9.23.
5. **Solextrude** the pline outline by 25.
6. Set **Color** to 2 (yellow).

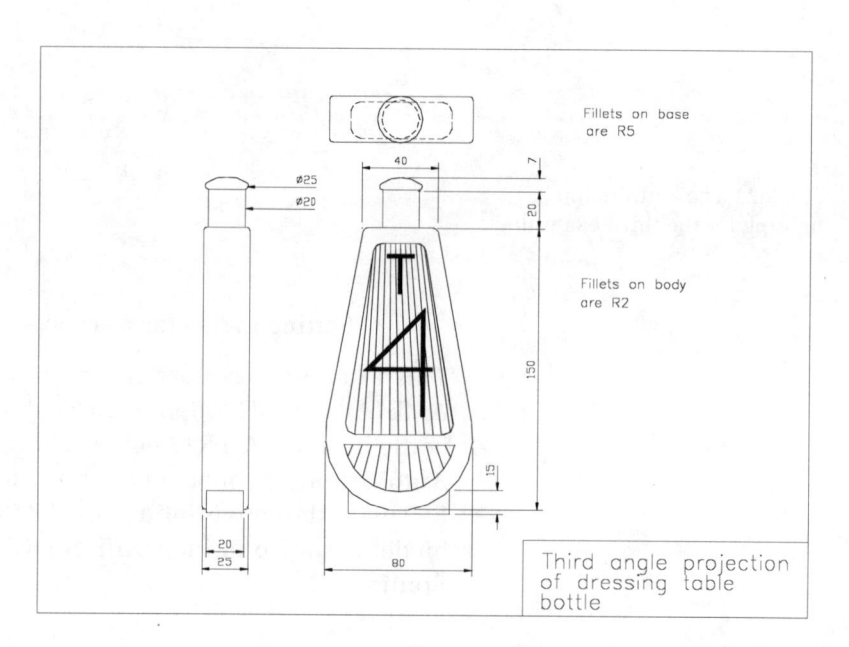

Fig. 9.23 An orthographic projection with dimensions of the dressing table bottle

7. With **Pline** draw the half outline of the cap as shown in Fig. 9.23.
8. **Solrev** the half outline.
9. Set the **UCS** to the World Coordinate System (WCS).
10. SOLMOVE the cap to its central position on the body.
11. Set **Color** 7 (white).
12. **Solbox** base to sizes given in Fig. 9.23.
13. Reset the **UCS** to **FRONT**.
14. **Solmove** so that the bottom of the base is resting at $y = 0$.
15. **Vpoint** $-1,-1,1$ (Fig. 9.24).
16. **Zoom** window to make the 3D model as large as possible.
17. **Solfill** front and back edges to R2. Fillet base corners to R5.
18. **Solunion** base to body.
19. **Solmesh** body/base and cap separately.
20. **UCS** World.
21. **Solucs** Make the front of the model; the new UCS and save the UCS as 'label'.
22. With **Pline** draw the two parts of the label. Top part in colour 4 (cyan) and bottom part in colour 3 (group).
23. **Rulesrf** the two parts of the label.
24. **Color** 1 (red).
25. **Trace** of width 3 to add the **T** and the **4**.
26. **UCS** World.
27. **Zoom** a (All).
28. **Move** the whole solid to a new position as in Fig. 9.25.
29. Add **AutoVision** lights as shown in Fig. 9.25.
30. **Render**.

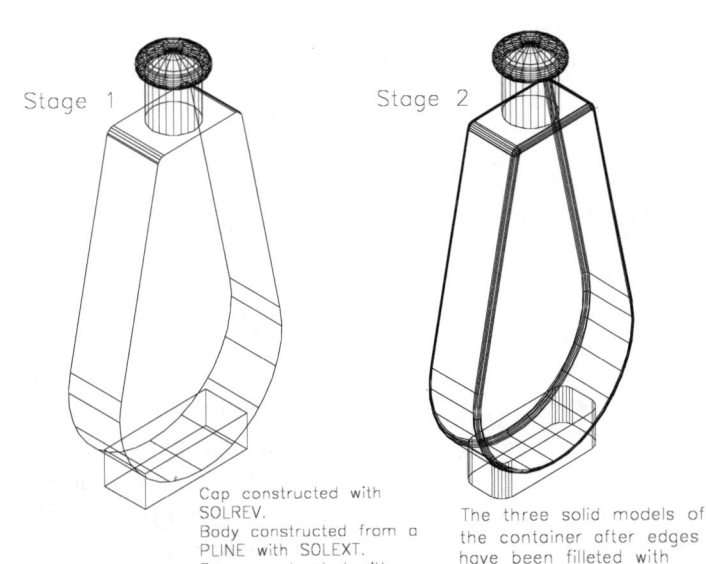

Fig. 9.24 The first two stages in constructing the AME model for the fourth example

Stage 1
Cap constructed with SOLREV.
Body constructed from a PLINE with SOLEXT.
Base constructed with SOLBOX.

Stage 2
The three solid models of the container after edges have been filleted with SOLFILL

158   An Introduction to 3D AutoCAD

Stage 3

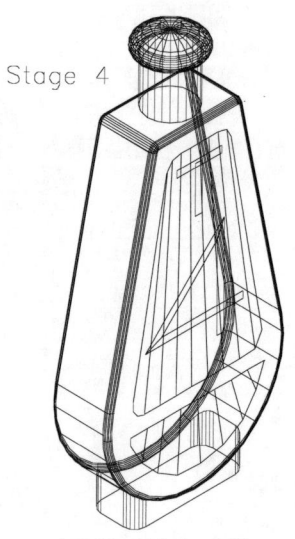

The three solid models after body and base have been acted upon by SOLUNION

Stage 4

Labels added — Plines Trace lines and Rulesurf

Fig. 9.25 The third and fourth stages in constructing the AME model for the fourth example

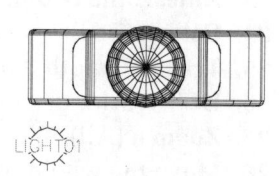

LIGHT01

Fig. 9.26 **AutoVision** lights added to the fourth example

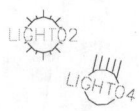

LIGHT02
LIGHT04
LIGHT03

Notes

1. When a drawing which includes AutoVision lights, materials etc. is saved to file, the AutoVision data is saved with the drawing data.
2. If the first of your renderings of a model does not seem to be very successful, try changing light positions, their intensities, their colours, or perhaps add further lights.
3. Another feature which may encourage a better rendering is changing the materials being attached to parts of the model.

4. The setting of the **Shadows** check boxes for the lights and also in the **Render** dialogue box could again affect the quality of a rendering.
5. **Spot lights** may also affect the rendering. Changing a **Distant Light** for a **Spot Light** or vice versa may result in a better rendering.
6. The best advice to the operator who wishes to produce renderings of good quality is to practise and experiment with a variety of settings.
7. Rendering inevitably takes some time, the more complicated the model being rendered, the more time is required. To save time, your first rendering could be with anti-aliasing off. In the **Render** dialogue box (Fig. 9.13) there is a button labelled **More Options....** *Left-click* on this button and in the dialogue box which then appears *left-click* in the **None** button under the **Anti-aliasing** name. This will enable more speed in rendering, but the result will not be so clean on its edges. When satisfied that lighting and materials render well, a final rendering could be made with one of the other anti-aliasing buttons set. Phong or High give the best results.

CHAPTER 10

Autodesk 3D Studio

Introduction

3D Studio is an Autodesk software package designed for constructing, rendering and animating 3D model drawings. It will also render and animate 3D models constructed in AutoCAD, whether drawn using the **Surfaces** commands, AME or those with the **Solids** commands in R13.

Selection device

Selection of commands is carried out within the 3D editor display screen with the aid of a mouse. An alternative is a puck or stylus with a graphic tablet, perhaps used in conjunction with a mouse. It is possible to operate the programs from the keyboard with the cursor keys, but this will be found to be slow. Most commands can be called by *entering* letters, or a combination of letters or a key and a letter from the keyboard. In this book, it is assumed that all working is performed with the aid of a mouse as the pointing device and that it has two buttons – left and right. To operate the mouse, buttons are clicked, i.e. they are pressed to achieve the required result. Note, however, that using the key alternatives is often quicker than clicking on commands with the mouse.

Cursors

Several types of cursor will be seen, according to the operation being performed at the time. Some of these carry arrows showing the direction of action which can be taken with the aid of the cursor. The cursor varies according to the type of action required. Cursors are moved with the aid of the mouse and actions initiated by clicking one or other of the mouse buttons.

Autodesk 3D Studio 161

Viewports

The program works with viewports. Their number and size can be varied as will be seen later (Fig. 10.15). When the program is first loaded, the 3D Editor appears with four equally sized viewports as shown in Fig. 10.1. The active viewport, that in which the operator is working at any one time, is outlined by a heavy white line. Switching viewports is carried out by clicking in the required viewport.

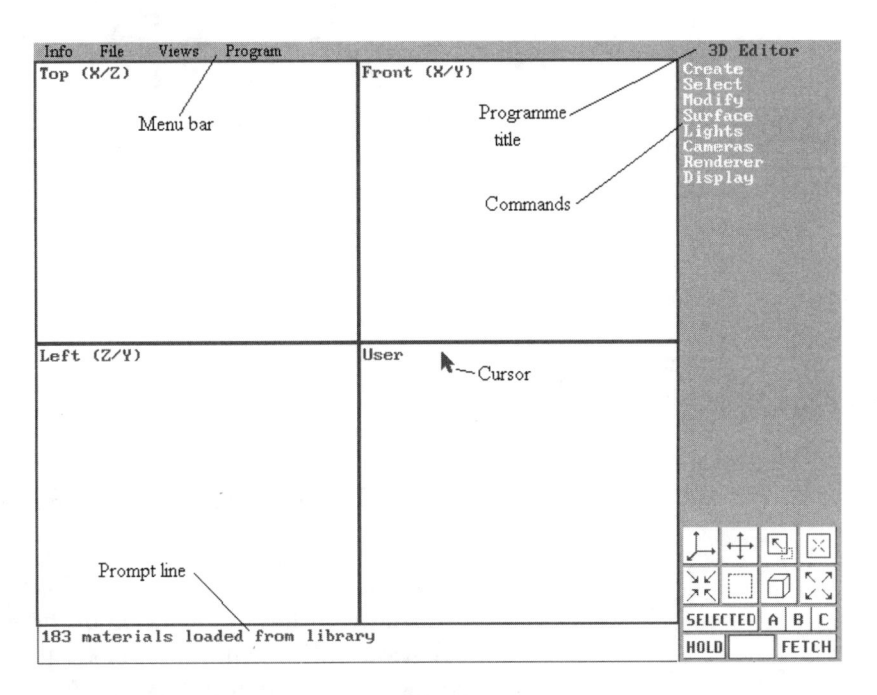

Fig. 10.1 The 3D Studio 3D Editor display

Dialogue and message boxes

Many operations performed in 3D Studio are associated with dialogue boxes, in which details can be entered from the keyboard, or message boxes displaying a message to which the operator can respond by clicking on buttons such as **OK**, **Create** and **Cancel**. Illustrations of a number of the boxes are included in this chapter.

Icon panel

A panel with eight icons will be seen at the bottom right-hand corner of the 3D Editor. Explanations of the responses to clicking on each of the icons are given in Fig. 10.2. In addition to the eight icon buttons, there are six buttons labelled **SELECTED**, **A**, **B**, **C**, **HOLD** and **FETCH** below the icon buttons. In this book, the purpose of these named and lettered buttons will not be explained, as they do not affect the simple explanations of renderings given in this chapter.

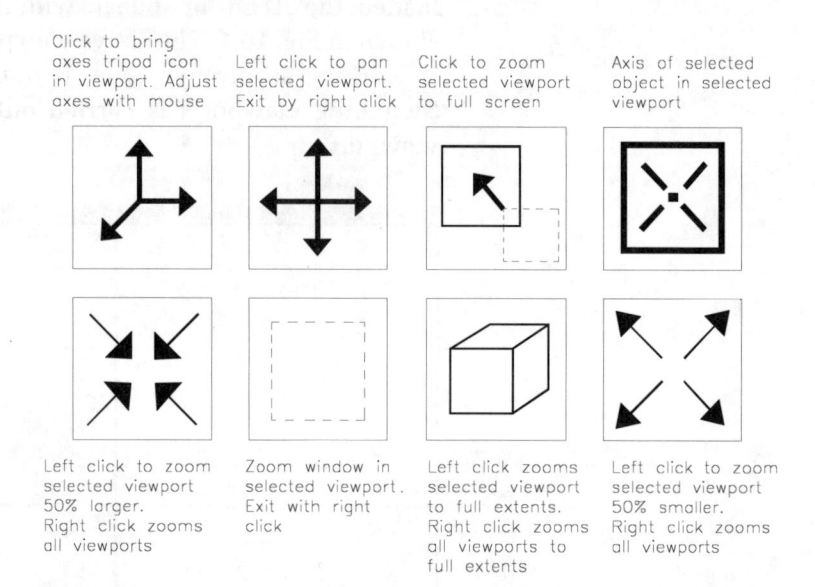

Fig. 10.2 An enlarged view of the 3D Studio icon panel

Calling AutoCAD and AutoSketch from 3D Studio

When configured to do so by a shell program, AutoCAD or AutoSketch, as well as MS-DOS, can be called from any of the four programs in 3D Studio, either by selection of the name of the software from the **Program** pull-down menu, or by pressing a function key – F6 for AutoCAD, F7 for AutoSketch, F9 for MS-DOS. To get back to 3D Studio from AutoCAD or AutoSketch, select **Quit** from the **File** pull-down menu of either program. 3D Studio will accept 2D DXF files from AutoSketch.

Programs in 3D Studio

3D Studio contains four basic programs:

1. 2D Shaper for creating 2D shapes which can be formed into 3D models.
2. 3D Lofter for converting 2D shapes into 3D models (by **lofting**).
3. 3D Editor for editing 3D models created in the 2D Shaper and 3D Lofter programs and including those from AutoCAD DXF files.
4. Keyframer for developing animations in 3D models.

It is not the purpose here to describe the full use and value of this software. To do so would require a whole book much larger than this one. In this book, it is only intended to show how the 3D Studio Editor program of 3D Studio can be used for the rendering of some varied examples of DXF files (*.dxf files) of 3D models created in AutoCAD. It is hoped that this will be a useful introduction to this excellent software. These examples show only a fraction of the methods available for creating, developing and demonstrating the possibilities for rendering 3D models in a computer environment. No attempt is made in this chapter to describe the animating of models with the software.

Filenames and their extensions

Both DXF and 3DS files (3D Studio files) from AutoCAD can be loaded into 3D Studio. All the examples shown here involve loading DXF files.

A number of types of file with the following filename extensions are used in 3D Studio:

1. *.shp* files – 2D Shaper files.
2. *.lft* files – 3D Lofter files.
3. *.3ds* files – 3D Editor and Keyframer files.
4. *.mli* files – Materials files.
5. *.prj* files – Project files, with components and settings in the same file.
6. *.dxf* files – Data Exchange Format files from AutoCAD or AutoSketch.
7. *.gif* files – For backgrounds and renderings.
8. *.cel* files – For backgrounds and renderings.
9. *.tga* files – Rendering image files.
10. *.tif* files – Bitmap files.
11. *.fli* files – Files from Autodesk Animator.

Of these – *.dxf*, *.3ds*, *.cel*, *.prj*, and *.tga* files will be referred to here.

Note about speed of rendering

Rendering takes time. The faster the speed of the Central Processing Unit (CPU) of the computer, the quicker will rendering take place. The fitting of a math co-processor in the computer is essential if using a computer fitted with 386 or 486SX operating chip. A suggested minimum Personal Computer (PC) equipment requirement for 3D Studio would be one fitted with an 80386 CPU chip running at 20 MHz with an 80387 math co-processor. However a computer fitted with an 80486 CPU running at 33 MHz, together with a Weitek co-processor would give greatly improved results. The best results would be with the fastest possible Pentium chip fitted, although a PC with an 80486 DX2 chip (running at 66 MHz) will be reasonably fast.

The 3D Editor of 3D Studio

The 3D editor program of 3D Studio contains the following command sets:

1. **Create:** This is for the creation of 3D models from basic primitives; changing their shape; development of complex models from the primitives created.
2. **Select:** This is for the selection of vertices, faces, elements and objects from 3D models.
3. **Modify:** This is for modifying vertices, edges, faces, elements and objects within 3D models.
4. **Surface:** This is for adding materials, smoothing and mapping surfaces and objects in 3D models.
5. **Lights:** This is for adding and adjusting the intensity, colour and position of lights for illuminating the environment of 3D models.
6. **Camera:** This is for including and adjusting cameras in the 3D model environment.
7. **Renderer:** This is for setting the rendering parameters and rendering a 3D model in its 3D Studio environment.
8. **Display:** This is for the displaying of various features connected with 3D models.

In this book, there is no intention of dealing with either the Create or the Modify command sets from the 3D Editor program. Here, only those parts of the 3D Editor for adding materials, adding lights and cameras and the rendering of 3D models from AutoCAD are mentioned.

Method of rendering a 3D model

The method of producing a rendered image of a 3D model used in this book is as follows:

1. *Left-click* on the name **File** in the menu bar and from the pull-down menu which appears load a DXF file into the 3D Editor display screen.
2. Make the views in each viewport a manageable size by *left-clicks* on the requisite zoom out or zoom in icons in the icon panel (bottom left corner of the 3D Editor display.

3. Add lights:
   (a) Ambient
   (b) Omni... usually one, although several may be added
   (c) Spot... several

   Usually four lights in all will be sufficient.
   Adjust each light by moving in each viewport as necessary.
4. Add camera. Adjust by moving in each viewport as necessary.
5. Select **Viewports** from the **Views** pull-down menu and change the bottom right corner viewport to a camera one. This allows changes of camera position and lens lengths to be adjusted while the results of the changes can be seen in the camera viewport from the viewing position of the camera.
6. Select **Renderer/Render View** and *left-click* in the camera viewport to check lights in rendering.

Notes

1. Rendering inevitably takes some time, depending upon the complexity of the model and of the rendering.
2. Check, before assigning materials to see whether lights are OK as to position, colour and strength.
3. Adjust or delete lights as necessary.
4. When a scene has been rendered, pressing the *Return* key of the keyboard brings back the 3D Editor display screen.
5. The sequences of clicking on 3D Studio commands and their options from in the command column of the 3D Editor display screen in order to arrive at the command to be used are shown in the following way:

   Surface/Material.../Choose

   In the order of selection of the commands and options.
6. When clicking on a command name shown in the command column followed by three fullstops (...) a set of options will appear in the column.
7. Rendering to **Wire** takes less time than rendering **Flat**, which in turn takes less time than rendering **Gourand**. **Phong** usually produces better rendering, but takes the longest time. **Metal** rendering also takes as long as does **Phong**. Thus to see the effects of lights and materials, a first trial rendering in **Flat** or **Gourand** may well save time. When satisfied that lights, materials an other details are satisfactory, then render in **Phong** or **Metal**.

Mapping, applying mapping coordinates and assigning materials

Material properties

No matter what the colour of the object or element in the drawing originated in AutoCAD, the rendering material and its colour will be determined by the materials selected in 3D Studio. If a material is not assigned to an object, an element or a colour, the colour in the rendered image will be neutral white (the default material), irrespective of its colour as set in AutoCAD.

If a material has only one of the properties **W**ire, **F**lat, **G**ourand, **P**hong or **M**etal, it need only be assigned to an object or an element in the 3D model being rendered. If a material has the mapping properties of **T**exture, **O**pacity or **B**ump, etc., mapping coordinates will also have to be applied to elements and objects in the 3D model. If mapping is not set and mapping coordinates not applied for such materials, the object or element to which the material has been assigned will not render.

In the 3D Studio Materials Libraries **3ds.mli**, each material will have a number of associated properties, showing in thirteen columns in the **Materials Selector** dialogue box:

Column 1: Shading when rendered – **F**(lat); **G**(ourand); **P**(hong); **M**(etal).
Column 2: **X** only if transparency is greater than **0**.
Column 3: **T1** if the material is assigned a **Texture#1** map.
Column 4: **T2** if the material is assigned a **Texture#2** map.
Column 5: **0** if the material is assigned an **Opacity** map.
Column 6: **B** if the material is assigned a **Bump** map.
Column 7: S if the material is assigned a **Specular** map.
Column 8: **H** if the material is assigned a **Shininess** map.
Column 9: **I** if the material is assigned a **Self Illuminated** map.
Column 10: **R** if the material is assigned a **Reflection** map.
Column 11: **2** if the material is assigned a **2-sided** map.
Column 12: **W** if the material is a **Wire** material.
Column 13: **F** if the material is a **Face map** material.

Applying mapping and assigning materials

1. Materials which are mapped can only be assigned to elements or objects in a 3D model after mapping coordinates have been applied. There are three types of mapping frames – planar, cylindrical and spherical. The mapping frame needs to be adjusted, moved, scaled, rotated etc., in relation to the element or object in the 3D model.

Then mapping coordinates must be applied. Only then can mapped materials be assigned to a part of a 3D model.
2. Some mapped materials may have to be tiled. Tiling determines the size of the repeat of the pattern in the material selected when a mapping material is used. Tiling must be set (e.g. 4 × 4 for a smaller repeat pattern than the 1 × 1 repeat set with the material). Tiling must be set before a material can be assigned.
3. Finally choose a material and assign it to the object or element which has had mapping coordinates applied.

The process of mapping and assigning materials follows a sequence of commands and options such as:

1. **3D Editor/Surface/Mapping.../Type**
    /Type/Cylindrical
    /Adjust/Move
    /Adjust/Scale
    /Adjust/Height
    /Adjust/Tiling
    /Apply/Object
2. **3D Editor/Surface/Material.../Choose**
    /Assign/By Name
    /Assign/Object
3. **3D Editor/Renderer/Setup.../Background**
    /Render

Those materials which are not **B**ump, **O**pacity, **R**eflection, **S**pecular or other form of maps do not need to have mapping coordinates applied to the elements, faces or objects required to carry the materials. The following is an example of applying mapping and assigning a material with a **B**ump map:

1. **Lights/Ambient**: accept the default values of 30/30/30 – a brighter general overall lighting would tend to affect other lighting and cause less sharpness of lighting effects.
2. **Lights/Omni.../Create**: accept values of 180/180/180 (white).
3. **Lights/Omni.../Move**: move to an overhead position in the top viewport.
4. **Lights/Spot.../Create**: accept values of 180/180/180 (white.
5. **Lights/Spot...Move**: move the spot light in each viewport to a better position.
6. **Lights/Spot.../Create**: repeat with a second spot light, but with values of 60/60/60 (still white but of less intensity).
7. **Cameras/Create**: in top viewport, accept 50 mm.
8. **Cameras/Move**: move to a good position.
9. **View pull-down/Viewports**; make the User Viewport the Camera Viewport.

10. **Cameras/Move**: adjust camera position to obtain a good view in the Camera Viewport.
11. **Display/Hide.../Lights**
12. **Display/Hide.../Cameras**
13. **Views pull-down/Redraw All**
14. *Right-click* on the **Zoom Extents** icon to zoom all viewports to extents.
15. **Surface/Mapping.../Adjust/Move**
16. **Surface/Mapping.../Aspect/Height**: adjust height and aspect of mapping.
17. **Surface/Mapping.../Apply.../Object**: apply mapping to required objects.
18. **Surface/Material.../Choose**: choose the required material from the library dialogue box which appears.
19. **Surface/Material.../Assign.../By Name**: assign to colour number.

Mapping coordinates and materials can be applied and/or assigned to an object by colour coding (using the coding 01 to 07 – red to white) or to a face or an element in a 3D model by clicking on the element.

Examples of rendering AutoCAD DXF files

Seven examples of 3D Studio renderings are described below. A variety of types of model are illustrated by these examples. They include a number of different materials, some of which have been mapped, and a variety of backgrounds. The results of some of the renderings are shown in the colour plates (between pages ??? and ???). Each was rendered with the Shading Limit set to **P**hong and with Anti-aliasing set **ON**. Before rendering, colours, lights, backgrounds and materials were first checked by rendering to **F**lat with Anti-aliasing **OFF**. This enabled faster rendering times than with **P**hong and Anti-aliasing **ON**. When satisfied a final rendering with **P**hong and Anti-aliasing **ON** was run.

The examples are:

1. A bevel gear – an AutoCAD **Rulesurf** model.
   DXF file – **bevgear.dxf**. A detailed description of the rendering is included below.
2. Two poppet valves – AutoCAD **Revsurf** model.
   DXF file – **valves.dxf**.
3. A glass bowl and its stand – AutoCAD **Revsurf** models.
   DXF file – **revsurf.dxf**.
4. A computer joystick – AutoCAD 13 **Solids** model.
   DXF file – **joystick.dxf**.

5. A silver vase – An AutoCAD **Revsurf** model.
   DXF file – **vase.dxf**.
6. A brick garage – an AutoCAD 13 **Solids** model.
   DXF file – **garage.dxf**.
7. A dressing table bottle – An AutoCAD 12 **AME** model.
   DXF file – **bottle.dxf**.

An example of rendering in 3D Studio

Introduction

1. As each of the actions described in the following procedures is carried out, prompts will appears at the prompt line in the 3D Editor display screen. These prompts describe the action to be taken by the operator to achieve the desired results.
2. The screen cursor (its position on the screen under the control of the mouse movements) changes shape according to the type of command being followed at the time.
3. Dialogue and message boxes appear to assist the operator from time to time. Each of these is shown by an illustration.
4. Selection of commands are shown as, for example:

   Lights/Omni.../Create

   To follow this instruction, first *left-click* on **Lights** in the Command Column, then when the sub-menu appears, *left-click* on **Omni...**, followed by a *left-click* on **Create**.
5. All of the model *bevgear* was constructed in AutoCAD in the colour 07 (white). In 3D Studio this becomes the **Object** Color07.

The procedure for rendering the bevel gear model

1. At the **C:> DOS** prompt, *enter* 3ds from the keyboard. The 3D Studio display screen appears showing the 3D Editor (Fig. 10.1).

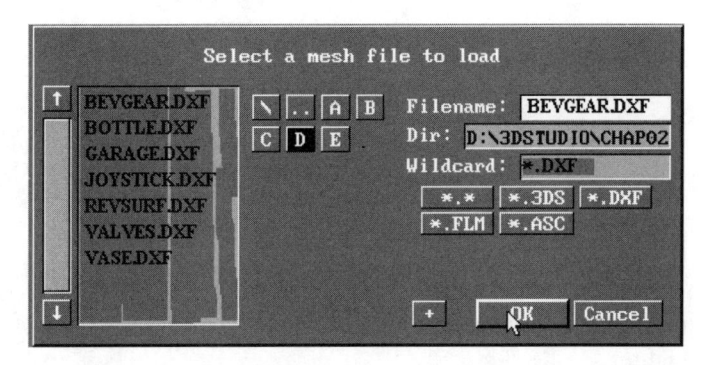

Fig. 10.3 The **Select a mesh file to load** dialogue box

170 An Introduction to 3D AutoCAD

2. *Left-click* on **File** in the menu bar. *Left-click* on **Load** in the menu which appears. The **Select a file to load** dialogue box appears (Fig. 10.3).
3. *Left-click* on the ***.DXF** button, then select the required directory and then *left-click* on the name **BEVGEAR.DXF** in the files list box.
4. The **Loading DXF File** dialogue box appears (Fig. 10.4). *Left-click* on **Color** and again on the **OK** button. A different view of the model appears in each of the 3D Editor viewports (Fig. 10.5).

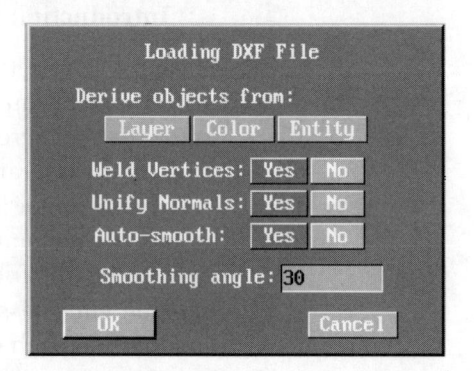

Fig. 10.4 The **Loading DXF File** dialogue box

5. **Lights/Ambient....** Dialogue box. *Left-click* on the **OK** button to accept **R/G/B** = 30/30/30.

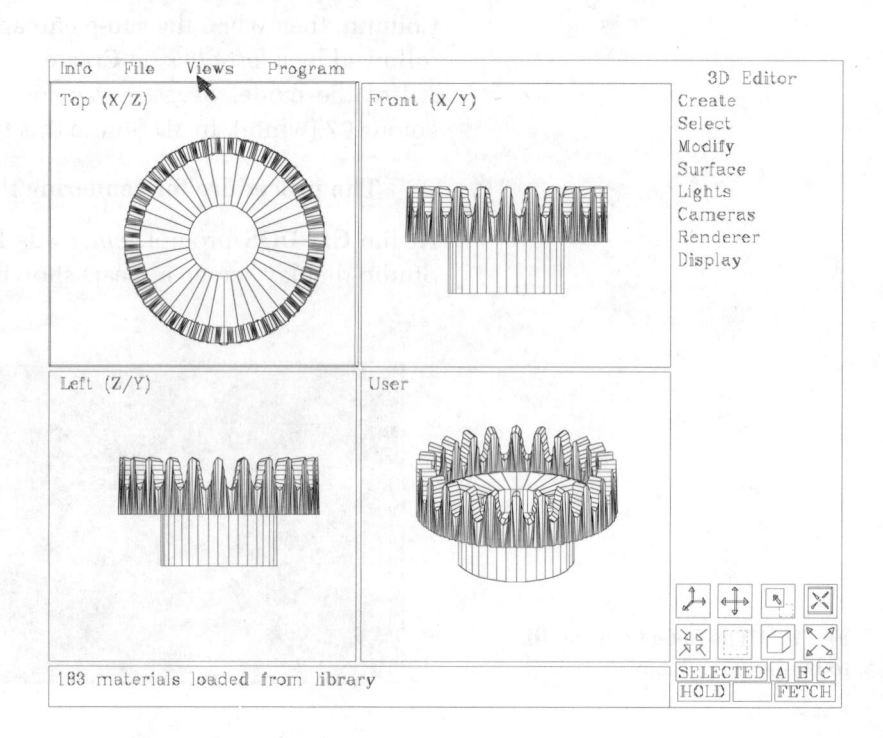

Fig. 10.5 The file **BEVGEAR.DXF** loaded into the 3D Editor

6. *Right-click* twice on the **Zoom** smaller icon in the icon display panel to reduce the size of the models in all viewports 100% smaller.
7. **Lights/Omni.../Create** Dialogue box (Fig. 10.6).
    (a) *Left-click* in the **Front** viewport to position the **Omni** light.
    (b) *Left-click* on **OK** to accept the R/G/B = 180/180/180 light and the accompanying H/L/S figures.
    (c) **Lights/Omni.../Move.**
    (d) *Left-click* in the **Front** viewport and move the **Omni** light as required.

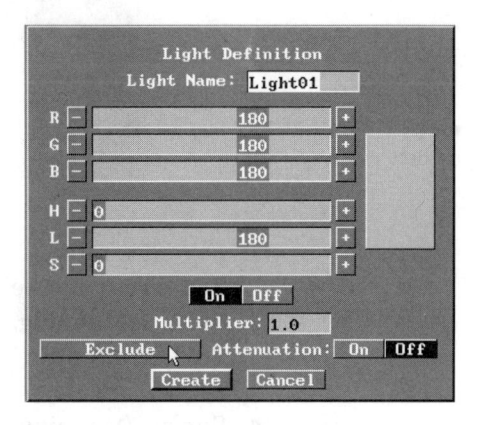

Fig. 10.6 The **Light Definition** dialogue box

8. **Lights/Spot.../Create**
    (a) *Left-click* in **Top** viewport to position the spotlight.
    (b) *Left-click* to position the spotlight's target. Dialogue box (Fig. 10.7).

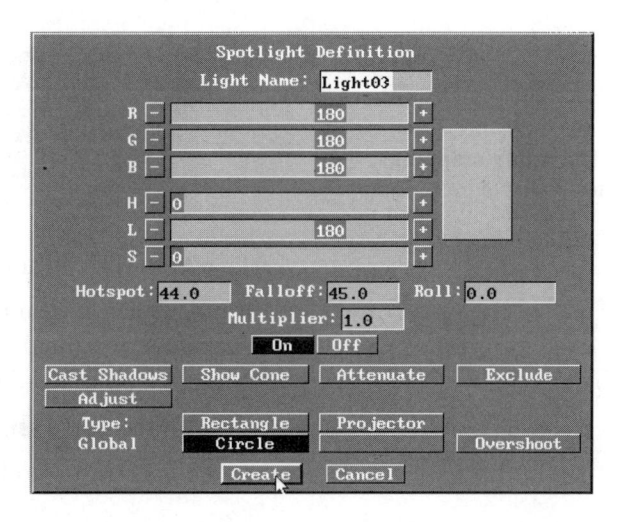

Fig. 10.7 The **Spotlight Definition** dialogue box

172 An Introduction to 3D AutoCAD

(c) *Left-click* on **Create** in the dialogue box to accept the default to accept R/G/B = 180/180/180 and the **Hotspot** and **Falloff** figures.

9. **Lights/Spot.../Move** move the Spotlight in **Front** and **Left** viewports to acceptable positions.

10. **Cameras/Create**

(a) Place a camera and the camera's target near the first spotlight. Dialogue box (Fig. 10.8)

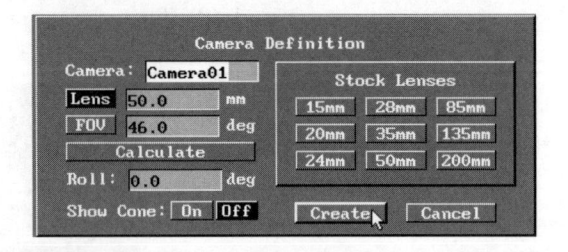

Fig. 10.8 The **Camera Definition** dialogue box

11. *Left-click* on the **Zoom extents** icon in the Icon panel. Views in **Top**, **Front** and **Left** viewports zoom to extents.
12. **Surface/Mapping.../Type/Cylindrical.**
13. **Surface/Mapping.../Adjust.../Move** and **Surface/Mapping.../Adjust.../Scale** – adjust mapping cylinder to fit around the model.
14. **Surface/Mapping.../Adjust.../Height** – adjust mapping cylinder for height.
15. **Surface/Mapping.../Apply.../Object.**

(a) *Left-click* on the model in the **front** viewport.
(b) Message box appears (Fig. 10.9).
(c) *Left-click* on the **OK** button.

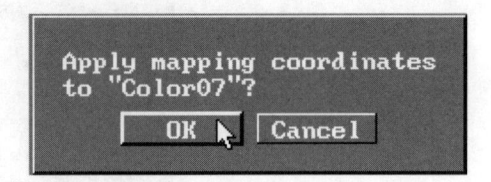

Fig. 10.9 The **Apply mapping coordinates** dialogue box

16. **Surface/Material.../Choose.**

(a) Dialogue box appears (Fig. 10.10). Go through the list box until the material named **WHITE PLASTIC 2S P 2** appears.
(b) *Left-click* on the name and also on the **OK** button.

17. **Surface/Material.../Assign.../By Name.**

(a) *Left-click* on the model.

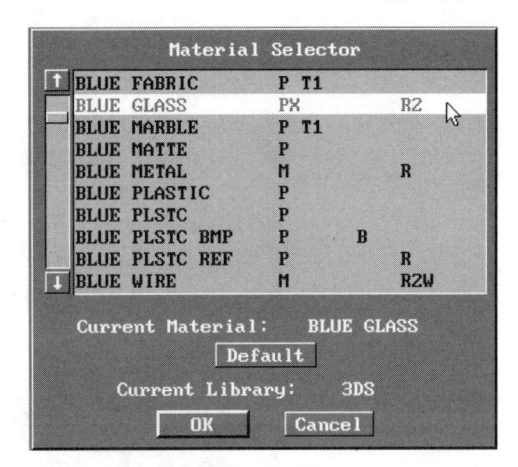

Dig. 10.10 The **Material Selector** dialogue box

(b) The **Assign WHITE PLASTIC** message box appears (10.11) *left-click* on the **OK** button.

Fig. 10.11 Mesage box asking whether the material should be assigned

18. **Renderer/Setup.../Background.**

   (a) Dialogue box (Fig. 10.12) appears.
   (b) *Left-click* on **Solid Color.**
   (c) Adjust slider bars so that R/G/B = 170/100/190 (magenta).
   (d) *Left-click* on **OK.**

Fig. 10.12 The **Background Method** dialogue box

174   An Introduction to 3D AutoCAD

19. **Renderer/Render.**

   (a) *Left-click* in the Camera Viewport. The **Render Options** dialogue box appears.

   (b) In the dialogue box, *left-click* on **Phong** and also in the **Anti-aliasing** box to set it **ON**.

   (c) *Left-click* on the **Render** button.

   (d) The **Rendering in Progress** dialogue box appears showing how far rendering has proceeded (Fig. 10.13)

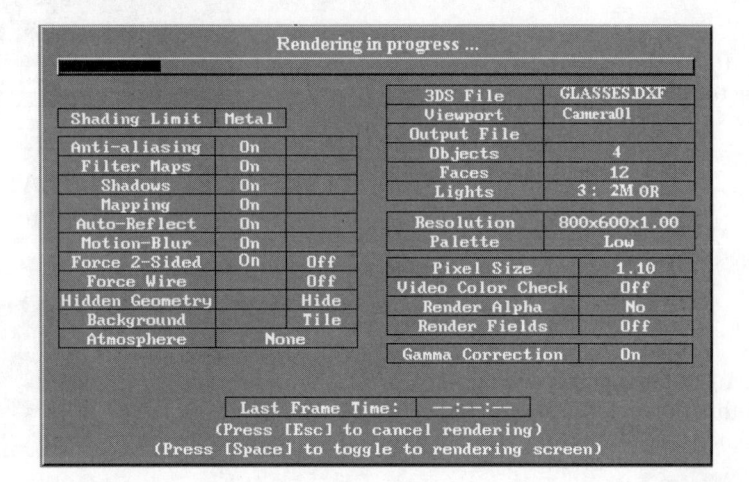

Fig. 10.13 The **Render Still Image** dialogue box changes to **Rendering in Progress** when rendering parameters have been set

20. *Right-click* and the 3D Editor display reappears.

Note: if the **Save Last Image** check box has been checked in the **Render Options** dialogue box, another dialogue box appears asking for a filename to which the rendered image can be saved (Fig. 10.14). To see the last rendered image again, that file – probably a ***.tga** file can be called back to screen. Other types of files can be saved, depending upon the operator's choice.

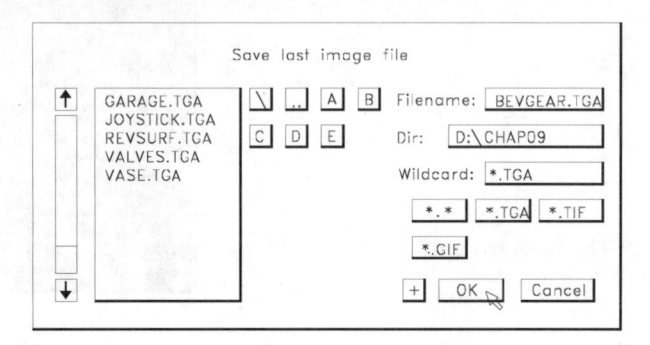

Fig. 10.14 The **Save last image file** dialogue box

Autodesk 3D Studio 175

21. Save the drawing and rendering details as **bevgear.prj** by a *left-click* on **Save Project** in the **File** pull-down menu. Saving a Project file with the extension **.prj** saves all settings such as lighting, materials and background details with the model drawing.

Viewports

Reference was made earlier to changing the viewports. *Left-click* on **Views** in the menu bar and on **Viewports** in the pull-down menu which appears. The **Select the viewport division method** dialogue box appears (Fig. 10.14) in which a choice of viewport layout can be made and in which the **Camera** viewport can be set.

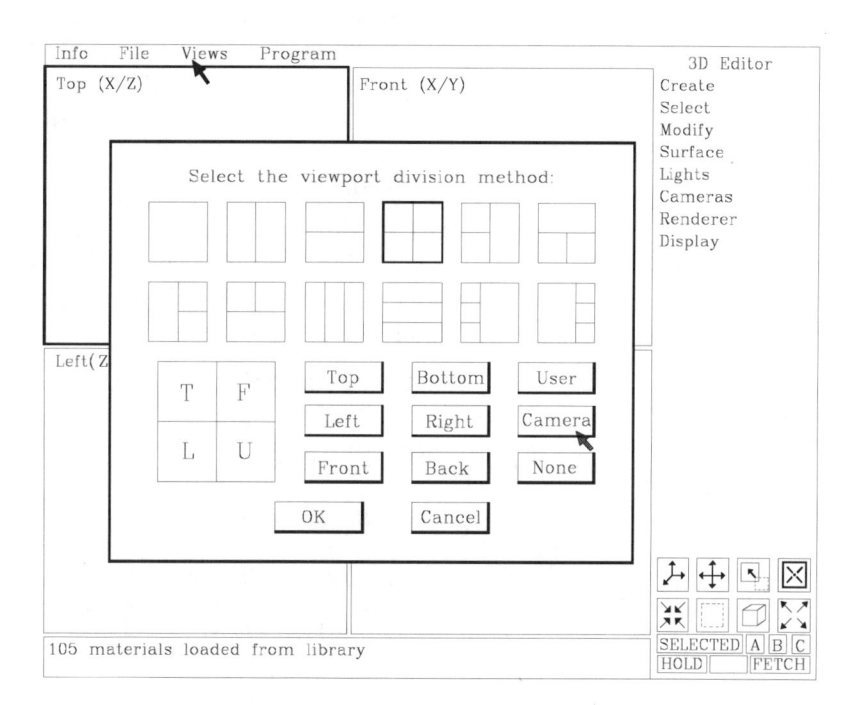

Fig. 10.15 The **Select the viewport division method** dialogue box

Further examples of mapping and assigning materials

Poppet valves

Lights

Light01: Ambient	default of 30/30/30
Light02: Omni	default of 180/180/180
Light03: Spot	default of 180/180/180
Light04: Spot	80/80/80 targeted from below

Materials

No mapping coordinates necessary
BLUE METALLIC   P
COPPER   P

Background

Solid background colour 160/160/160 (grey)

Bowl and plastic stand

Lights

Light01: Ambient   default of 30/30/30
Light02: Omni   default of 180/180/180
Light03: Spot   60/60/60
Light04: Spot   40/40/40 targeted from below and behind

Materials

The two-sided material Green Glass and the texture map Palm Tree both needed mapping coordinates applied. Mapping coordinates were applied to the bowl with cylindrical type and to the mat with planar type.

GREEN GLASS   P X 2
PALM TREE TRUNK P T1 B
RED PLASTIC   P

Background

Bitmap *browntile.cel* tiled 4 × 4

This rendering is shown in Plate XI

Joystick

Lights

Light01: Ambient   default of 30/30/30
Light02: Omni   default of 180/180/180
Light03: Spot   50/50/50
Light04: Spot   40/40/40 targeted from below

Materials

DARK BROWN MATTE	P
COPPER	P
RED PLASTIC	P
GREEN PLASTIC	P
YELLOW PLASTIC	P

Background

Solid background colour 140/140/140 (grey)

Vase

Lights

Light01: Ambient	default of 30/30/30
Light02: Omni	default of 180/180/180
Light03: Spot	default of 180/180/180
Light04: Spot	default of 180/180/180

Materials

The reflection map Chrome Gifmap was assigned to the vase (Object Color02) after mapping coordinates had been applied through a cylindrical type of mapping.

Background

Bitmap *Clouds.cel*

The rendering of this example is shown in colour plate XII

Brick garage

Lights

Light01: Ambient	default of 30/30/30
Light02: Omni	default of 180/180/180
Light03: Spot	default of 180/180/180
Light04: Spot	default of 180/180/180

Materials

Color01: RED PLASTIC	P	Door
Color02: WHITE PLASTIC	P	Woodwork
Color03: CONCRETE TILE	G T1	Floor
Color04: BUMPY BROWNBRICK	P T1 B	Front wall

Color05: BUMPY BROWNBRICK   P T1 B   Side walls
Color06: DARK WOOD INLAY   P T1   Roof
Color07: GLASS   P X 2   Windows

Background

Solid background colour 150/150/150 (grey)

The rendering of this example is shown in colour plate X.

Dressing table bottle

Lights

Light01: Ambient   default of 30/30/30
Light02: Omni   65/80/65
Light03: Spot   default of 180/180/180
Light04: Spot   60/75/60

Materials

Color01: RED PLASTIC   P   Letters on label
Color02: GOLD   P   Cap
Color03: AQUA BUMBPFLI   P B   Label
Color04: GREEN GLASS   P X 2   Bottle body

Background

Solid background colour 140/70/120

The rendering of this example is shown in Plate XIII.

CHAPTER 11

AutoCAD Designer

Introduction

Designer is an Autodesk software package which runs inside either AutoCAD R12 Dos (Designer Release 1.1) or AutoCAD R13 (Designer 1.2). The software is a 3D parametric drawing tool, which can be used to construct 3D models based on features (extrusions, sweeps, holes, fillets etc.) from which dimensioned views in orthographic projections – either First or Third angle – can be speedily produced. The command system is practically identical in both the AutoCAD R12 and R13 versions, with some enhancements in the R13 version. As with the methods of describing constructions for producing 3D models in other parts of this book, the following pages show the use of commands *entered* from the keyboards. When using Designer, commands begin with **ad**, thus a Designer extrusion will require calling the command **adextrude**.

The contents of this chapter contain only very brief descriptions of constructing two 3D models in Designer, together with accompanying First angle orthographic projections. The intention is only to show that Designer is yet another software tool for the construction of 3D model drawings within AutoCAD.

Calling Designer commands

Commands may be called either by selection from the Designer pull-down menu (Fig. 11.1) or by *entering* the command name at the command line. To *enter* the command **Extrude** at the command line:

Command: *enter* adextrude *right-click*

And the **Designer Extrusion** dialogue box appears on screen (Fig. 11.2). Parameters for setting the extrusion can then be made in the dialogue box. When the required settings have been made, a *left-click* on the **OK** button of the dialogue box results in options appearing at the command line.

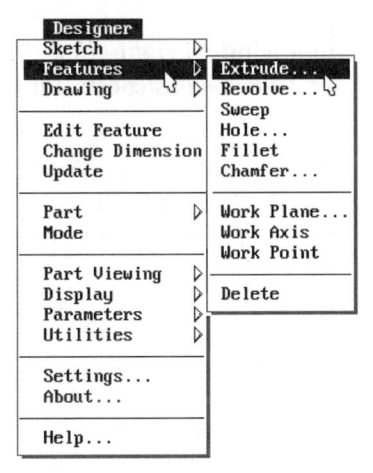

Fig. 11.1 Selecting the **Extrude** comand from the **Designer** pull-down menu

180 An Introduction to 3D AutoCAD

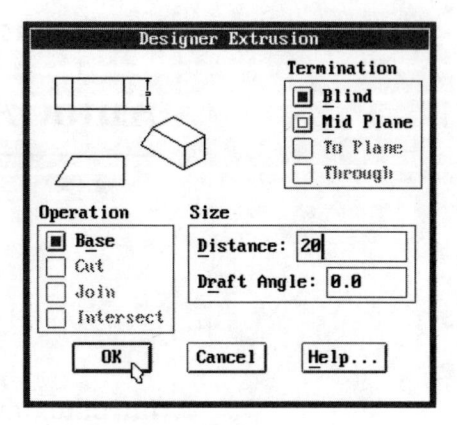

Fig. 11.2 The **Designer Extrusion** dialogue box

As can be seen from Fig. 11.1, several of the commands in Designer result in the appearance of a dialogue box – as shown by the fact that some of the command names are followed by three fullstops (...).

First example

1. The first stage in constructing a Designer 3D model is always to draw a sketch. This sketch is then formed into what is known as a **Sketch Profile**. The Sketch Profile can then be changed into a feature such as an extrusion. The forming of a simple extrusion is shown in Fig. 11.3. After drawing the sketch outline with AutoCAD commands such as **Pline**, **Line**, **Circle**, **Arc** etc., the sequence of commands would be:

Command: *enter* adprofile *right-click*
Select objects: select the sketch within a window *right-click*
Solved under constrained sketch requiring 2 dimensions/constraints.
Command:

If the parametric features of Designer are to be used, it is important at this stage to fully dimension the Sketch Profile. Failure to do so will destroy the parametricity of the 3D model being constructed.

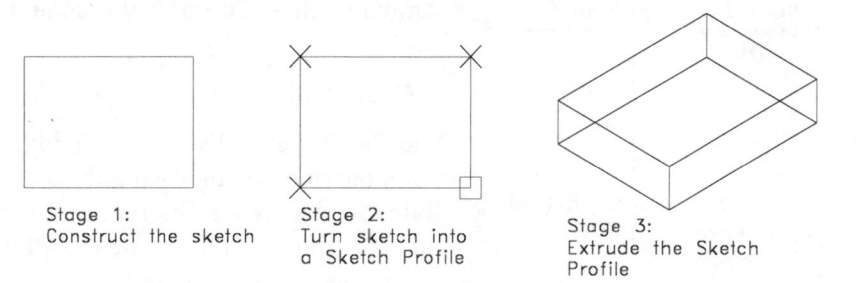

Fig. 11.3 Three stages in forming an extrusion

Stage 1: Construct the sketch

Stage 2: Turn sketch into a Sketch Profile

Stage 3: Extrude the Sketch Profile

For this first example we are not attempting to use the parametric facilities of the software. To form the extrusion:

Command: *enter* adextrude *right-click*

The **Designer extrusion** dialogue box appears. Figure 11.2 shows the settings made in the dialogue box for this first example. *Left-click* on the **OK** button and the Sketch Profile extrudes (Fig. 11.3).

2. Two major features of constructing Designer 3D models are **Work Planes** and **Sketch Planes**. To add these to the extrusion, place the model so far constructed in an isometric viewing position by:

Command: *enter* adpartview *right-click*
View option Front/Right/Left/Top/Bottom/Isometric/<Sketch>:
enter i (Isometric) *right-click*
Command:

And the model assumes an isometric viewing position.

Command: *enter* adworkpln *right-click*

And the **Designer Work Plane** dialogue box appears. In the dialogue box set check boxes as shown in Fig. 11.4, followed by a *left-click* on the **OK** button.

When the prompts appear asking for a face and an edge to be selected, *pick* an appropriate face and edge. The work plane appears on the isometric view (Fig. 11.5). When the first work plane has been established offset a second work plane central to the isometric view of the extrusion.

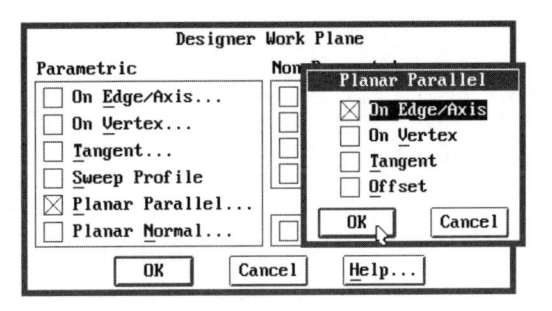

Fig. 11.4 The **Designer Work Plane** dialogue box

3. Now form a **Sketch Plane** by:

Command: *enter* adskpln *right-click*
Select work plane or planar face: *pick* the offset work plane
Select work axis or straight edge: *pick* any edge parallel to the work plane

182 An Introduction to 3D AutoCAD

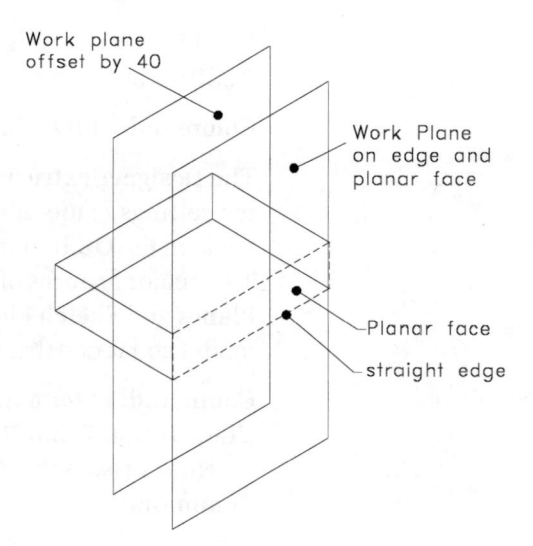

Fig. 11.5 Two work planes for the first example

Rotate/<Accept>: an ucsicon appears to indicate the direction of the x and y axes. *Enter* r (Rotate) until the icon is showing the directions required. When satisfied *right-click*.

4. Place the model in a Sketch position with **adpartview** by accepting the default **<Sketch>**.
5. Draw a sweep profile on the Sketch Plane with **Pline** and **Fillet** (Fig. 11.6).

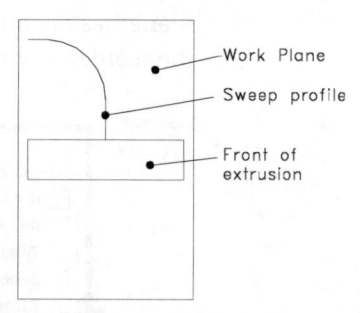

Fig. 11.6 The Path Profile for the sweep

6. Call **adpath** and change the sweep path sketch into a **Path Profile**.
7. Form yet another Work Plane at the end of the Path Profile, using the **Sweep Profile** option in the **Designer Work Plane** dialogue box (as seen in Fig. 11.4).
8. Call **adpartview** (Isometric) and form a Sketch Plane from the Sweep Work Plane. On this Sketch Plane draw a circle at the end of the Path Profile (Fig. 11.7).
9. Change the circle into a Sketch Profile with **adprofile**.
10. Place the model in an Isometric view with **adpartview** and call **adsweep**. When the command line prompts for **adsweep** appear,

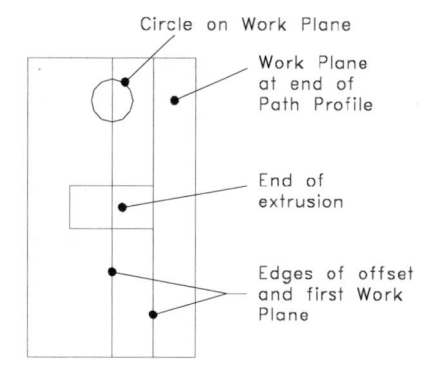

Fig. 11.7 The circle for the Sketch Profile of the Sweep

pick the Path Profile and the Sketch Profile in turn and the sweep forms.
11. Add another Path Profile and circular Sketch Profile to form a hole through the first sweep.
12. With **adchamfer** chamfer the edges of the base and the inner lip of the sweep. The resulting 3D model is as shown in Fig. 11.8.

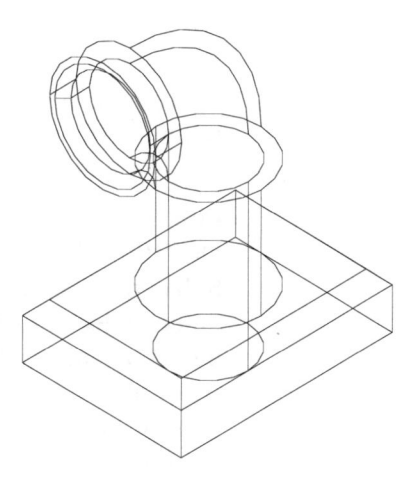

Fig. 11.8 The 3D model of the first example

13. To set an orthographic projection of the model call **adview**. In the **Designer Drawing View** dialogue box check that the **Base** check box is checked and, following prompts which then appear at the command line, a base view (a Front view) of the model appears in a new screen (the **Drawing Mode** screen). In a similar fashion by checking the **Ortho** and **Iso** check boxes of the dialogue box in turn, a complete orthographic projection, together with an isometric view within a drawing sheet, can be produced in the **Drawing Mode** screen. Figure 11.9 shows the first example in such an orthographic projection. If the Sketch profiles and Path

184 An Introduction to 3D AutoCAD

profile for the model had been dimensioned, dimensions would appear with the orthographic projection. However, in this example dimensions were added with the aid of other Designer commands.

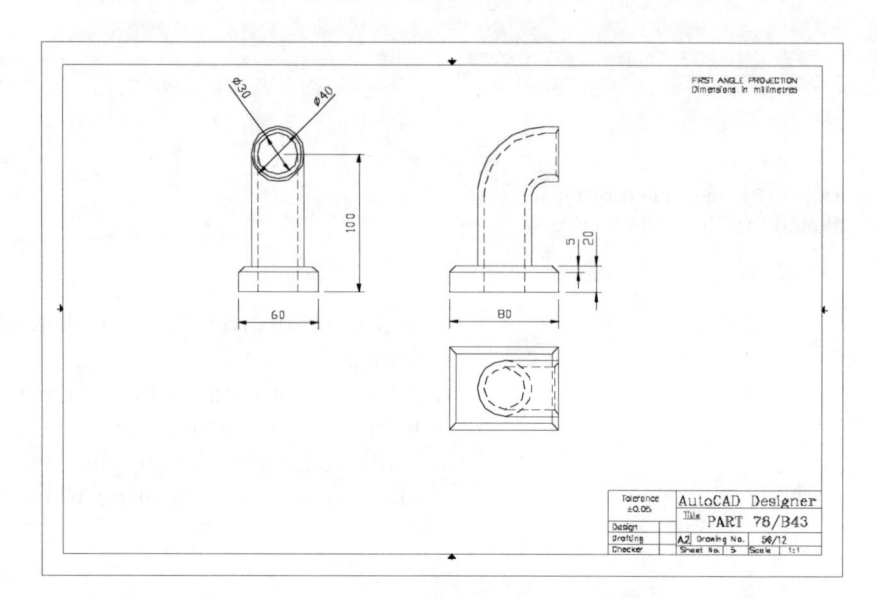

Fig. 11.9 The first example – the orthographic projection in the **Drawing Mode** screen

14. Designer models can be rendered with AutoVision, but only if the wireframe model is acted upon to form surface meshes. In Designer this is carried out with the command **admesh**:

    Command: *enter* admesh *right-click*
    ON/OFf <OFf>: *enter* on *right-click*
    Select parts to mesh.
    Select objects: *pick* the model
    Select objects: *right-click*
    Allowable deviation between facets and model <0.1>: *right-click*
    Command:

    And the model meshes (Fig. 11.10).
15. Designer meshed models can be rendered either in AutoCAD Render or in AutoVision. Figure 11.11 shows a rendering of the model in AutoVision.

    Notes

It is appreciated that the description of the construction of the first example of a Designer 3D model given above is brief. Also the stages in the sequence may suggest to those who have not worked with Designer to be rather time consuming. However, it will be found that

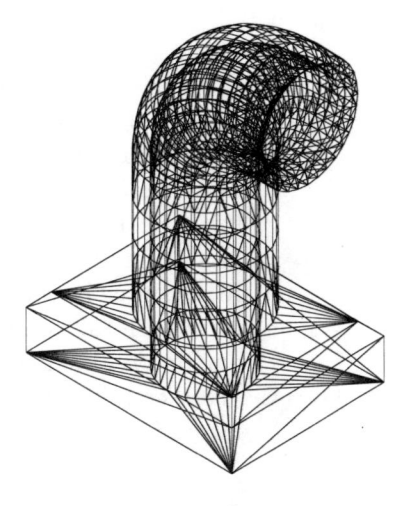

Fig. 11.10 The meshed model of the first example

Fig. 11.11 The first example after rendering in AutoVision

when working with the software the construction of a 3D model in Designer is not as time consuming as would at first appear.

Second example – parametric possibilities

This second example is included to demonstrate the parametric functions of Designer. The model of the first example was not dimensioned. By not including dimensions, it was not possible to demonstrate the parametric functions. This second example, however, will be fully dimensioned, commencing with fully dimensioning the Sketch Profile on which the model is based.

Designer dimensioning

Dimensioning in Designer can be of three types, shown in the dimensioning of the Sketch Profile of the second example in Fig. 11.12: Numeric – the left-hand drawing; Parametric – the centre drawing; Equation – the right-hand drawing. In order to ensure that the model has full parametric possibilities each dimension in the model, including features such as extrusion, holes, chamfers and fillets, must be related to all others. This is carried out, as indicated in Fig. 11.13, by setting up each dimension in a relationship with one major dimension. In this example the dimension **d0** of 100 was taken as the base dimension to which all others were related by a form of equation.

Fig. 11.12 Numeric, Parametric and Equation dimensions in the Sketch Profile of the second example

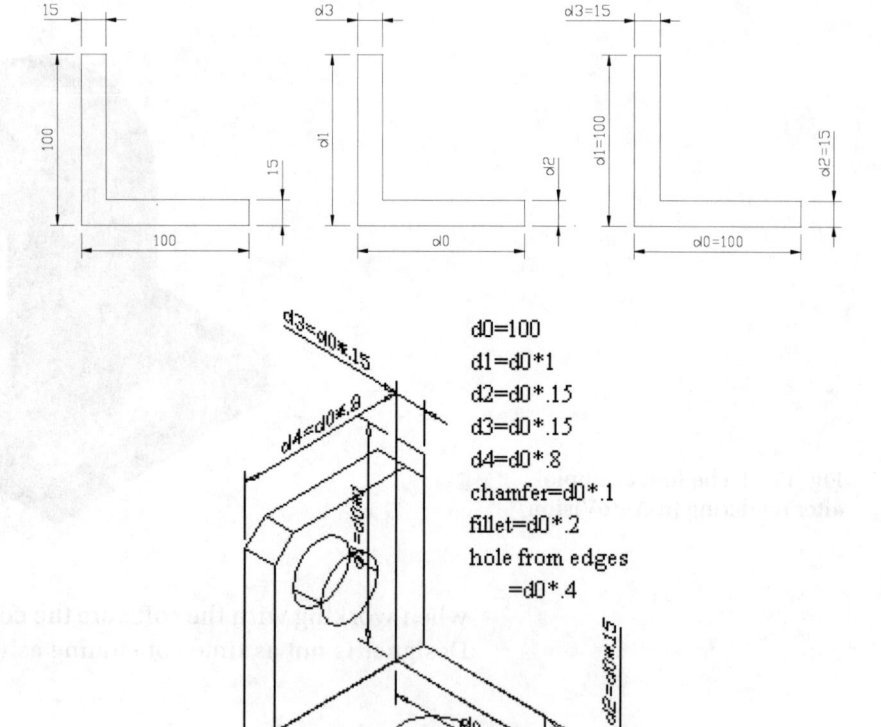

Fig. 11.13 All the dimensions of the second example in parametric form

d0=100
d1=d0*1
d2=d0*.15
d3=d0*.15
d4=d0*.8
chamfer=d0*.1
fillet=d0*.2
hole from edges
=d0*.4

The equation can take a form such as d0/2 (division); d0*.5 (multiplication); d0+1.25 (addition); d0−.25 (subtraction). Other forms of equation may take the form of trigonometrical ratios, angular ratios and the like. If the base dimension of d0 (in this example) is changed with the aid of the command **adeditfeat**, all other dimensions change. When the model is then acted upon with the command **adupdate**, not only will the model change to its new (parametric) dimensions, but so will the associated orthographic views in the **Drawing Mode** screen.

Note

When making all dimensions in a model parametric, do not forget that the settings in the various dialogue boxes must also be related to the main dimension. Thus the hole, which was originally of a diameter 30, is set in the **Designer Hole** dialogue box as d0*.3. So also were the distances of the hole from the two edges to which its centre related (d0*.4). Similarly the chamfer sizes were set in the **Designer Chamfer** dialogue box as d0*.1, and the fillet to d0*.2 in the **Designer Fillet** dialogue box.

Examples of parametrics in the second example

Original model: Figure 11.14 shows two orthographic views of the original model for the second example. To change the screen from the **Part Mode** in which a 3D model is constructed to the **Drawing Mode** in which the orthographic views appear, the command **admode** is used.

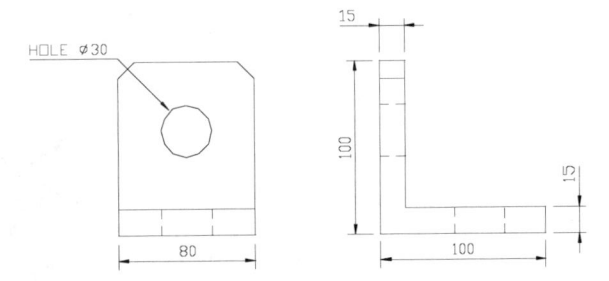

Fig. 11.14 Two orthographic views of the original 3D model of the second example

First change: Fig. 11.15 shows the same orthographic views after the dimension d0 (100) was changed with **adeditfeat** to 80 and then updated with **adupdate**. When **admode** was then called to go back into **Drawing Mode**, it was seen that the orthographic views, with their dimensions, had also updated to the new parametric dimensions.

Second change: Fig. 11.16 shows the same orthographic views after the dimension d0 (now 80) was changed with **adeditfeat** to 120. After **update** and calling **admode**, the **drawing Mode** views had changed as shown in Fig. 11.16.

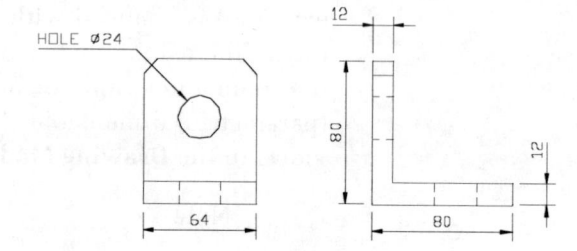

Fig. 11.15 First change

The models for the second example

Figure 11.16 shows the original model after **admesh**. Fig. 11.17 shows all three models after being rendered in AutoVision.

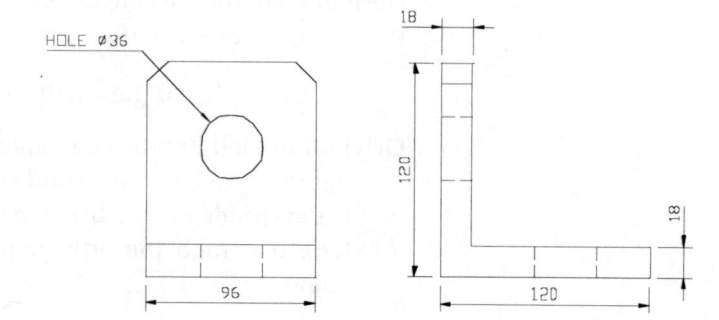

Fig. 11.16 Second change

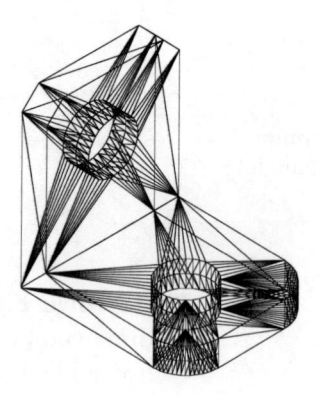

Fig. 11.17 The original model after **admesh**

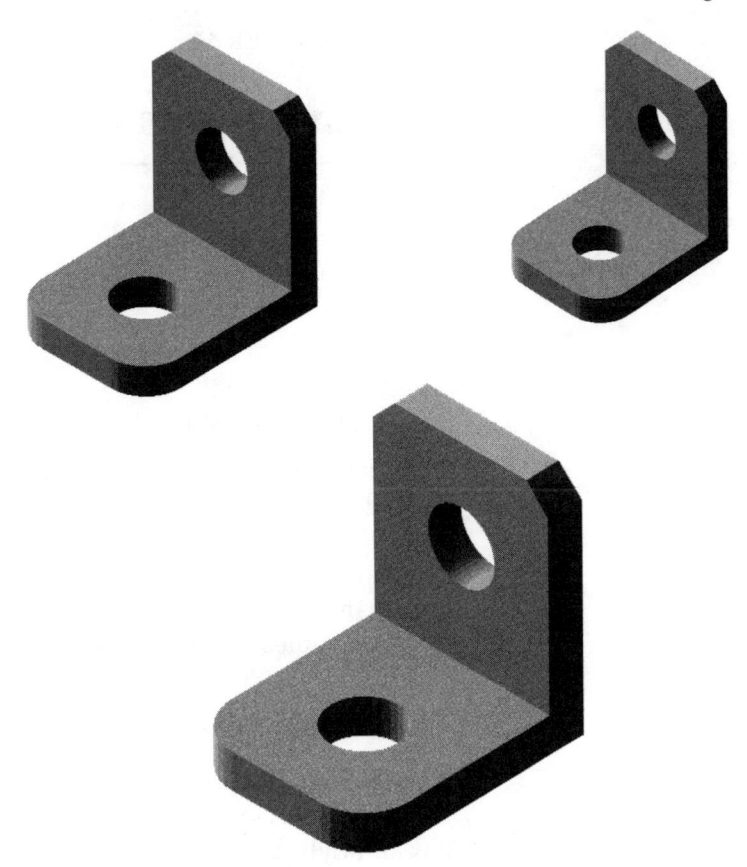

Fig. 11.18 The three parametric models of the second example after renderings in AutoVision

CHAPTER 12

Examples of 3D models

Introduction

Nine examples of a variety of 3D models drawn in AutoCAD and one created in 3D Studio are given in this chapter. These show a variety of methods of construction, either with the AutoCAD **Surface** command systems, with the Advanced Modelling Extension (AME) or with the AutoCAD R13 **Solids** tools. 3D Studio renderings of some of the examples are shown in the colour plates section.

Example 1 – a stile

A **Vpoint** parallel projection view of the model is given in Fig. 12.1. The model was constructed with the aid of two R13 **Solids** tools – **Box** and **Cylinder**. All parts of the construction were acted upon by **Union** before being transferred to 3D Studio via a *.3DS file.

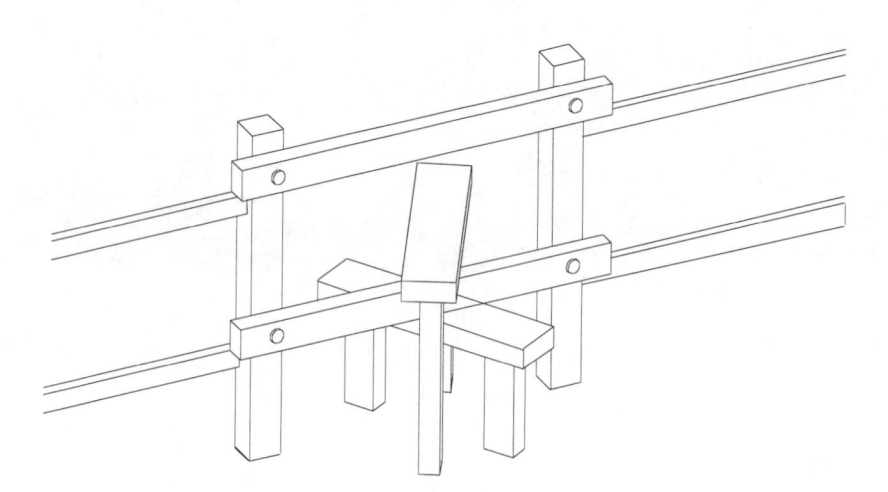

Fig. 12.1 Example 1 – a stile

The 3D Studio rendering parameters were:

Lighting

Light01:   Ambient   default of 30/30/30
Light02:   Omni   default of 180/180/180
Light03:   Spot   default of 180/180/180

Materials

Color01:   BLUE METALLIC P
Color07:   BROWN MATTE   P

Background

VALLEY_L.TGA

The results of the rendering are shown in Plate XV

Example 2 – a tiled table

Figure 12.2 is a **Dview** (**Di**stance) perspective projection of the model. The model was constructed in AutoCAD with the aid of AME. The table frame consists of a number of **Solbox**es, with the outer corners of the legs **Solfill**ed. The frame **Solbox**es were acted upon by **Solunion** to form a single Boolean solid model. A single tile constructed with **Solbox** had a pattern added to its top surface with **Pline**s of 1 unit thickness. The single tile was then **Copy**ed to obtain the 15 tiles for the table top. In order to keep the tiles as separate

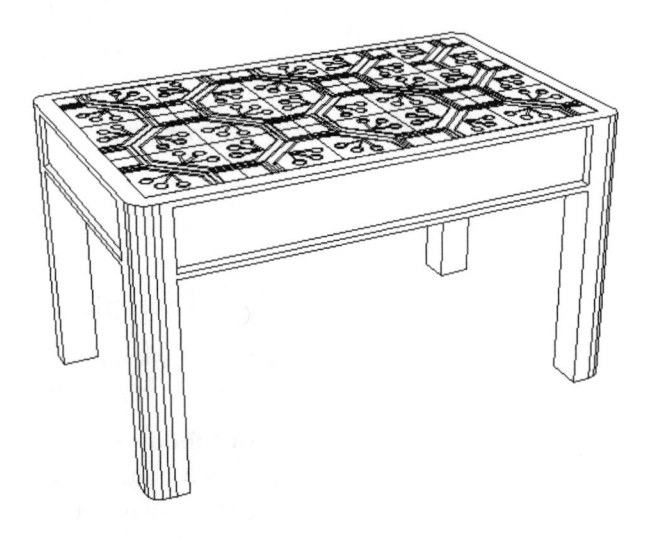

Fig. 12.2 Example 3 – a tiled table

units, they were not acted upon by **Solunion**. The whole model was given surface meshes with **Solmesh** before **Dview** was called.

Example 3 – a machine part

Figure 12.3 is a four viewport AME model with dimensions added to the orthographic views in three of the viewports. The model was constructed from **Solbox**es, with **Solfill**s and **Solcyl**s. The holes in the base were created by using **Solsub** to subtract **Solcyl**s from the base. Three UCS systems were used: ***WORLD***; one viewing from the front (UCS **FRONT**); another viewing from the end (UCS **END**). The four views were positioned with the aid of **Vpoint**, after turning **UCSfollow** off in each viewport. Note that when adding dimensions to AME models in orthographic views, **Osnap**s cannot be used – if used there is no surety that the snapping will be at the intended position.

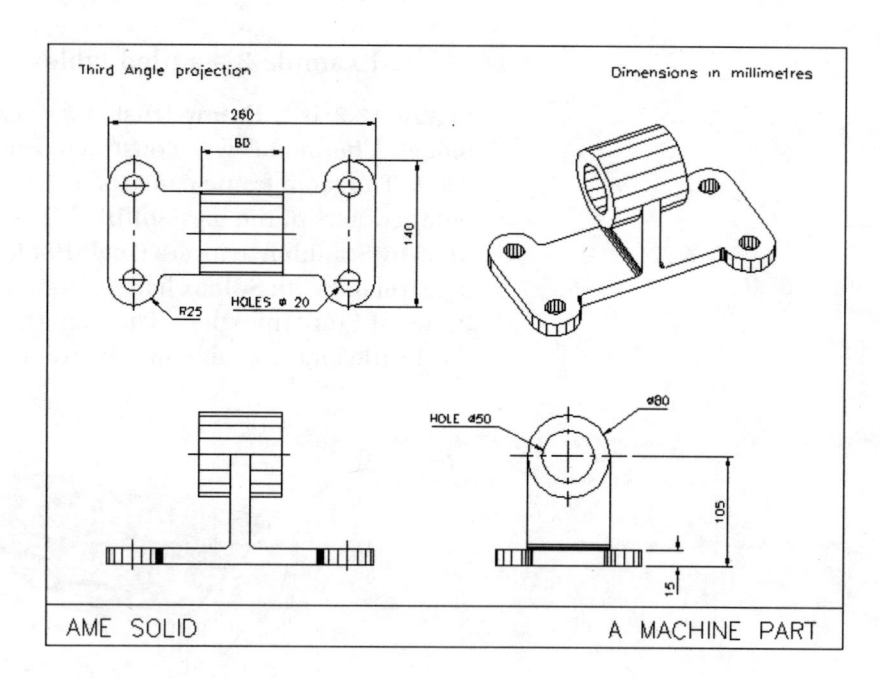

Fig. 12. 3 Example 3 – a machine part

Example 4 – a support bracket

Figure 10.4 is a three-viewport screen of this R13 **Solids** model. The model was constructed by following the sequence:

1. **UCSfollow** ON (1).
2. **UCS** 3 point – the UCS as viewed from the front.
3. **UCS** – save as **Front**.

Examples of 3D models

4. **Arc** – draw the double arc of Part A.
5. **Pline** – add plines to form the flat end of Part A. Join the right-hand ends of the arcs with a pline.
6. **Pedit** – join plines and arcs into a continuous pline.
7. **Extrude** – extrude the pline to its required height with angle to Z at 0.
8. In a similar manner form the rib – i.e. as an extrusion from a pline outline.
9. **UCS** – *WORLD*.
10. **Move** – move the two extrusions to suitable positions.
11. In a similar manner form the open front end and the 'shelf' of the bracket – i.e. as extrusions from pline outlines.
12. **Cylinder** – two cylinders for the bolt hole.
13. **UCS** – restore **Front** – check that the parts of the model are positioned correctly in relation to each other. If not, use **Move** to reposition them.
14. **Subtract** – subtract the two bolt holes from extrusion A.
15. **Union** – all parts.
16. **Tilemode** – OFF (0). Places screen in PSpace.
17. **Limits** – set PSpace limits to 420,300.
18. **Zoom** – All.
19. **Layer** – make a new layer **VPORT** – Colour 2 (Yellow).
20. **Mview** – 3; **T**op; **F**it.
21. **Mspace** – **Ucsfollow** OFF (0) in each viewport in turn.
22. **Vpoint**- Top: −1.−1.5,−1; Bottom: 0,−1,0; Bottom right: 1,0,0.
23. **Zoom** – to 1 in each viewport in turn.

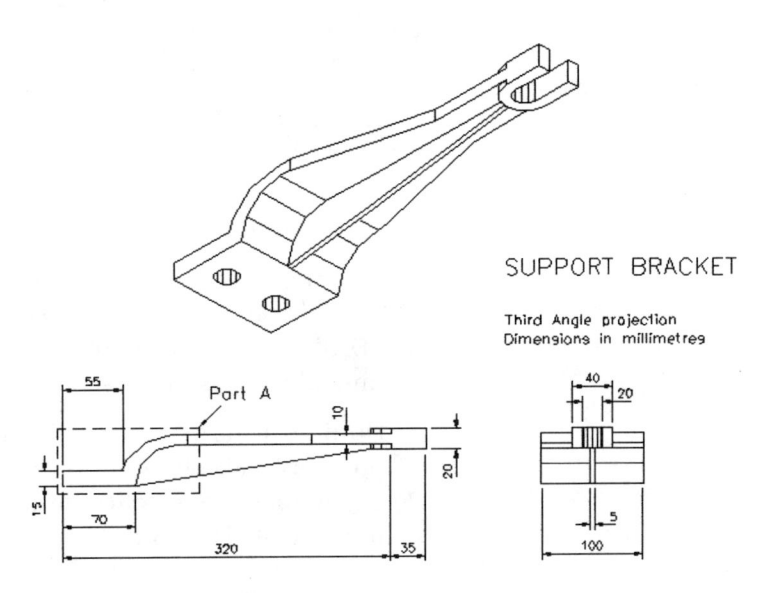

Fig. 12.4 Example 4 – a support bracket

194 An Introduction to 3D AutoCAD

24. **Move** – move viewports to suitable positions.
25. **Layer** – set layer 0 current.
26. **Mview** – Hideplot – ON – turn on in each viewport in turn.
27. **Layer** – turn layer **VPORT** OFF.

Example 5 – a machine part

Figure 12.5 is a four-viewport screen of this model. It has been constructed from **Solbox**es, **Solcyl**s and **Solext**rusions, on a number of different UCS planes. **Solsub** and **Solunion** and **Solmesh** were called to complete the model. The methods of placing the model in four viewports followed the routines given for Example 4 above. Finally the model was acted upon by **Solprof** and the layers 0 and 1-PH-2 turned off to produce profile only views.

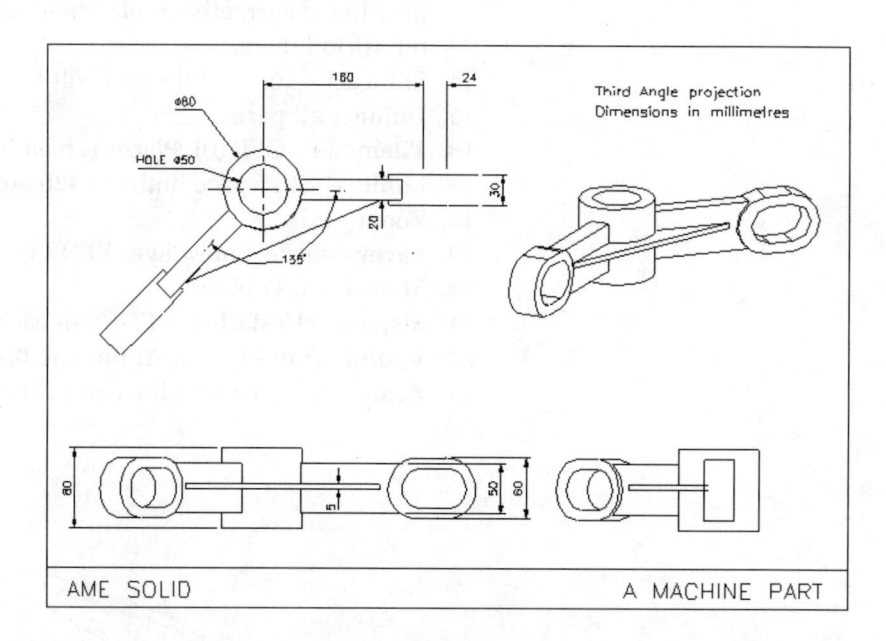

Fig. 12.5 Example 5 – a machine part

Example 6 – 3D AutoCAD

A rendering of this model is shown in Plate XIV. Figure 12.6 shows the model as it was formed in 3D Studio. The model was then saved as a DXF file and opened in AutoCAD. The procedures for creating the model were as follows:

1. Outlines of the four parts of the model were drawn in the 2D Shaper program of 3D Studio.
2. The outlines were 'lofted' to give them thickness in the 3D Lofter program of 3D Studio.

3. Lights, a camera, materials and rendering backgrounds were added in the 3D Editor program of 3D Studio.
4. The views of the model in the 3D Editor of 3D Studio were saved as:

    (a) A project file (extension **.prj**), which includes all details of the model, its lights, camera, materials and rendering background.
    (b) A DXF file (extension ***.dxf**).

5. The DXF file was loaded into AutoCAD.

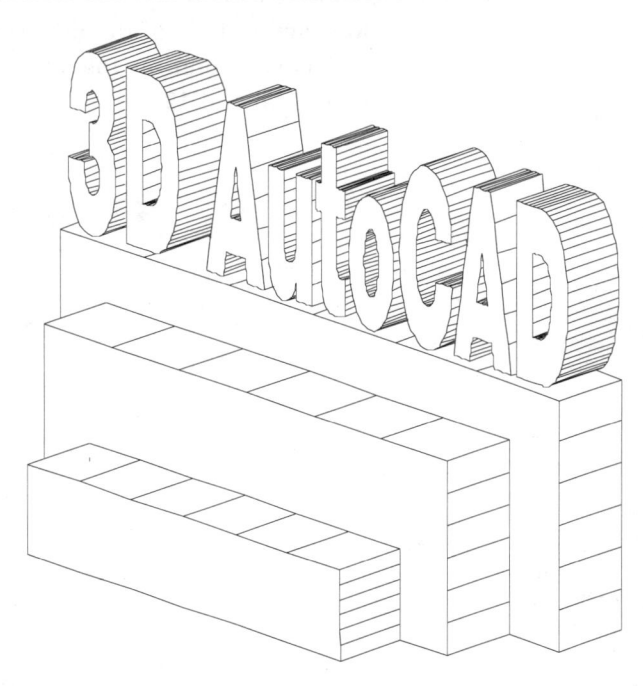

Fig. 12.6 Example 6 – a model created in Autodesk 3D studio

Details of lighting, camera materials and rendering background for the model:

Lighting

Light01: Ambient	default of 30/30/30
Light02: Omni	default of 180/180/180
Light03: Spot	default of 180/180/180
Light04: Spot	60/60/60

Materials – assigned to named objects

Letters:	GOLD	P
Back:	RED PLASTIC	P
Middle:	BLUE PLASTIC 100	P
Front:	GREEN MATTE	P

196   An Introduction to 3D AutoCAD

Rendering background

TREETRUNK.CEL

Example 7 – a coffee jug

Figure 10.7 shows two views of this model with the lid lying by the side of the body of the jug, the second with the lid in place. This model was constructed with the **Surface** commands **Edgesurf** and **Revsurf**. Details of the **Edgesurf** edges and the **Revsuf** path curves and axes of rotation, together with the **Surftab** settings, are given in Figs. 12.8 and 12.10.

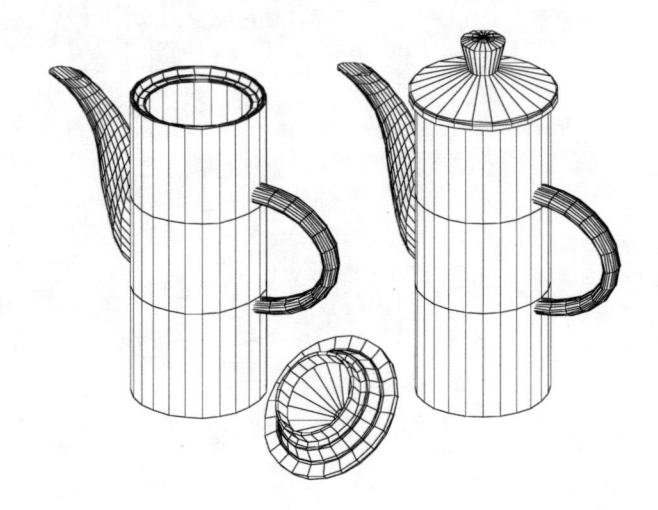

Fig. 12.7 – Example 7 – two views of a coffee jug

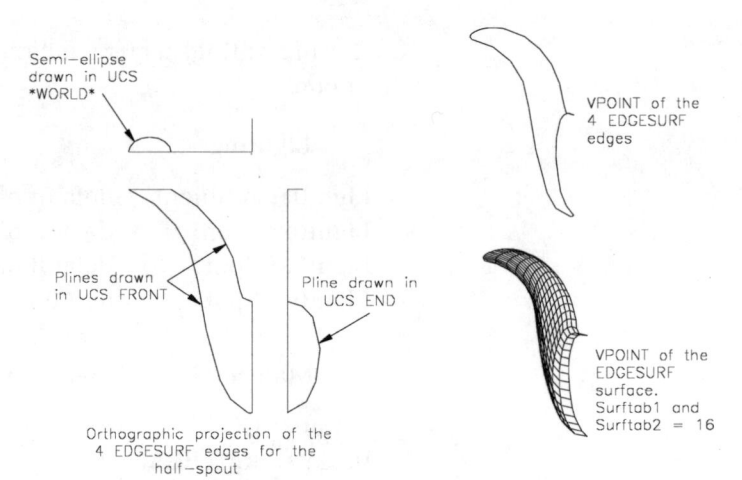

Fig. 12.8 Example 7 – constructions for the spout

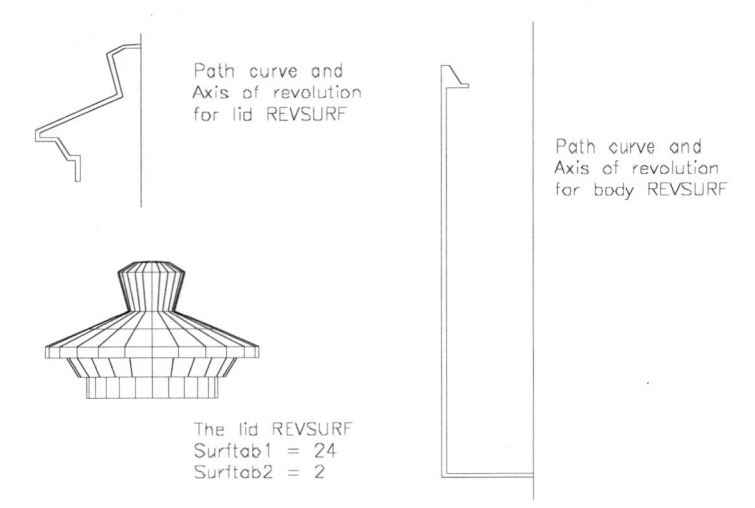

Fig. 12.9 Example 7 – constructions for the body and lid

Example 8 – a door handle

Figure 12.10 is a **Solprof** view of this model. Constructed from **Solbox**es, **Solcyl**s and **Solcone**s, with edges of the backplate **Solfill**ed. The handle is an AME extrusion from a pline outline. The given illustration is a profile only view, obtained by calling **Solprof**. Layers 0 and 1-PH-2 have been turned off.

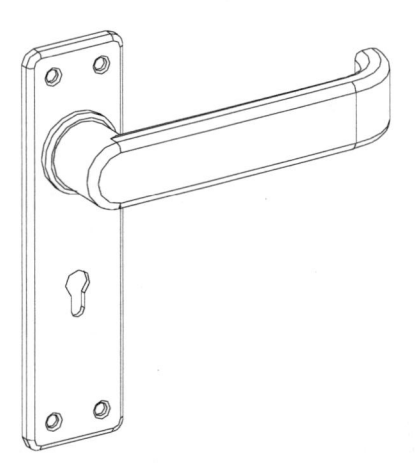

Fig. 12.10 Example 8 – a door handle

Example 9 – photographic developing tongs

Fig. 12.11 is a **Solprof** view of this model, with layers 0 and 1-PH-2 turned off. Its construction was base on **Solext**rusions from pline outlines. Several UCS planes were formed to position the parts in correct relationship to each other. Details of the pline outlines for

198 An Introduction to 3D AutoCAD

the extrusions are given in Fig. 12.12. Further details of the construction are given in Fig. 12.13.

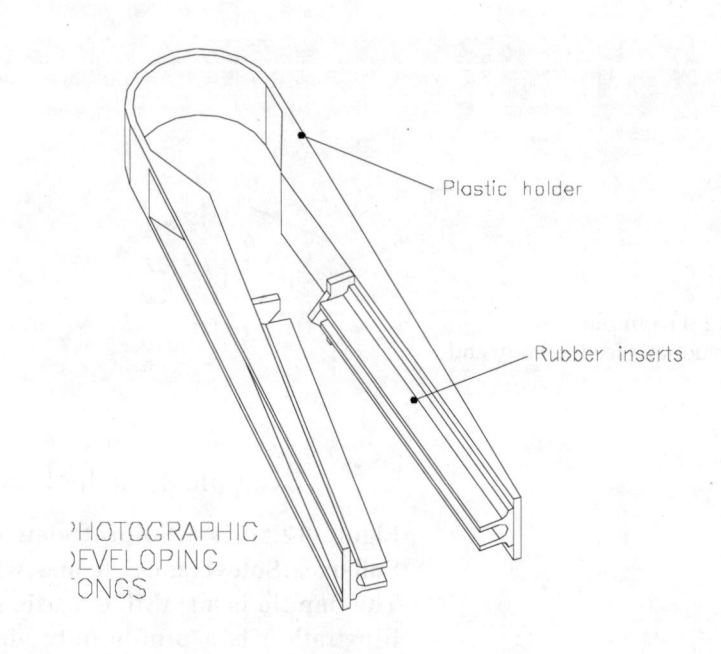

Fig. 12.11 Example 9 – photographic tongs

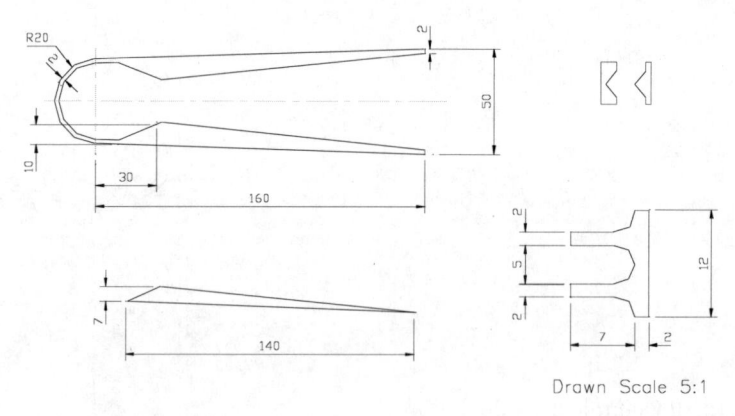

Fig. 12.12 Example 9 – pline outlines for the extrusions

Dimensions of body, inserts, rubber inserts and stops – PLINEs for SOLEXT

Drawn Scale 5:1

Examples of 3D models 199

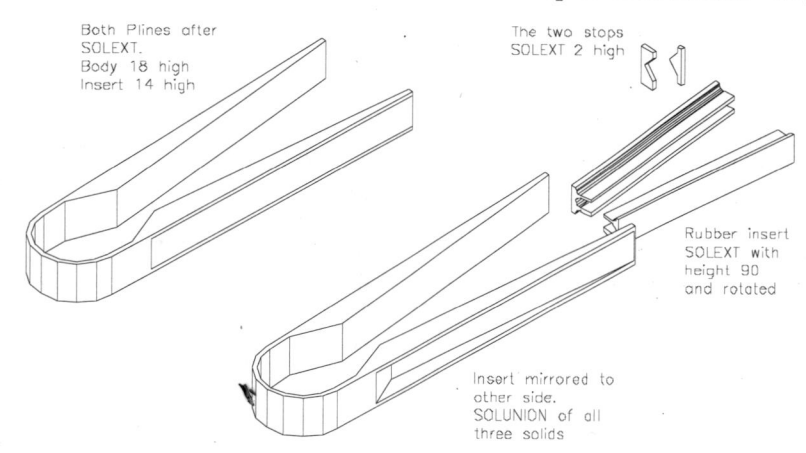

Fig. 12.13 Example 9 – stages in constructing the solids

Example 10 – pipe grips

Figure 10.14 is a **Solprof** view of an exploded projection of this model. Details of the pline outlines from which the **Solext**rusions were developed are given in Fig. 12.15. When the extrusions had been created, **Solcyls**s were **Solsub**tracted from both parts. Two extrusions were needed for the body, together with an extrusion created from a double arc (constructed in UCS **END**). The given drawing is a profile one after calling **Solprof** and turning layers 0 and 1-PH-2 off.

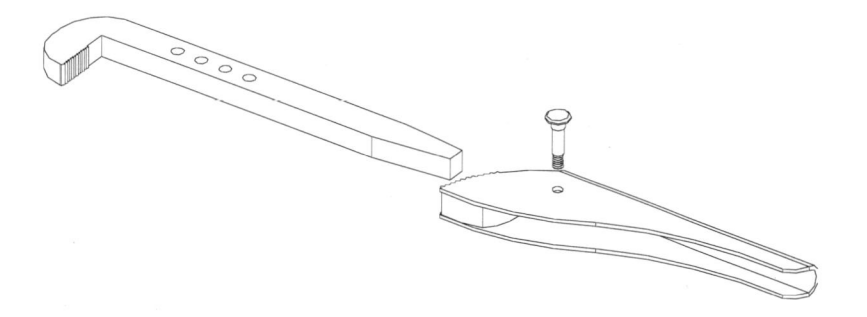

Fig. 12.14 Example 10 – pipe wrench

Note

Any of the examples shown in this chapter could have been constructed in either AutoCAD R12 or AutoCAD R13 using AME (R12), the **Solids** tools (R13) or, in some cases the **Surfaces** tools (either R12 or R13).

200 An Introduction to 3D AutoCAD

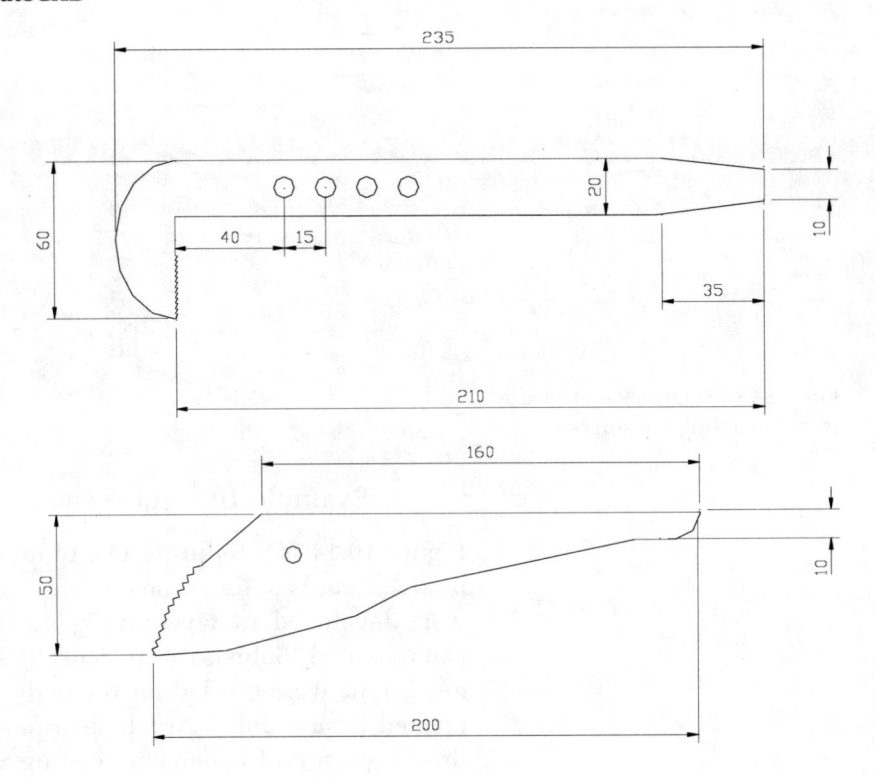

Fig. 12.15 Example 10 – pline outlines for extrusions

Index

.xy filter 8

2D coordinates 5
2D Shaper program 162

3D AME models 97
3D coordinates 5
3D Editor program 162
3D Lofter program 162
3D model examples 190
3D models in R13 124
3D models in viewports 95
3D Objects 21, 44, 122
3D solid models 82
3D solids with R13 122
3D Studio 160
3D Studio ambient lights 165
   animations 162
   cursors 160
   file types 163
   icon panel 161
   materials 165
   omni lights 165
   programs 162
   renderings 164, 166
   selection device 160
   shell programme 162
   spot lights 165
   viewports 175
3d.lsp 44
3dface 10, 16, 20, 21, 23
3dline 7, 20
3dmesh 16, 40
3dpoly 40, 42

abbreviations for commands 4
absolute coordinates 7

acad.dwg 73
acad.pgp 4
admesh 188
Advanced Modelling Extension
   see AME
ambient light 147
ambient lighting in
   3D Studio 165
AME 82
   Convert 82, 132
   primitives 83
   tools 83
   variables 86
animations in 3D Studio 162
applying mapping 166
assigning materials 166
AutoCAD
   background 152
   Designer 179
Autodesk 3D Studio 160
AutoLisp 40
AutoVis pull-down menu 146
AutoVision 145
   lighting 147

backgrounds 146
Boolean
   operations 132
   operators 88
Boundary Hatch dialogue
   box 131

calling commands 2
Camera option of dview 136
circle 3
   sub-menu 3
Clip option of dview 143

Color Wheel 152
colours 146
Command prompt 2
coordinate origin 5
copy 25
current
  elevation 17
  thickness 17
cursors in 3D Studio 160

Designer 179
  commands 17
  Drawing View dialogue
    box 183
  Extrusion dialogue box 180
  parametric possibilities 185
  renderings 189
  sketch planes 181
  work planes 181
dialogue and message boxes in
  3D Studio 162
disk capacity 91
Distance option of dview 140
distant light 147
Draw
  menu 4
  pull-down menu 20, 83
dview 136
  options 141
Dviewblock 135

Edge Defined Path 21
edgesurf 16, 29
elev 17
elevation tool 18, 38
examples of renderings in
  3D Studio 166
eXit option of dview 144
extruded surface 22

file types in 3D Studio 163
filters 8
flat rendering 165
flyouts 4, 122

Gourand rendering 165

hide 10, 23, 85
Hide option of dview 143
HideEdge 27
hideplot 74

icon panel in 3D Studio 161
icons 4
Invisible prompt of 3dface 25

keyboard 2
Keyframer program 162

light intensity 147
lights 146
  for a scene 147
limits 6
line 2, 7
Load Modeler 82

M and N vertices 41
mapping coordinates 166
materials 146, 150
  in 3D Studio 165
Materials
  dialogue box 151
  Library 150
menu bar 2
menus 2
Metal rendering 165
methods of rendering in
  3D Studio 164
mirror 25
Model
  pull-down menu 82
  Space 73
Modify toolbar 124
modifying lights 148
mouse 1
MSpace 70, 72
mview 74

new UCS 57

Off option of dview 143
omni lights in 3D Studio 165

pan 6
Pan option of dview 142
Paper Space 73
parallel projection 13
parametricity 180
perspective view 140
pface 16, 43
Phong rendering 165
plotter 2
point light 147
pointing device 1
Points option of dview 138
polygonal surface meshes 21
printer 2
problems with solcham and solfill 102
programs in 3D Studio 162
PSpace 70
   icon 51
pull-down menu 2

R12 1
   compared with R13 82
R13 1
   examples of 3D models 124
solid models 122
regen 27
Region Modeler 83
relative coordinates 9
Release 12 *see* R12
Release 13 *see* R12
renderings 146
revolved surface 22
revsurf 16, 32
rotate option of vpoint 13
ruled surface 21
rulesurf 16, 36

saveasr12 82
saver12dwg 82
sections for 3D solids 115
selection
   device in 3D Studio 160
   methods 4
shade 145
shadedge 145
shadows 146

shell program for
   3D Studio 162
ShowEdge 27
Sketch Planes 181
slice tool 136
sliders in dview 139
solaxes 103
solbox 83, 84
solcham 100
   problems 102
solchp 105
solcone 83, 84
solcyl 83, 84
solext 86
solfeat 108
solfill 101
solfill problems 102
solhangle 115
solhpat 115
solhsize 115
Solid fill 18
Solids
   toolbar 124
   tools 17, 122, 124
solint 90
solmesh 85
solmove 103
solprof 109
   examples 111
solpurge 107
solrev 87
solsect 113
solsep 106
solsphere 83, 85
solsub 89
soltorus 83, 85
solucs 107
solunion 88
solvar 86, 117
solwdens 86
solwedge 83, 85
speed of rendering 163
sphere 45
spot lights 147
   in 3D Studio 165
Super Video Graphics
   Array 146

surface meshes 85
Surfaces
    toolbar 10, 20, 46
    tools 28
Surftab1 28
Surftab2 28
SVGA 146

tabsurf 38
tabulated Surface 21
Target option of dview 137
Tiled Viewport Layout 70
tilemode 70
tool
    name abbreviations 4
    tips 122
toolbars 4, 122, 124
tools 2
Twist option of dview 142

UCS 6, 50, 59
    3point 55
    Orientation dialogue box 52
    origin 53
    Presets 52
    right hand rule 56
    tool 52
UCSfollow 50
    settings in viewports 72
UCSicon 50
Undo option of dview 143
User Coordinate System
    see UCS

variables 28
VDU 1
View pull-down menu 11, 135
Viewpoint Presets 12
viewports 70, 77
    and 3D models 95
    in 3D Studio 175
    in PSpace 77
visual display unit *see* VDU
vpoint 11, 16
    icon 15
    settings in viewports 72

WCS 17
Windows version 4
wire rendering 165
wireframes 85
work planes 181
workstation 1
World Coordinate System
    see WCS

x,y,z 5

zoom 7
Zoom option of dview 139